Indicative Trauma Impact Manual

ITIM for Professionals - First Edition 2023

A non-diagnostic, trauma-informed guide to emotion, thought, and behaviour.

By the same author

Taylor, J. (2022) Sexy but Psycho: How patriarchy uses women's trauma against them, Hachette, Little, Brown Publications, London

Taylor, J. (2022) Implementing trauma-informed approaches to VAWG: A guide for statutory services, VictimFocus

Taylor, J. & Shrive, J. (2021) 'I thought it was just a part of life': Reporting new data on violence committed against women and girls in the UK since birth, VictimFocus

Taylor, J. & Shrive, J. (2021) Real Stories of Women: Honouring the voices of women who become pregnant or have children conceived in sexual violence, VictimFocus

Taylor, J. & Shrive, J. (2021) Public perceptions and attitudes towards women who become pregnant or have children conceived in sexual violence, VictimFocus

Taylor, J. (2020) Why Women are Blamed for Everything: Exposing the culture of victim blaming, Hachette, Little, Brown Publications, London

Taylor, J. (2020) The Reflective Journal For Parents and Carers: Supporting your child after sexual abuse, VictimFocus

Taylor, J. & Shrive, J. (2020) The Primary School & Home School Guide: Ethical sex and relationships education for young children, VictimFocus

Taylor, J. (2020) Woman in Progress: The Reflective Journal for Women and Girls Subjected to Abuse and Trauma, VictimFocus

Taylor, J. (2020) The Reflective Journal for Researchers and Academics, VictimFocus

Taylor, J. (2019) The Reflective Journal for Practitioners Working in Trauma and Abuse, VictimFocus

Indicative Trauma Impact Manual

ITIM for Professionals - First Edition
2023

A non-diagnostic, trauma-informed guide to emotion, thought, and behaviour

DR JESSICA TAYLOR
JAIMI SHRIVE

© VictimFocus Ltd 2023

Copyright Notice: All content in this book is the intellectual property of the authors and may not be reproduced or used without permission. This includes text, images, and other media. If you wish to use any of the content in this book, please contact the authors for permission.

First published in paperback in Great Britain in 2023 by VictimFocus

The moral rights of the authors have been asserted.

All rights reserved. No part of this publication may be reproduced, stored in a retrieval system, or transmitted in any form or by any means electronic, mechanical, photocopying recording or otherwise without the prior written permission of the publisher.

ISBN: 978-969-30-9235-6 (paperback)
ISBN: 9798388381262 (Trade paperback on Amazon)

Printers used by VictimFocus use paper from well-managed forests and other responsible sources.

VictimFocus Ltd

www.victimfocus.com

Foreword

Welcome to the Indicative Trauma Impact Manual (ITIM), First Edition.

We're delighted to have published this, and we thank you or your organisation for purchasing this manual.

Drawing upon decades of literature, data, practice wisdom, lived experiences, and conversations with professionals working in abuse, mental health, and trauma, we identified a gap that desperately needs addressing; a trauma-informed, non-pathologising practical manual for professionals.

This book presents a new way for professionals (those who hold cases, and those who do not), to understand psychological trauma and distress, the impacts of this, and how we can support those struggling with trauma and distress in the best way possible, without suggesting or implying that the person is disordered, abnormal, irrational, or mentally ill.

For many years, academics and activists have debated the validity and meaning of psychiatric diagnosis of anyone who is in a state of trauma or distress, due to the overlap in perceived 'symptoms' of 'mental illness' and natural distress. Where does natural distress end, and mental disorder start? Who decides when trauma responses become abnormal? Who decides how long it is acceptable to grieve? Or have nightmares?

Some academics have demonstrated that the criteria and lists of symptoms for mental disorders overlap so heavily, that a person in distress can be diagnosed with over 10 mental disorders at any one time (Middleton, 2013).

Decades of misunderstanding, working from outdated and debunked theories, and little alternatives has led to mass psychiatric treatment of, and labelling of hundreds of responses to trauma and distress. At the point of writing this manual, 26% of the adult UK population are prescribed antidepressants, benzodiazepines, z-drugs, pregabalin, and opioids (PHE, 2023). Further, at the end of 2022, NHS Digital reported that 18% of children aged 7 to 16 years old, and 22% of young people aged 17 to 24 years old had a 'probable mental disorder'.

This is where the Indicative Trauma Impact Manual (ITIM) comes in.

We have created and written the ITIM to serve as a tool for professionals who want to work in a more trauma informed, anti-pathology approach.

We hope that this manual enables the changes of policy and practice, to prevent the gatekeeping of services and provisions for those who are in need of support due to their distress and trauma, and validates the struggle, harm, oppression, and fear that so many face.

This is the first edition of the ITIM, and we expect to make revisions, updates, and increase in quantity of the content of this manual as the years come. Our peer review process was an incredibly important part of the ITIM, and has included many ideas for the Second Edition, and translations.

This is the very beginning, and so we welcome all feedback and enquiries.

Everything must start somewhere.

Contents

	How to use this book	9
	Disclaimer	13
1.	Introduction to ITIM	15
	- History of pathologisation and medicalisation of human suffering	16
	- Theories and practical models of mental health	21
	- Anti-Pathologising Trauma Informed Services (APTI)	29
	- VALIDATE Model	30
	- Core Values of APTI Services	31
2.	Basic human emotions	39
3.	Distressing experiences and traumas *(Alphabetical)*	45
	A-E	45-81
	F-J	82-102
	K-O	102-111
	P-T	111-151
	U-Z	151-155
4.	Trauma responses and coping mechanisms *(Alphabetical)*	157
	A-E	157-198
	F-J	198-232
	K-O	232-242
	P-T	242-289
	U-Z	289-294
5.	Signs of trauma in infants and toddlers	295
6.	Physical responses to trauma and distress	299
	- Distress and trauma related flare-ups of pre-existing illnesses or conditions	326
	- Health issues that may be ignored, minimised, or pathologised	329

Indicative Trauma Impact Manual (First Edition)

7.	Useful tools and resources	351
	- Exploring coping mechanisms tool	352
	- Baseline trauma tool	354
	- Ecological model of trauma and distress	358
	- Maslow's Hierarchy of Needs	360
	- Mapping out traumas and stressors	361
	- Beliefs about self tool	362
	- Counterfactual thinking tool	363
	- Exploring intersectionality in trauma and distress	364
	- Understanding the trauma response	365
	- Exploring trauma responses	366
	- Belief in a Just World tool	367
	- Trauma self-blame tool	368
	- Harmful responses to trauma tool	369
8.	Side effects, withdrawal, and complaints about medication	371
9.	Understanding bias and oppression in psychiatry	379
10.	Understanding approaches to supporting traumatised and distressed people	387
	About VictimFocus	407
	With Thanks to Reviewers	408
	Bibliography	409

How to use this book

The Indicative Trauma Impact Manual (ITIM) is a reference book, suitable for:

- Medical professionals
- Social workers
- Therapists and counsellors
- Support workers
- Emergency services professionals
- Academics and students
- Teachers and education professionals
- Caseworkers
- Legal professionals
- Psychologists and Psychiatrists
- Health care professionals
- Any other professionals working with people in distress, trauma, or crisis

The manual describes, explains, and explores everything from acceptance to xenophobia in an A-Z of traumas, experiences, emotions, thoughts and behaviours that are common in traumatised and distressed people. This edition also includes diagrams, theories, and peer reviewed evidence throughout.

This book can be used to understand the wide range of trauma responses, coping mechanisms, experiences, emotions and thoughts that may arise. It is designed to be non-medical, and does not support diagnostic or medical labelling. The ITIM is a handbook for professionals to consider the presence, meaning and impact of hundreds of human experiences. It is not possible for this to be exhaustive, and professional will need to use their own judgement, training and knowledge when working with, and safeguarding, their clients.

Limitations and notes about this manual

As a resource specifically pertaining to distress and trauma, this guide does not give information or guidance relating to changes in behaviour, thoughts or emotions that may arise from brain injury, concussion, brain tumour, stroke, aneurism, or neuro-surgery.

Whilst other theorists and practitioners may choose to take a medical or biological position, this manual does not consider the trauma responses, coping mechanisms, or distressing experiences listed in this book to be genetic, hereditary, innate, predisposed, or caused by chemical imbalances in the brain.

This book works from the foundation and current understanding that there has been no singular gene found to underpin, cause, or explain any 'psychiatric disorder', that there is no conclusive evidence of a 'serotonin chemical imbalance' in the brain, that many of the original 'dopamine' theories are being retracted or rejected, and there are no objective measurable tests for any 'psychiatric disorders'.

Instead, it is suggested that experiences of abuse, violence, oppression, discrimination, inequality, and chronic distress harm the human being, resulting in natural and common changes in behaviour, thoughts, emotions, health, beliefs, and motivations.

A note on medicalised language

The authors of the ITIM are committed to the use of factual, accurate language and as such you may notice words and phrases throughout this manual that are more commonly associated with psychiatric/medical model of mental health. This is due to the original meaning of words such as 'anxiety' and 'depression' becoming so interlinked with the pathologisation of human emotion, and their overused 'disorder' descriptions, that their original meaning has become distorted.

As such, we do not see a need to alter this language and rather to explain how it can be used to understand human emotion, trauma responses, and coping mechanisms more accurately.

For example, where we may have said that a traumatic experience may leave someone feeling 'distressed and anxious', we do not use this language to mean 'anxiety disorder' or the colloquial 'anxiety' (to mean a mental health issues). Similarly, if we discuss people feeling depressed and low, this does not mean the person 'has depression' (to mean a depressive disorder).

Trauma does not excuse harm committed towards others

It is important to the authors that this resource is not used to excuse those who commit abuse, violence, hatred and harm towards others, in the name of their own trauma or distress. We argue that whilst the trauma of a person may be valid and the person may be in need of significant support, they still make an active choice to harm others. When this harm is criminal, they are still making a choice to break the law and to harm and traumatise someone else.

Many people who have been subjected to distress and trauma never go on to harm others people, and so we do not accept the suggestion that trauma and distress alone causes someone to abuse or violate another person, or their rights to safety.

A trauma-informed approach should not ignore, minimise or obscure the harm some people choose to inflict on others, and should not be used to excuse those choices. There must be accountability, and the trauma of the victim must be the priority where harm has been committed.

Ideas about how this book can be used:

- A counsellor dips in and out of this book when thinking about the different coping mechanisms their client is using in day-to-day life

- A student uses this book to explore an alternative way of thinking and writing about trauma, coping mechanisms and experiences
- A support worker in a charity uses this book to think about how many of the traumatic or distressing experiences their client has been subjected to across their lifespan
- A teacher uses this book to think about how many of the children in their class are displaying signs of potential neglect or abuse
- A psychologist reads this book to explore an alternative approach to supporting their client, who after many years and psychiatric diagnoses from others, says that nothing is working
- A nurse uses the chapter in this book to learn about illnesses and medical issues that are often pathologised in people who are deemed to have mental disorders
- An individual reads through this book to gain further understanding of their own experiences, responses and coping mechanisms

Disclaimer

Medical Disclaimer: The information provided in this book is for educational purposes only and is not intended as medical advice. It is not a substitute for professional medical advice, or treatment. Always seek the advice of your doctor or other qualified healthcare provider with any questions you may have regarding a medical condition. Never disregard professional medical advice or delay in seeking it because of something you have read in this book. If you think you may have a medical emergency, call your doctor or 999/911 immediately.

Specific Disclaimers

• Changes to psychiatric medication and treatment must be done so with the support and advice of a registered healthcare provider. It is not advisable to suddenly stop taking prescribed medication, as it is common for medication to have side effects and withdrawal effects. However, if your client expresses a wish to stop taking medication, or to reduce dosages, please seek support and advice about safe medication tapering for your clients.

• Chest pain and cardiac symptoms should be taken seriously and anyone experiencing chest pain or other cardiac symptoms should contact their registered healthcare provider.

• The advice of registered healthcare professionals should be sought for all suspected health conditions or medical symptoms. This manual should be used as a guide to trauma responses, coping mechanisms, and manifestations of such by professionals after relevant health conditions have already been ruled out.

CHAPTER 1

Introduction to ITIM

Understanding trauma responses and coping mechanisms: An alternative to pathologisation

The ITIM is best understood as a resource for professionals who want to think about, explore, examine, and understand trauma, distress and human suffering without using medicalisation or pathologisation.

The dominant model of mental health is the 'medical model'. It is so dominant that many people (including professionals) are not aware that there are any other theoretical models of mental health at all. They assume that the science around mental health is settled, and that mental disorders have been proven to be caused by genetics, serotonin, dopamine, brain injury, neurodivergence and illnesses.

It is so dominant in fact, that millions of people can name psychiatric disorders and medications, and some even feel they can distance-diagnose other people with mental disorders based on what they say, do, think, or feel.

Psychiatric language has become so embedded into day-to-day conversations that people no longer describe their fear, sadness, despair, worry, forgetfulness, distress, or helplessness. Instead, they say, 'my anxiety is playing up', 'my depression is bad today', and 'I think I am a bit ADHD'.

There is widespread poor emotional literacy, in children and adults. People who have been informed that they have mental disorders and personality disorders may not be able to confidently describe or identify their valid, natural, normal emotions, thoughts and behaviours, as they have been framed as 'symptoms' of a mental illness. Once their mental and emotional life has been recast as disordered and abnormal, some people can have difficulty processing their distress, and trauma.

A disorder is defined as a 'state of confusion', and medically, a disorder is defined as 'a condition characterised by lack of normal functioning of physical or mental processes'.
Whilst we do not support or use this term in our work, theory or practice, it is unfortunately the term for what psychiatry and psychology currently consider to be 'abnormalities' or 'syndromes' in behaviour, thought and emotion.

The 'D' in many mental health issues stand for disorder, for example, personality disorder (PD), eating disorder (ED), post-traumatic stress disorder (PTSD), generalised anxiety disorder (GAD), bipolar disorder (BD) and so on. This is important to note, as whilst we are encouraged to believe that mental health is an accepted and normal issue in a modern and progressive society, these issues are still being classified as psychiatric disorders of abnormal functioning of the mind.

For example, we still label people who are experiencing natural and normal responses to trauma with 'PTSD' which frames their trauma responses as mental disorders. Instead, we could remove the 'D' from the label easily, and simply talk about trauma responses, or post-trauma responses. There is no need or use for the framing of the disorder, as the responses are in no way disordered.

The ITIM is an ambitious provision of descriptions, explanations and ideas about hundreds of common trauma responses, feelings of distress, and coping mechanisms whilst avoiding psychiatric categorisation, pathologisation and labelling.

History of pathologisation and medicalisation of human suffering

From the late 1800s onwards, physicians and men in other positions of power (including slave owners) such as Dr Samuel A.

Cartwright, began to suggest mental illnesses that could explain behaviours and emotions. Cartwright invented the mental illness 'drapetomania', which he described to be a mental disorder of Black enslaved people who wish to be freed.

He argued that they were obsessed with being White and required hard labour and lashes to cure them of their mental illness.

Further than this, white medical researchers and psychiatrists developed the concept of 'dysaethesia aethiopia' which they described as a depressed, lethargic, dullness of enslaved Black people.

And as the development of psychiatric disorders continued, the racist diagnosis and treatment of Black people deepened, with schizophrenia becoming well known as the 'Black man's disorder' by the 1970s. Academics and practitioners added the term 'aggressive' to the diagnostic criteria of schizophrenia and then directly marketed antipsychotics to Black people who they felt were 'out of control' (Smith, 2020).

By the 18th century, one of the most common psychiatric diagnoses used to control, imprison, and violate women was that of hysteria. Fast forward a century or two, and in the early 1900s, Sigmund Freud who is widely described as the 'father of modern psychology', suggested that women and girls had deeply embedded unconscious 'penis envy' in their psyche, and were innately mentally ill due to another invented illness called 'hysteria'. Hysteria was based on the belief that the female uterus was causing insanity, disobedience and behavioural issues in women and girls, due to causing imbalances in the body. This powerful concept led to mass womb extractions, forced sterilisations, abusive treatments and lifelong imprisonment for women who did not conform or behave.

As the years wore on, gay men and lesbian women were diagnosed with 'sexual deviation' and 'sociopathic personality disturbances'. Dr Edmund Bergler wrote about homosexual people in 1956, 'For me, they are sick people requiring medical help…Homosexuals are essentially disagreeable people...their shell is a mixture of superliciousness, fake aggression and whimpering.'

Thanks to these comments and ideas about homosexuality being a mental disorder, many gay men and lesbian women were subjected to 'aversion therapy'. This so-called treatment involved the use of electro-convulsive therapy, chemical emetics, LSD, insulin to induce coma, and frontal lobotomies to attempt to 'cure' people of their same-sex attraction (Carr and Spandler, 2019).

Into the 1960s, and through to the 1990s, Black rights activists and protestors were diagnosed with 'protest psychosis' and imprisoned. It was theorised by Bromberg and Simon in 1968 that participation in the civil rights movement, or in any of the Black power movements, was part of 'volatile schizophrenic symptoms in the Black community'.

In fact, the power and perceived 'hostility' of the Black power movement was frequently theorised by white psychiatrists to be caused by schizophrenia. Today, 90% of all psychiatric care beds in the US are in prisons, which are disproportionately populated by Black men (Segrest, 2020).

Elsewhere, women and girls were being diagnosed with 'histrionic personality disorder'. This disorder was much more commonly diagnosed in women, and a review in 1983 by Kaplan argued that it was a disorder based on bias, stereotype and the pathologisation of femininity. Later, the popular diagnosis used to pathologise women was 'borderline personality disorder' and then 'emotionally unstable personality disorder', both of which are significantly more likely to be diagnosed in women and girls, and have come under frequent and robust criticism for the overt misogyny in theory and practice. Ussher (2013) argued that these personality disorders had become 'catch all diagnoses' used against women and girls, similar to the way 'hysteria' had been used as the 'wastebasket of mental health'.

Psychiatry and psychology have a long and shameful history of creating illnesses and disorders with no medical evidence base, diagnosing people with life-changing and stigmatising disorders, and then treating them with dangerous, harmful, and sometimes fatal 'treatments' and substances.

In 1952, the 'bible of psychiatry' was first published – the Diagnostic and Statistical Manual of Mental Disorders (generally shortened to the 'DSM').

The aim of the DSM was to provide a manual for doctors and psychiatrists to recognise and diagnose people with mental disorders.

Whilst we don't use the term 'mental disorder' in public anymore, it is still in the title of the DSM to this day, and we must never lose sight of the fact that everything contained within the DSM is perceived to be a disorder of the mind, of personality, or of behaviour (regardless of how many times we say 'mental health' instead).

Between 1950 and 1973, there was significant criticism of the DSM and psychiatric diagnostic criteria in general, with studies showing that psychiatrists using the DSM often did not agree on the correct diagnosis for a patient.

In 1974, the third DSM (DSM-III) was published with the aim of creating more standardised, robust criteria for diagnosis of mental disorders. The goal was to structure them and publish them to look like illnesses with 'symptoms' and 'tests' and 'recommended treatments' and 'medications'.

The authors of the DSM-III claimed that they had created a scientific and objective manual which was 'ideology free'.

Despite the claims, studies showed that the new DSM was just as unreliable as the others, but it had a major difference: it positioned itself as a medical manual which referred to medication, drugs, and dosages. It sounded more scientific, and it was perceived as more scientific. Many people regard the DSM to be the most influential and robust manual of mental disorders and illnesses, and its global impact cannot be understated.

Every revision of the DSM has increased the numbers of diagnosable mental disorders exponentially.

DSM Version	Year	Number of mental disorders
DSM-I	1952	128
DSM-II	1968	193
DSM-III	1980	228
DSM-III-R	1987	253
DSM-IV	1994	383
DSM-IV-TR	2000	383
DSM-V	2013	541

Despite the list of mental disorders growing, and the number of annual prescriptions and psychiatric diagnoses increasing, more people are beginning to question the validity of the medical model, and the concept of mental disorders.

Some professionals are looking for an alternative to medicalisation of the human experience, and many of them are turning to a trauma-informed approach to mental health.

Definition of a trauma-informed approach

An approach to understanding human distress and mental health which considers that a change in behaviour, thought, or emotion arises from past or current trauma, distress, oppression, or harm. Within this context, trauma can be variable and dynamic. Whilst trauma was historically considered to be a one-off, life-threatening event, it is now accepted to encompass any event or set of events that cause deep distress, disturbance, oppression, fear, harm, or injury.

How is this approach different to current approaches to mental health and human distress?

A trauma-informed approach is opposed to the labelling, medication, pathologisation and problematising of humans. Instead of seeking what is 'wrong' with the individual (whether that is called a 'mental health issue' or a 'disorder'), the trauma-informed approach supports the individual from the perspective that their responses to distress are normal, natural, justified, understandable, and valid. Therefore, a trauma-informed approach does not engage in systems or narratives which seek to position the individual as having an internal issue that needs to be diagnosed, treated, managed, or solved with therapy, medication, or social isolation.

What are the different theoretical approaches to mental health and human distress?

When we talk about being 'trauma-informed', we are talking about a theoretical and philosophical approach to understanding mental health, disorder, illness, distress, oppression, and abuse. It is one of several theoretical approaches. It is quickly becoming more popular but is not the most dominant approach to understanding human distress.

To move towards a trauma-informed approach is to move towards revolutionary paradigm change. Whilst this may feel particularly huge and/or insurmountable, there are already many trauma-informed pilots, police forces, education providers, social work projects, charities, and private services that have successfully implemented change. Change is possible.

Theories and practical models of mental health

There are several main theories of mental health that have been proposed over time. Here are some of the most commonly recognised:

Biological theory: This theory posits that mental disorders are caused by imbalances in neurotransmitters, genetics, or other biological factors in the brain.

Psychodynamic theory: This theory suggests that mental disorders are caused by unconscious conflicts and repressed emotions from early childhood experiences.

Cognitive-behavioural theory: This theory proposes that mental disorders are caused by distorted or irrational thinking patterns and negative behaviours.

Humanistic theory: This theory emphasises the importance of self-actualisation and personal growth, and suggests that mental disorders occur when people are unable to achieve their full potential due to environmental factors.

Sociocultural theory: This theory posits that mental disorders are influenced by social and cultural factors, such as poverty, discrimination, and trauma.

1. Medical model

Biological model of mental illness (medical model)

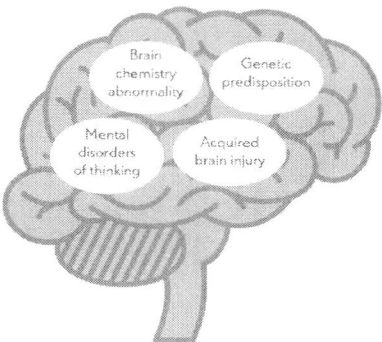

Taylor (2022)

The 'medical model' is shorthand for a theory of mental health which suggests that mental illnesses, diseases, and disorders should be identified, treated, and managed in the same way as physical injuries, illnesses, diseases, and disorders. This model describes and responds to mental illness as 'a set of mental disorders caused by or linked to brain diseases which require pharmacological treatments to target presumed biological abnormalities' (Deacon, 2013). The medical model tends to assume that mental health issues are caused by biological and neurological issues in the brain.

Some people lean towards 'brain chemistry' explanations and some talk about 'neuroscience' explanations. Some talk about 'hereditary mental illness' and 'genetics'. This approach places the mental health issues and illnesses securely and exclusively in our brains. It posits that mental illness is 'just like physical illness' and should be treated as such. It is more heavily used in psychiatry but is now prominent in psychology and some areas of psychotherapy too.

2. Social model

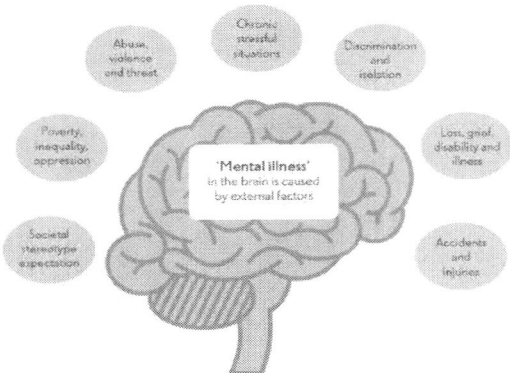

Taylor (2022)

The 'social model' is shorthand for a theory of mental health which suggests that humans are impacted by their context, environment, and experiences. Instead of suggesting that behaviours, feelings, and thoughts are mental illnesses or disorders, the social model encourages us to look at the factors surrounding the person to consider what might be causing their distress.

The social model usually does not support psychiatric diagnosis but can sometimes be used to argue that social factors are 'causing' mental illnesses.

The social model of mental health locates the cause or root of a so-called mental health issue within the social environment or context of the person, instead of inside the person themselves. The social model opposes all biological models.

Rather than suggesting that mental health or illness is in the brain or body of the person, those who subscribe to this model examine the factors around the person. Every and any
contextual, social, cultural, or environmental factor could be the cause of distress or mental health issues, including accommodation, poverty, oppression, abuse, discrimination, peer, and family issues.

Whilst this model doesn't support biological models of mental health, it is often used this way. It is not commonly used in psychiatry. It is more common in psychology, social work, and psychotherapy.

3. Biopsychosocial model

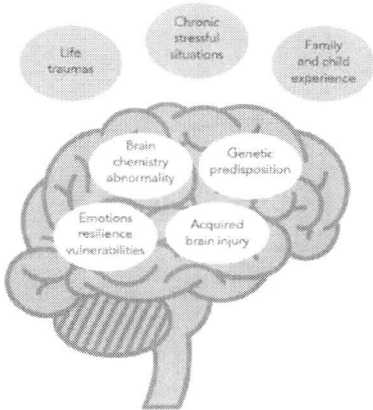

Taylor (2022)

The biopsychosocial model is an interdisciplinary approach to understanding mental health by looking at the way biological factors in the medical model, socio-environmental factors in the social model and other psychological factors intersect.
The biopsychosocial model of mental health was developed in part to address some of the gaps of a purely biological, biomedical model of mental health.

In 1977, George Engel argued that the biomedical model ignored many other factors that could be contributing to mental illness. There are three domains to explain mental illness:

- Biological factors (genetics, brain chemistry, disease, brain injury)

- Psychological factors (emotions, resilience, interpretation, vulnerabilities)
- Social factors (life trauma and stressors, family, and child experiences)

The original arguments were that mental illnesses were made up of complex interplay between these three domains, with many connections between and within them, however, as time has gone on, this model has become gradually more medical and biological, with the other intersecting factors being minimised.

4. Trauma-informed model

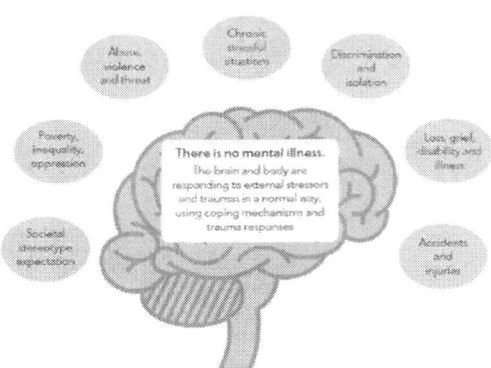

Taylor (2020)

An approach to understanding mental distress and mental health which considers that a change in behaviour, thought or emotion arises from past or current trauma. Within this context, trauma can be variable and dynamic.

Whilst trauma used to be considered a one-off, life-threatening event, it is now accepted to encompass any event or set of events that cause deep distress, disturbance, fear, harm, or injury.
The trauma-informed approach to mental health, illness and distress argues that there are undeniable and consistent strong

correlations between all so-called 'mental health issues' and human trauma, distress and oppression.

Therefore, it is argued that 'disorders', 'illnesses' and 'diseases' are likely to be natural physical and psychological manifestations of human trauma and distress, in response to events and experiences in our lives – not brain abnormalities or mental illnesses.

Other useful terms to remember as you work through this book

Deficit-based approaches

An approach to social issues, mental health, abuse, and oppression which uses the negative events, experiences and so-called 'deficits' in a person's life to predict their risk level, future or present behaviours, thoughts, or circumstances. A trauma-informed approach would strongly oppose deficit-based approaches, and would not use the negative events in someone's life to judge, assess or predict their future.

Strength-based approaches

The opposite to deficit-based approaches, the strength-based way of working in social issues, mental health, abuse and oppression focuses on the strengths, skills, talents and wisdom of the person instead of defining them by their 'deficits'. There is a current push towards strength-based approaches in many fields including social care, policing and mental health practice.

Pathologisation

To characterise a behaviour, thought or feeling as medically or psychologically abnormal. This includes the practice of seeing those behaviours or thoughts as medical symptoms as an indicator of a disease or disorder of the mind.

Anti-Pathologising Trauma Informed Services (APTI)

Developed by VictimFocus, APTI is a conceptual approach to all forms of human support services ranging from health services to community charities. Much can be gained from adopting an anti-pathologising, trauma-informed approach to supporting humans in distress.

Pathologisation is common, even within services which claim to be trauma-informed. This is why we have chosen to prioritise anti-pathologisation in trauma-informed services in our approach.

Underpinning approach

APTI approaches could apply to many organisations, community groups, clinical services, modalities, and techniques, if it is possible to adapt them so that they become trauma-informed, anti-pathologising, anti-oppressive in policy, practice, ethos, and theory. APTI is best considered an approach to culture change that would require systemic redesign, consistent and confident leadership, an increase in education, and a change in service delivery.

To support professionals in causing change, we have created the VALIDATE acrostic on the next page. We chose the word 'validate' to support our work, due to the way so many people talk about their need for validation of their traumas, distress, experiences, sensations, concerns, questions, and needs. In many cases where people have felt let down or wronged by services, it is due to not being validated, or being ignored. One of the most powerful impacts of APTI approaches is to validate and de-pathologise normal, natural responses to human distress.

The APTI service should aim to VALIDATE the client, their experiences, and their needs:

V – Victim focussed: The service is focussed on the rights, wellbeing, journey, experiences, and needs of anyone who is a victim of harm. They should advocate for and protect victims of any form of harm.

A – Anti-pathology: The service rejects the pathologisation of their clients and does not support the pathologisation of responses to human trauma. The service does not seek to, or support the psychiatric diagnoses, medication, restraint, or forced treatment of humans who have been traumatised and distressed by experiences.

L – Logical: The service provides logical and rational approaches to traumatised people, which demonstrably consider what is in the best interests of their clients. Similarly, the service believes that trauma responses to distressing experiences are logical, rational, and explainable.

I – Informed: The service is well-informed, well-educated and provides an evidence-based approach to trauma, distress, abuse, harm, and oppression. The service is committed to teaching their clients and/or wider community about trauma, harm, distress, and oppression.

D – Dynamic: The service is dynamic and flexible in the way it responds to people in need. The service understands that everyone needs something unique and tailored to their trauma.

A – Anti-oppressive: The service is committed to anti-oppressive practice and theory, and rejects any theory, resource, practice or policy that oppresses, stereotypes, harms, silences or ignores marginalised groups of people.

T – Trauma informed: The service is trauma-informed and understands the impact trauma and distress has on humans.

E – Ethical: The service strives to 'do no harm', and to abide by ethical guidelines in all of their work to avoid abuse, harm, exploitation, bullying, discrimination and violence.

Core values of APTI services

1. Trauma and distress are universal experiences. At one time or another, every human will experience, or be subjected to, some kind of experience that significantly distresses or traumatises them. These experiences will manifest differently in each person, with many common overlaps within and between people, and traumas.
2. Humans live in a global society which frequently causes them ongoing indirect and direct harm through large systems of power and control such as colonialism, capitalism, socialisation, tradition, culture, religious beliefs, racism, misogyny, homophobia, classism, poverty, deprivation, segregation, war, drought, instability, and inequality.
3. Trauma responses, coping mechanisms, and related changes in thoughts, beliefs, feelings, and behaviours are highly likely to be natural, common, understandable, and explainable.
4. The professional who is providing the service or support is likely to also have significant experiences of trauma and distress themselves, in addition to vicarious trauma from repeated exposure to distressing disclosures and work environments. It is important that the professional acknowledges and understands their own trauma and coping mechanisms, and does not seek to deny, or minimise them in order to appear authoritative.
5. People deserve access to support services which validate, support, explore, listen, mentor, and guide them without seeking to diagnose them as mentally disordered, or in need of psychiatric medication.
6. The relationship is often the 'intervention'. In many cases, the action of a human supporting, listening, providing a safe space, and validating the feelings and experiences of another human is the most impactful part of the service (whether it is traditional psychotherapy, or joining a local art class).
7. The client should never be under pressure or expectation to disclose or discuss trauma or distress in a trauma-informed service. Much useful support can be provided

without disclosure and detail. Similarly, there should never be an expectation that the client needs to 'deep dive' back into years of traumatic memories and experiences in order to move forwards.

8. Professionals must accept that therapeutic input is not always needed or desired, and that people require different approaches at different times of their lives. There is no one-size-fits-all. Some people benefit greatly from one-to-one talking therapy, but for some, this can be deeply traumatic and unnerving. However, there are many other alternative approaches, and we must ensure we do not support the 'medication or therapy' myth.
9. Support of the client avoids individualising the distress into the mind of the person, and instead explores external stressors and traumas that are having an impact on the life of the person.
10. Professionals should be advocates for their clients and be willing to support them to remove or correct inaccurate, misleading, harmful and biased information or diagnoses from their medical and support records. This may include accompanying or supporting the client to advocate for themselves in asking for their medical files, case records, care records, or documentation in order to challenge malpractice or misdiagnosis.

Understanding and addressing the role of oppression

An anti-pathologising, trauma-informed approach must include a thorough and demonstrable understanding of the role of oppression and institutional discrimination in human distress and trauma (both historically and currently). Rather than seeing the client as an individual who is experiencing 'symptoms' and 'signs' of an illness or disorder of the mind, a trauma-informed approach must consider that millions of people will be subjected to daily, chronic, ongoing distress and trauma due to being exposed to oppression and oppressive systems, institutions, beliefs, narratives, and social norms.

This means moving away from individualising and internalising the suffering into the human, and avoiding the location of 'issues' within the brain. Instead, the practitioner should step back, and take stock of the often numerous, and overwhelming, pressures, traumas, distress, fears, and difficulties a person may be facing.

During this process, examining intersectionality of trauma and oppression should be considered a basic starting point, as no matter what the person has been through in their life, inequality, oppression and protected characteristics will play a role in those events, experiences, and the response they received from support networks, professionals and wider society.

Dynamic approaches and techniques

Becoming APTI as a service or as a professional does not necessarily mean adopting a new modality, technique, approach or discipline. For some people, it is simply a different way of thinking about the conceptualisation of trauma, distress, pathologisation and validation.

Secondly, due to how unique all humans, all traumas and all trauma responses are, it is useful to have multiple approaches, resources, perspectives and techniques that can be used, mixed, or considered for each client as they work through their own journey of processing and understanding their trauma.

It is worth reflecting on whether you use any resources, techniques or approaches that are incompatible with APTI core values, though. For example, if your service uses resources which tend to shock and retraumatise the client into behaving or thinking differently, this would not be a technique that could be supported by APTI approaches.

Similarly, if it is your practice or within your service to assess and then diagnose people with mental disorders and recommend medication or other invasive treatments for their 'disorder', this would not be compatible with APTI approaches, as they would be theoretically opposing approaches to human distress.

The role of the professional

Within an APTI service, the role of the professional needs careful and reflective consideration. There has been significant professionalisation of support services over the past century, which has resulted in consistent and evidenced power dynamics when people seek support for distress and trauma. Peer, equal, reciprocating support is not a core service in most areas, and one-to-one therapies, support services, helplines and community groups are now most often staffed by trained/educated professionals. Additionally, they are often regulated and governed by safeguarding legislation, laws, regulatory bodies and other professional codes.

Whilst this development has been largely positive, it has meant that many people find themselves seeking support from professional services that can be highly structured, regulated, and controlled, which does not mirror the kind of safe space for compassionate and human support they were looking for.

For example, it is common to be receiving a support service for one hour per week, with a professional who the client knows very little personal information about, in a service where they are too scared to explain their entire feelings or situation in case the information is passed to third party agencies under safeguarding or mental health protocols, and where they know their case files or notes could be requested by a court or lawyers during an investigation.

In this way, it is important that professionals understand that whilst they can do everything possible to be as trauma-informed, welcoming, safe, supportive and compassionate as possible, they still play a role in an establishment or system of power.

There are then some key considerations:

1. The professional is not above, or immune to trauma and distress. It is very likely that they have their own trauma histories and distress, and this is likely to be triggered or impacted by their direct work with those in distress.
2. The professional is just as likely as the client to have been exposed to, subjected to, or to have experienced trauma, abuse, distress, loss, and harm. In this way, there is no 'them' and 'us' in the service or in professional practice. The dichotomy of 'professional' or 'survivor' is also technically inaccurate, too; as most professionals will also have been through trauma and distress.
3. The professional needs to acknowledge the power dynamics within the relationship with the client and address them authentically without minimising them.
4. The professional needs to remain sensitive to the way 'building rapport' and 'building relationships' with the client are likely to be triggering and uncomfortable experiences for some clients, due to the similarity with the grooming process which occurs in most forms of abuse, control and harm.

The use of resources and interventions

APTI approaches will not use resources, interventions, materials, media, or tactics which aim to shock, harm, traumatise, distress, or create negative/harmful associations. Resources must not be used in order to shock or harm a person into changing their behaviour, feelings, or thoughts.

Implementing APTI approaches in your work

Implementing APTI approaches to the work you do as a professional may range from simply adopting and changing your own practice as an independent practitioner (if you can do this), to very large systemic processes of consultation and change (if you belong to a large organisation or institution).

It is likely that this process will take time, and it is therefore important to consider examining the following:

1. Policies which relate to trauma, vicarious trauma, wellbeing, mental health, distress, risk assessment, and referrals
2. Relationships and referral pathways to partner organisations, and whether they also uphold APTI core values. If they do not, how to work with them in a way that does not pathologise your client further
3. Training and education of staff, management, and volunteers
4. The use of interventions, resources, techniques, and approaches (and whether they are APTI)
5. Referral forms, questionnaires, psychometric measures
6. Service design and delivery models (and whether they are APTI)
7. Monitoring and reporting of service performance, client progress, or data collection of clients and their experiences
8. Whether the service or approach could meet the VALIDATE acrostic (p. 31)

CHAPTER 2

Basic human emotions

The basic human emotions are often considered to be happiness, sadness, anger, fear, surprise, and disgust. Some researchers also include other emotions such as shame, guilt, love, and envy as basic emotions, while others consider these to be more complex emotions that arise from a combination of the basic emotions. The basic emotions are universal across cultures and are believed to have evolutionary significance in helping humans to respond to environmental and social stimuli in adaptive ways.

Fear

Fear is an emotion that is triggered by the perception of danger or threat, either real or imagined. It is a natural and adaptive response to situations that may pose a potential harm or risk to an individual's physical or emotional well-being. Fear is typically accompanied by physical sensations such as increased heart rate, rapid breathing, sweating, and tension in the muscles. It can range in intensity from mild unease to intense panic, and can be experienced in response to a variety of stimuli, such as specific objects or situations, memories, or thoughts.

Sadness

Sadness is a basic human emotion that is often triggered by feelings of loss, disappointment, or grief. It is a natural and common response to challenging life experiences such as the death of a loved one, the end of a relationship, or a significant change in one's life circumstances. Sadness can be characterised by a range of emotions including feelings of sorrow, melancholy, regret, and hopelessness. It is typically accompanied by physical sensations such as lethargy, fatigue, and a decreased appetite. Sadness is a normal and healthy response to difficult life situations and can serve as a catalyst for self-reflection, personal growth, and healing.

Anger

Anger is a basic human emotion that is often triggered by feelings of frustration, disappointment, or perceived injustice. It is a natural and adaptive response to situations that threaten our well-being or our sense of control over a situation. Anger can range in intensity from mild irritation to intense rage, and can be expressed in a variety of ways, such as verbal outbursts, physical aggression, or passive-aggressive behaviour. It is typically accompanied by physical sensations such as increased heart rate, rapid breathing, and tension in the muscles. While anger can be a normal and healthy response to challenging situations, uncontrolled or prolonged anger can be harmful to one's health and relationships. It is important to learn healthy ways of expressing and managing anger, such as through assertiveness, conflict resolution, and relaxation techniques.

Disgust

Disgust is a basic human emotion that is often triggered by experiences that are perceived as unpleasant or repulsive. It is a natural and adaptive response to situations that threaten our sense of hygiene, safety, or moral values. Disgust can be characterised by feelings of aversion, nausea, and revulsion. It is typically accompanied by physical sensations such as gagging, nausea, and avoidance behaviours. Disgust can be elicited by a variety of stimuli, such as certain tastes or smells, bodily fluids or functions, or social norms and taboos. While disgust can serve a protective function by helping us avoid potentially harmful substances or behaviours, excessive or irrational disgust can interfere with daily life and relationships.

Guilt

Guilt is a complex emotional state that is often triggered by feelings of responsibility or remorse for a past action or inaction. It is a natural and common response to situations where we believe we have violated a moral or ethical code, or failed to meet our own or others' expectations. Guilt can be characterised by feelings of shame, self-blame, and regret. It is typically accompanied by physical sensations such as tension in the muscles, racing thoughts, and a decreased appetite. Guilt can be adaptive, serving as a signal that we need to repair relationships or make amends for our actions. However, excessive or irrational guilt can interfere with daily life and relationships.

Enjoyment

Enjoyment is a positive emotional state that is often triggered by experiences that bring us pleasure or satisfaction. It is a natural and rewarding response to situations that enhance our well-being, such as spending time with loved ones, engaging in hobbies or interests, or achieving personal goals. Enjoyment can be characterised by feelings of happiness, contentment, and fulfilment. It is typically accompanied by physical sensations such as relaxation, smiling, and laughter. Enjoyment can have a positive impact on our physical and mental health, helping to reduce stress, improve mood, and increase resilience. It is important to prioritize enjoyable experiences in our lives and to practice self-care and relaxation techniques to support a balanced and fulfilling lifestyle

Apathy

Apathy is a lack of interest, motivation, or emotion towards a particular person, object, or situation. It is characterised by a feeling of indifference or disconnection, and a lack of concern or involvement in one's surroundings or activities. Apathy can result from a variety of factors, such as low mood, chronic stress, helplessness, or exhaustion. It can be accompanied by physical symptoms such as fatigue, lethargy, or a lack of appetite.

Injustice

Injustice is not usually considered to be a core emotion, but we have included it here as it underpins so many of the experiences and trauma responses. Injustice is a situation in which someone is treated unfairly or without the rights they deserve. It is a violation of fairness, equity, or moral or legal principles. Injustice can occur on an individual level, such as in the form of discrimination or prejudice, or on a systemic level, such as in the form of social or economic inequality. Injustice can result in feelings of anger, frustration, or powerlessness, and can have a negative impact on one's psychological and emotional well-being. It is important to recognise and challenge instances of injustice, and to advocate for fairness, equity, and social justice.

Surprise

Surprise is a basic human emotion that is often triggered by unexpected or sudden events or stimuli. It is characterised by a sudden feeling of astonishment, disbelief, or amazement. Surprise can range in intensity from mild curiosity to shock or awe, and can be accompanied by physical sensations such as a rapid heartbeat, widening of the eyes, or an open mouth. Surprise can be elicited by a variety of stimuli, such as a surprise party, an unexpected gift, or a sudden change in circumstances. While surprise can be a positive and enjoyable experience, it can also be a negative or stressful one, depending on the nature of the surprise. Overall, surprise is an adaptive response that helps us to quickly process new information and adapt to changing situations.

Envy

Envy is an emotion that is characterised by a feeling of discontent or resentment towards someone who possesses something that one desires but does not have. It is a complex emotion that can include feelings of jealousy, bitterness, or covetousness. Envy can arise from a variety of situations, such as seeing someone with material possessions, social status, or personal qualities that one desires but does not have. Envy can be accompanied by physical sensations such as tension in the muscles, a feeling of tightness in the chest or stomach, or a sense of restlessness. While envy is a common human emotion, excessive or irrational envy can lead to negative outcomes such as social isolation, aggression, fear, low mood, and hopelessness.

CHAPTER 3

Distressing experiences and traumas

This section contains an A-Z of distressing and traumatic experiences and abuses that a person may have been subjected to in their lifespan. It is by no means an exhaustive list, as trauma should always be regarded personal and individual.

It may be that whilst reading this section, the professional notices that their client has been subjected to several, many or even hundreds of traumas. Some may be acute and singular, whereas others, such as childhood sexual abuse, may be made up of hundreds of traumas, alongside years of ongoing fear, distress, injury, harm, and impact.

Ableism

Ableism is a form of discrimination or prejudice against people with disabilities. It can be traumatic because it can lead to exclusion, marginalisation, and social isolation of people with disabilities. Ableism can also cause people with disabilities to internalise and accept negative stereotypes and feel a sense of shame or inadequacy. It can prevent them from accessing necessary resources and accommodation, including healthcare, education, and employment opportunities, leading to a lower quality of life. Additionally, ableism can contribute to the stigmatisation and dehumanisation of people with disabilities, leading to harmful attitudes and behaviours towards them.

Arguably then, being subjected to ableism daily is traumatic and distressing. Whether that is comments and actions, or significant physical barriers to access (lack of ramps, lack of access to rooms and buildings through doorways etc), ableism marginalises and erases people with disabilities from public life.

Abortion

Abortion is the medical or surgical process of terminating a pregnancy (also referred to as a 'termination'). In a medical abortion, the pregnant woman can take prescribed medication which will cause the death and miscarriage of the foetus. In a surgical abortion, the woman will undergo an operation which causes the death and removal of the foetus.

For some women and girls, abortion will be a confusing, distressing, frightening and traumatic experience. The trauma may be rooted in the decision (whether she was forced/pressured, was unsure, or freely made the decision), the disclosure (whether she told someone, or had to keep it a secret), the response (whether she was supported, or criticised), the process (seeking medical advice, the way she was treated by her doctor, the environment of the clinic or hospital, the advice and support she was given), and the procedure (the pain, the sensation, the bleeding, the wounds, and the recovery).

In addition to all the above, due to the cultures, religions and traditions around conception, pregnancy, birth, motherhood and gender roles, there are often other complex layers of trauma which arise from the judgement and commentary of others. Abortion is frequently polarising, and so women who make the decision to have an abortion have rarely done so in a neutral society. Women may be framed as evil, murderers, selfish, abusive, irresponsible, or disgusting for seeking an abortion. For religious women and girls, they may also have added trauma around the way their religion or beliefs conflict with their right to access abortion.

Even when an abortion is sought and successful, women may struggle with feelings of loss, grief, regret, guilt, self-hatred, fear, anger, and sadness. It is important to remember that for many women, abortion is a life-saving and vital service – and some women may not have any residual trauma from their experience.

Abortion (lack of access to, or prevention of)

Not being able to access abortion can be traumatic for a variety of reasons. It can be traumatic for women who are experiencing an unwanted or unplanned pregnancy and are unable to access the medical care they need to terminate the pregnancy safely. This can lead to feelings of powerlessness, shame, and stigma. Additionally, being denied access to abortion can result in women having to continue with an unwanted pregnancy, which can have long-lasting physical and emotional effects. It can also be traumatic for those who are seeking abortion care but face barriers such as financial, geographical, legal, or cultural barriers. The experience of navigating these barriers can result in feelings of frustration, fear, and hopelessness.

Accidents

Accidents may include falls, trips, incidents at work, in public and private spaces which cause harm or injury to the person. The accident may have caused minor injuries, right the way through to life-changing injuries and impacts on day-to-day life.

Having an accident can be traumatic for several reasons. Trauma is defined as a psychological and emotional response to an event that threatens an individual's safety or well-being, and an accident can trigger this response in several ways.

An accident can be sudden and unexpected, leaving the person feeling a sense of shock and disbelief. The suddenness of the event can make it difficult for them to process what has happened, and can leave them feeling disoriented and confused.

Of course, an accident can be physically and emotionally painful. People who have experienced an accident may suffer from physical injuries or pain, which can be distressing and overwhelming. This physical pain can also trigger emotional responses, such as fear, or panic.

Having an unexpected accident can also lead to a sense of loss of control. People who have experienced an accident may feel that they have lost control over their environment or their own bodies, which can lead to feelings of helplessness and vulnerability. For lots of people, predictability of life is an important part of feeling stable and in control. An unexpected and life-changing accident can shake the stability of the person, who may become scared of the potential of other unpredictable events.

Accidentally killing or seriously injuring someone

Accidentally killing someone can be traumatic for several reasons. For many people, this is one of the worst things they can imagine doing. Whether it was an accident at work, a car crash, or a mistake that caused someone to lose their life, the impact can be lifelong remorse, guilt, shame, shock and disbelief.

People who have accidentally killed someone may feel responsible for the person's death, even if it was not their intention. This sense of guilt and remorse can be overwhelming and can lead to feelings of shame and self-blame.

Even though a death may be genuinely accidental, the event can lead to legal consequences. people who have accidentally killed someone may face legal charges and consequences, which can add to their distress and trauma. This is particularly true for those who are convicted of manslaughter, those who are found guilty of negligence which lead to the accidental death of someone, or those who accidentally kill someone when losing control of their car.

Adoption

Adoption can be traumatic for several reasons, both for the child who is being adopted and for the birth parents who are giving up their child.

For the child who is being adopted, some reasons why adoption can be traumatic include:

Separation from birth parents: Separation from birth parents can be a deeply traumatic experience, as it can trigger feelings of loss, grief, and abandonment. Children who are adopted may experience a sense of confusion, identity issues, and a feeling of being disconnected from their biological roots.

Attachment and relationships: Children who are adopted may have difficulty forming relationships and attachments to their adoptive parents or other people, as they may have experienced traumatic separation and loss in the past.

Loss of culture and identity: Adoption may mean that children lose access to their birth culture and language and may struggle with identity issues as a result.

For the birth parents who are giving up their child, some reasons why adoption can be traumatic include:

Separation from child: Giving up a child for adoption can be a traumatic experience, as birth parents may experience feelings of loss, grief, and a sense of abandonment.

Stigma and shame: Birth parents who give up their child for adoption may experience stigma and shame from their family and society, which can lead to feelings of guilt and self-blame.

Lack of control: Giving up a child for adoption can be a traumatic experience for birth parents, as they may feel that they have lost control over their lives and their child's future.

It is important to note that not all adoptions are traumatic, and many adopted children and birth parents go on to live fulfilling lives. However, for some people, adoption can be a traumatic experience that has a significant impact on their psychological and emotional wellbeing.

Anaphylactic responses

An anaphylactic response, also known as anaphylaxis, is a severe and potentially life-threatening allergic reaction. Anaphylaxis occurs when the body's immune system overreacts to an allergen, which is a substance that the body perceives as harmful. Common allergens that can trigger anaphylaxis include foods, medications, insect stings, and latex.

During an anaphylactic response, the body releases a flood of chemicals, including histamine, that can cause a range of symptoms, such as:

- Skin reactions, such as hives, itching, and flushing.
- Swelling of the face, lips, tongue, and throat.
- Difficulty breathing, including wheezing and shortness of breath.
- Low blood pressure, which can cause fainting or dizziness.
- Rapid or weak pulse.
- Nausea, vomiting, and diarrhoea

Anaphylaxis is a medical emergency, and for some people, can be fatal. For this reason, having an allergic reaction can be especially traumatic for people. Some people will try hard to avoid all allergens, so when they have a reaction, it is often sudden and unexpected. The suddenness of the event can make it difficult for people to process what has happened, and can leave them feeling disoriented and confused.

Anaphylaxis can include physical pain, and painful urgent injections. For some people, anaphylaxis may include terrifying symptoms such as difficulty breathing, swelling, and low blood pressure.

Suffering from unexpected anaphylactic reactions can lead to a deep sense of loss of control and stability. For some people, they may feel frightened of any subsequent reactions, and may become hypervigilant in order to protect themselves from potentially fatal reactions. This can lead to people feeling vulnerable, anxious, helpless, and low.

Assault

Assault is a type of violent crime that involves intentional physical harm or the threat of physical harm to another person. Assault can take many forms, such as hitting, kicking, choking, or using a weapon, and can occur in a variety of settings, such as in the home, on the street, or in a workplace.

Assault is often traumatic due to the shock and disbelief of being attacked and harmed by another person. Much violent assault is committed by someone known to the victim, so trauma from assault is rarely as simple as just the physical injuries and impact.

It is common for people to experience long-lasting trauma responses from assaults. It is important for professional to refrain from making value or impact judgements based on the 'seriousness' of the assault or of the injuries. Assaults will have unique impacts on each person, and the severity of the injuries are not necessarily aligned with how much psychological trauma the person will experience.

Asthma attacks

Having asthma attacks can be traumatic for many people. Asthma is a chronic condition that affects the airways in the lungs, making it difficult to breathe. During an asthma attack, the airways become inflamed and narrow, which can cause shortness of breath, wheezing, chest tightness, and coughing.

The physical symptoms of asthma attacks can be severe and can make it difficult to carry out daily activities. The sudden onset of an asthma attack can be frightening, and people may feel a sense of panic and fear as they struggle to breathe. The physical symptoms can also be painful and uncomfortable, leading to feelings of helplessness and distress.

Second, asthma attacks can impact a person's emotional wellbeing. The fear of having an asthma attack can cause daily distress, leading to feelings of uncertainty and worry about the future. This can also lead to social isolation, as people may avoid activities that could trigger an asthma attack, such as exercise or outdoor activities.

Asthma attacks can have a significant impact on a person's quality of life. Asthma attacks can lead to missed school or work, decreased productivity, not being able to participate in activities and opportunities, not being able to travel safely, and financial burdens from time off work, medical procedures, or medications.

Attacked by an animal

Being attacked by an animal can be sudden and unexpected, leaving people injured, and in shock. If the animal was wild or not known to the person, there is the trauma of unpredictability and random harm to process. However, if the animal is a beloved pet, or an animal well known to the person, there may be an additional layer of shock and trauma due to having an emotional connection to the animal that has attacked them.

If the injuries are serious, most people understand that animals will be destroyed on the basis that they are dangerous, and so this complicates the trauma (especially if the animal was a pet).

Being attacked by an animal can cause ongoing psychological distress. People who are attacked by an animal may experience ongoing fears and phobias related to the event, such as a fear of animals, a fear of going outside, or a fear of certain locations.

Attending scene of a violent death or crime

For professionals and the public, attending the scene of a crime can expose people to a range of disturbing and distressing smells, sensations, sights, and sounds. This can include witnessing violent acts, seeing blood or injuries, or hearing screams or cries for help. These sights and sounds can be traumatic, overwhelming and can trigger feelings of fear, helplessness, or disgust.

If attending crime scenes is part of an occupation, it may be a common and repetitive trauma to be exposed to serious violence and injury on a daily basis. This includes the personal danger and risk the professional is at, when attending these scenes.

Attending the scene of a crime can be emotionally draining. People who attend the scene of a crime may feel that they are responsible for managing the situation or helping others, which can be a heavy burden. This emotional drain can lead to feelings of exhaustion, burnout, or compassion fatigue.

Arrested

Being arrested is often traumatic, especially for those who have never been arrested before. If the person knows why they are being arrested and knows they have committed crime, the immediate distress may be connected to a fear of consequence, outcomes, and the process of being prosecuted.

However, if the person knows they have not committed a crime, or is completely unaware of what crime they are being arrested for, or know they are being wrongfully arrested, the trauma is likely to be connected to feelings of fear, injustice, lack of control, helplessness, hopelessness and fear of consequence. Being arrested causes a sudden and unexpected loss of control over the person's life. They may be raided or have their house searched, have their possessions seized, be physical restrained, be publicly arrested, remanded in custody, and kept in a custody suite for hours or days.

Further, the person may be interrogated, strip-searched, subjected to police brutality, or arrested and detained abroad in a country where they do not speak the native language.

Baby from rape (having a)

Having a baby from rape can be traumatic for many reasons. For someone who has been raped, the pregnancy can serve as a constant reminder of the trauma they were subjected to by the rapist or abuser. It can bring up feelings of shame, guilt, regret, self-blame, and anger, and can cause significant psychological distress.

In addition, the pregnancy can create a range of practical and logistical challenges. The woman or girl may struggle with decisions about whether to terminate the pregnancy, and the socio-cultural issues surrounding abortion. She may also feel obliged to keep the baby, as she may be told that it is not the child's fault that they were conceived in rape. The woman may also experience significant distress about how to financially support the child or may worry about how to explain the child's origins to others.

Finally, there is the possibility of ongoing contact with the perpetrator of the rape if they choose to assert parental rights or seek access to, or custody of the child. This can be extremely traumatic and can cause ongoing distress and feelings of vulnerability that last the entire childhood period (a minimum of 18 years).

Bereavement

Bereavement is a life changing and traumatic because it involves a significant loss, and can trigger a range of complex emotions, such as grief, sadness, guilt, anger, regret, and injustice. When a person experiences the death of a loved one, they may feel like they have lost an important part of their life and may struggle to adjust to a new reality without that person.

Bereavement can also be accompanied by physical symptoms such as fatigue, insomnia, or loss of appetite. The experience of bereavement can be particularly traumatic if the death was sudden or unexpected, if the person was young or had a significant impact on the person's life, or if the person had a close and supportive relationship with the deceased. The grieving process can be long and difficult, and can involve a range of emotions that can be difficult to process.

It is important to consider that bereavement can be a complex experience for people who have become estranged from the deceased, were abused by the deceased, or had unfinished business with the deceased.

Most people describe grief as something that stays with them for the rest of their lives, and this should be considered normal.

Blackmail

Being blackmailed is often a traumatic experience because it can trigger feelings of fear, self-doubt, threat, shame, and helplessness. Blackmail involves being threatened with the exposure of embarrassing, private or damaging information, often in exchange for money or other favours. Blackmail is therefore always based on a power dynamic. This can lead to a loss of control in life, relationships, finances, or circumstances, as the blackmailer may hold significant power over the person being blackmailed.

The fear of the consequences of the information being exposed, such as loss of reputation, relationships, or employment, can be highly distressing and can trigger feelings of fear, hopelessness, helplessness, worry, uncertainty, injustice, confusion, anger and isolation. Blackmail can also be associated with feelings of shame or guilt, as the person may feel like they have done something wrong or inappropriate, that is being used against them.

If a person has a history of trauma or abuse, being blackmailed can be particularly triggering, as it often mirrors abusive power dynamics and threat.

Blamed for someone's suicide

Being blamed for the suicide of a third party can lead to lifelong feelings of guilt, shame, and self-blame. This can happen in several circumstances including when abusers, sex offenders and perpetrators kill themselves when awaiting trial or during police investigation. This may also happen when someone is perceived as 'not doing enough' to prevent the suicide of another person, especially where the person sought help, or told people they were suicidal prior to their death.

People who are blamed for someone else's suicide may feel that they are responsible for the person's death, even if they did not cause or contribute to it. These feelings of guilt and self-blame can be overwhelming and can lead to ongoing psychological distress and trauma responses.

People who are blamed for someone else's suicide may be ostracised or isolated by others, leading to a loss of family, friends, and social support.

Boarding schools

Boarding schools can be a traumatic experience for some people because they involve a significant separation from family and home environment, which can trigger feelings of loss, homesickness, and loneliness.

The boarding school environment can be highly structured and regimented, which can lead to feelings of powerlessness or a loss of autonomy.
The experience of being away from home and family for an extended period of time can also lead to feelings of disconnection, and can make it difficult for a person to form close relationships or develop a sense of belonging.

If a person is also subjected to bullying, sexual abuse or mistreatment while at boarding school, this will exacerbate feelings of isolation, distress, and trauma.

Boarding school trauma can be particularly pronounced for those who have been subjected to previous trauma or abuse. Overall, the experience of boarding school can be challenging and can have a lasting impact on a person's psychological and physical well-being.

Body shaming

Body shaming refers to the act of criticising, mocking, or ridiculing someone's physical appearance, often based on harmful societal beauty standards or expectations. Body shaming can take many forms, such as negative comments about a person's weight, shape, skin colour, or other physical features. Body shaming can occur in many contexts, including social media, workplace, schools, and personal relationships.

Body shaming can have long-lasting negative effects on a person's self-esteem, body image, and psychological wellbeing. It can lead to feelings of shame, guilt, and inadequacy. Body shaming can also lead to social isolation, withdrawal, self-harm, self-loathing, a desire for cosmetic surgery, and can contribute to the perpetuation of societal beauty standards and stereotypes.

Bullying

Being bullied is generally associated with childhood. It is important to remember that bullying behaviours and experiences continue into adulthood, and are not confined to childhood. Further, it is worth considering the similarities between bullying and abuse, and why there is a different name for a set of behaviours that are clearly abusive. Bullying is rarely defined as abuse, which can minimise and trivialise the experience for both children and adults.

Bullying involves repeated and intentional acts of violence, aggression, abuse, intimidation, harassment, targeting, or mistreatment, often directed towards a person who is perceived as weaker or vulnerable. This can lead to a sense of isolation, as the person being bullied may feel like they are alone or unable to defend themselves.

Bullying can also be associated with feelings of shame, self-blame or humiliation, as the person may feel like they are being targeted for being different or for something they cannot change.

Burglary

Being a victim of burglary is a traumatic violation of privacy, safety, security, and stability. It is likely to cause long-term feelings of fear, worry, vulnerability, and hyper-vigilance.

For many people, home is their safe-space. To learn that someone has broken in and been through their things to steal valuables is highly traumatic. This is only worsened if the person and/or their family was in the house at the time of the burglary.

Financially, there is a significant impact to burglary, especially if the person loses valuables that are not insured or cannot be replaced.

Capitalism

There are various perspectives on why capitalism can be traumatic for some people. One perspective is that the capitalist economic system leads to inequality, exploitation, and social division, which can cause distress, trauma, and a sense of injustice for those who are disadvantaged or marginalised. The central focus on profit and competition can also lead to a culture of individualism and self-interest, which can erode social bonds and create a sense of isolation or disconnection. In addition, the pressures and demands of the capitalist system can lead to overwork, burnout, desensitisation, commodification, and other forms of distress that can negatively impact a person's wellbeing.

From a trauma-informed perspective, capitalism can be traumatic for those who have been subjected to previous trauma or abuse, as it can reinforce feelings of powerlessness, helplessness, and victimisation.

The emphasis on competition and individualism can create a culture of blame and shame, which can exacerbate feelings of self-doubt and inadequacy. The economic insecurities and uncertainties of the capitalist system can also trigger feelings of fear, particularly for those who have experienced poverty, inequality, discrimination, or instability in the past.

Catcalling

Being catcalled can be a traumatic experience because it can trigger feelings of fear and objectification. Catcalling involves unsolicited and often sexually explicit comments or gestures directed towards a person, usually in public or on the street. Even though catcalling can happen to anyone, it happens much more to women and girls. YouGov (2021) found that 97% of women had been catcalled.

Catcalling is a form of harassment that can create a sense of vulnerability, commodification, dehumanisation, and powerlessness. The experience of being catcalled is often associated with feelings of objectification, as the woman or girl may feel like they are being reduced to their appearance or sexual desirability, rather than being seen as a whole person. In this sense, catcalling sexualises, dehumanises and dementalises the person.

Catcalling can also be accompanied by physical gestures or actions, such as stalking, harassment and sexual assault, which can cause significant trauma and distress. Unfortunately, due to the social acceptability and commonality of catcalling, many women and girls are not taken seriously when they disclose or report being targeted. For similar reasons, men and boys responsible for this behaviour are rarely apprehended or brought to justice, which causes feelings of injustice.

Catfished

Being catfished can be a traumatic experience because it involves being deceived and manipulated by someone who has created a false identity online.

This can lead to feelings of shock, betrayal, anger, and confusion, particularly if the person has invested time and emotional energy into the relationship or communication. The experience of being catfished can also be associated with feelings of humiliation or shame, as the person may feel like they have been tricked or made to look foolish.
In some cases, the person may also be exposed to further forms of manipulation or exploitation, such as financial scams or blackmail.

Child sexual abuse and exploitation

Child sexual abuse is common, and highly traumatic because it involves sexual activity with a child, which is a violation of their rights, their body, the law, and the child's physical and emotional boundaries. A child under 16 years old cannot consent to sexual activity. Sexual abuse can cause a wide range short and long-term trauma responses and coping mechanisms.
Being subjected to child sexual abuse can lead to feelings of disgust, self-loathing, shame, guilt, and self-blame, as the child may feel (or be made to feel) responsible or complicit in the abuse. The abuse can also create feelings of fear, and mistrust, particularly if the abuser was someone in a position of trust or authority over the child.

Child sexual abuse can often be associated with long-term physical pain, injuries, sexual harm, psychological trauma, and ongoing health problems.

Children's homes (group homes)

Being in a children's home can be a particularly traumatic experience because it involves being separated from family, friends, and familiar surroundings, which can be unsettling and distressing for children.
Children in care may have experienced previous traumas, such as injuries, illnesses, bereavement, and loss, or may have been subjected to abuse, neglect, exploitation, trafficking, and other harms. Whilst removing a child from their family may be vital to protecting them from further harm, it is often distressing, disruptive and traumatic to be taken to live in a care service.

Children's homes can also be associated with feelings of stigma, shame, and isolation, particularly if the child feels like they are different or 'not normal' compared to other children who live with their birth families. Children in care may experience feelings of powerlessness, helplessness, or a lack of control over their lives, as they may not have input into decisions about their care, support, protection plans, locations, access to technology, or placements.

The quality of care in children's homes can vary widely, and some children may be subjected to further neglect, abuse, or exploitation whilst in the care of statutory or private care services. This can further compound feelings of trauma and distress, particularly if the child is not protected from abusive professionals and services (or is framed as lying, attention seeking, or making malicious complaints).

Overall, being in a children's home can be a highly distressing and traumatic experience for children, particularly as they are very likely to have experienced previous traumas, or been subjected to other forms of abuse or harm before. policies and procedures in place to protect children from harm and to promote their well-being.

Civil unrest

Civil unrest should be categorised as traumatic because it involves a breakdown of social order, often resulting in violence, destruction, collapse, distress, and instability in communities. This can create fear, powerlessness, aggression, and uncertainty for people and communities who are affected by the unrest.

Civil unrest can also be associated with a range of related traumas, such as loss of life or injury, damage to property, disruption of services and businesses, lack of access to money and resources, and displacement of people from their homes. These events can lead to significant feelings of trauma, grief, and loss, particularly for those who have been directly affected by the unrest.

Civil unrest can also create a sense of powerlessness or lack of control over a person's life, particularly if people are unable to protect themselves or their families from harm. The experience of being caught up in civil unrest can also be associated with feelings of anger, frustration, and helplessness, particularly if the unrest is related to issues of social injustice or inequality.

Overall, civil unrest can be a highly traumatic experience for people and whole communities, particularly if it is prolonged or has a lasting impact on day-to-day lives.

Classism

Classism is specific to areas in the world where the class system is established and powerful. For example, the UK still has an influential and obvious class system, whereas other countries do not have an equivalent form of discrimination based on social class. Classism can be particularly traumatic because it involves discrimination and prejudice based on social class (which arguably, is inescapable as the person is born into their social class), which can result in feelings of embarrassment, blame, shame, humiliation, and exclusion for people who are marginalised or oppressed. Usually, classism presents as a hatred, stereotyping, and mistreatment of people from 'lower' social classes such as the 'working class' population and the so-called 'underclass' population.

Common comments and assumptions about those from lower social classes include that they are lazy, do not want to work, contribute nothing to society, 'scrounge' off the state, are stupid, unhealthy, uncivilised, and uncultured.

Classism can severely limit opportunities for education, employment, healthcare, and housing, which can lead to feelings of powerlessness, helplessness, despair, and a lack of control. People who are subjected to classism may also internalise negative beliefs about their own worth or value in the world, leading to feelings of low self-esteem, self-blame, self-loathing, and self-doubt. This can also contribute to a sense of isolation and a lack of social connection, as people may feel like they do not belong anywhere, or are not accepted by others.

This is particularly difficult for those who were born into lower social classes who find themselves in environments or areas of higher social classes, as they are likely to be openly mocked, discriminated against, put down, underestimated, and undervalued.

An example of this might be a young adult from a poor, working-class area who gets into a top university based on their exemplary grades, but then is bullied for their accent, background, upbringing, hometown, dialect, and lack of resources. Another example of this might be an adult who becomes wealthy through self-employment or setting up a successful business, who is never accepted into circles of people who were born into wealth, or have established social positions, as they are seen as 'less than' or of 'new money' and 'trashy'.

Classism is likely to be felt as distressing, traumatic, abusive, harmful, rejection, humiliation, and embarrassing. This can be particularly true for people who are subjected to ongoing or chronic discrimination based on their social class.

Coercive control

Coercive control is a form of abuse. It is traumatic and distressing because it involves a pattern of abusive behaviours that are designed to control or manipulate another person, which can result in significant psychological harm, feelings of fear, helplessness, and isolation.
Coercive control often involves emotional, psychological, or financial abuse, and may frequently include physical or sexual violence.

People who are subjected to coercive control may feel like they are constantly walking on eggshells or living in a state of fear, as they may be afraid of the consequences of not complying with the abuser's demands. Coercive control can also create a sense of isolation and a lack of social connection, as the abuser may try to cut off the person from friends, family, or support networks.

This can make it difficult for people to seek help or support, and can contribute to a sense of hopelessness or despair.

It is important to consider that some abusers will also infiltrate a support network instead of isolating the person from their support network. This way, they can control the whole family, and friend network, so if the person ever discloses the coercive control, others have been groomed, too.

Overall, coercive control can be a deeply traumatic experience for people who are subjected to it.

Conversion therapy

Conversion therapy is a harmful and abusive practice that aims to change a person's sexual orientation or gender identity, which can be traumatic because it involves invalidating a person's sense of self and identity, and can result in significant psychological harm. Conversion therapy is based on the false assumption that being lesbian, gay, bisexual, transgender or non-binary is a mental disorder, a crime, or a sin, that can be cured or changed. Conversion therapy can involve a range of harmful practices, such as electroshock therapy, aversion therapy, and talk therapy that aims to shame or guilt people into changing their sexual orientation or gender identity. These practices often work by trying to create a negative association between the sexuality or identity, and the outcomes/consequences/feelings. Due to this highly abusive practice, it is common for people to suffer significant psychological harm.

People who are subjected to conversion therapy may also experience a sense of betrayal, particularly if they are forced into it by family members, religious institutions, or medical professionals. This can lead to feelings of anger, resentment, humiliation, shame, and a sense of loss of trust in those around them.

Criminal damage

Criminal damage can be traumatic because it involves the destruction or damage of property, which can create a sense of violation, loss, and vulnerability for people who are affected by it. Criminal damage can also be associated with a range of negative consequences, such as financial loss, disruption of services, and a loss of a sense of safety and security.

People who are directly affected by criminal damage may experience a range of emotions, such as fear, anger, frustration, and a sense of powerlessness. They may also experience feelings of trauma, particularly if they are threatened, or physically harmed during the incident.

Criminal damage can also create a sense of community-wide trauma, particularly if it is part of a larger pattern of criminal activity or social unrest in the area. This can lead to feelings of worry, fear, and a loss of trust in policing, institutions and community organisations.

Cults (being abused or harmed in/by)

Being abused is a profoundly traumatic experience. In addition, cults often use coercive and manipulative tactics to control their members, which can leave people feeling trapped and helpless. Cult members may be subjected to physical, emotional, or sexual abuse, or may be forced to engage in harmful, criminal, abusive or dangerous activities. This abuse can be very traumatic and can lead to long-lasting physical and psychological effects.

Due to the collective and powerful nature of cults, they can cause a loss of identity and a sense of isolation. People who are abused in a cult may be separated from their families and friends, and may be subjected to a strict set of rules and beliefs that can contradict or compromise their own values and beliefs. This loss of identity and isolation can lead to feelings of confusion, loneliness, and a loss of authenticity.

Cult leaders may use techniques such as brainwashing, gaslighting, threats, rewards, promises, or other psychological manipulation to control their members.

Much like leaving abuse, leaving a cult can be difficult, dangerous, and traumatic. People who have been abused in a cult may face barriers to leaving, such as fear of reprisal, financial dependency, or a lack of support from family and friends. Sometimes, people who leave cults find themselves totally isolated and outcast.

It is also worth considering the way they might need to re-evaluate and reprocess their understanding of the world, religions, politics, sexuality, and many other personal and social issues once they have left the cult. This can be both liberating and terrifying.

Cyber stalking

Cyber stalking is a form of online harassment that involves repeatedly contacting or harassing someone through electronic communication, such as email, social media, or messaging apps.

Cyber stalking can be traumatic for several reasons:

Intrusion and invasion of privacy: Cyber stalking involves a persistent and unwanted intrusion into a person's personal life, which can leave them feeling targeted, violated, frightened, and vulnerable.

Fear and intimidation: Cyber stalkers often use threats, intimidation, blackmail, and harassment to control and manipulate people, which can lead to feelings of fear, helplessness, hopelessness, and anger.

Loss of control: People who have been subjected to cyber stalking may feel like they have lost control over their own lives, as the stalker may be able to monitor their online activity, track their movements, or interfere with their occupations, activities, opportunities, businesses, and personal relationships.

Isolation and shame: People who have been subjected to cyber stalking may begin to feel isolated and ashamed, as they may be reluctant to share their experiences with others due to fear of judgement or stigma. Further, the stalker may deliberately threaten or spread rumours to family and friends, to ensure they have no support.

Death of your child

The death of a child can be an incredibly traumatic experience for parents and families, as it involves the loss of a loved one and a significant disruption to the family unit. The death of a child can be sudden and unexpected, which can make it even more difficult to process and cope with. It is common for people to struggle with the trauma of losing their child for many years. Some people will report that the trauma of losing their child stayed with them for their entire life.

For many parents who lose their child, there is a sense of injustice, and of shock. Most parents never envisage losing their child, and expect to die before their children. It is particularly traumatic for parents who nurse their children through terminal illness, or through an experience which causes them to die, as children may ask questions about their death, or their recovery. Depending on the age of the child, the parent may be coping with the loss of an infant, who they would not have been able to communicate with, or the loss of a teenager, who was likely to have an understanding of death, fear, finality, loss, and trauma.

Parents and family members who experience the death of a child may experience a range of intense and overwhelming emotions, such as grief, anger, sadness, guilt, and a sense of helplessness. The loss of a child can also lead to a sense of disorientation and a loss of purpose or meaning in life, as parents may struggle to come to terms with the fact that their child is no longer with them.

The death of a child can also be traumatic because it may involve feelings of guilt, particularly if parents feel like they could have done something differently to prevent the death. This can contribute to feelings of self-blame and a sense of responsibility for the loss, which can be difficult to overcome.

Death or illness of pets

The death of a pet can be a traumatic experience for people and families, as pets often play an important role in people's lives and can provide a profound sense of companionship, comfort, and joy. Pets often become a part of the family, and their death can create a sense of emptiness and a disruption to the daily routine.

Some people struggle with the loss of their pet, as they cannot communicate with them. For example, some people are asked to make a choice as to whether to euthanise their pet if they become old, unwell, or terminally ill. It is often a very difficult experience for people to sit with their pet whilst they are euthanised, and it can cause lifelong feelings of guilt and shame.

When pets die in accidents or of natural causes, people can feel deeply traumatised by finding their dead pet, and not being able to be there with them in their final moments.
People who experience the death of a pet may experience a range of intense and overwhelming emotions, such as grief, sadness, guilt, and a sense of loss.

The death of a pet can also be traumatic because it may involve feelings of guilt or regret, particularly if people feel like they could have done something differently to prevent the death, spot an illness sooner, or protected their pet better. This can contribute to feelings of self-blame, shame, and a sense of responsibility for the loss, which can be difficult to overcome.

Death threat

Receiving a death threat can be a traumatic experience because it involves the threat of fatal violence and harm, in order to deliberately frighten, control, or harm the person and their families. Death threats can be particularly traumatic if they are unexpected, repeated, or if the person making the threat is known to the person.

Death threats are a common experience, as they tend to be frequent in cases of stalking, harassment, domestic abuse, trafficking, exploitation, and other interpersonal crimes. They are also an unfortunately common experience for people in the public eye, such as politicians, celebrities, influencers, and business people.

People who receive death threats may experience a range of intense and overwhelming emotions, such as fear, anger, helplessness, hopelessness, and a sudden sense of vulnerability. It is common for people to experience an acute shock response, have a panic attack, and become extremely frightened for their life and their safety.

Death threats can also create a sense of social isolation, particularly if the individual is afraid to share their experience with others or feels like they are not being taken seriously. This can contribute to feelings of shame, guilt, and a sense of powerlessness.

It is important for professionals to consider that death threats should always be taken seriously, despite their own beliefs as to whether they will be followed through or not. It is highly traumatic for someone to receive an intention to kill, and a threat to be killed, by someone who wants to either frighten them, threaten them into doing something, or will eventually follow through on their threat.

Debt

Being in debt is a traumatic experience for many people, as it can create life-changing financial insecurity, shame, and a loss of control. Debt creates a precarious and unpredictable experience to live in, which may result in losing accommodation, possessions, safety, security, items of personal and sentimental value.

People who are in debt can also find themselves in difficult financial circumstances through no fault of their own, and through other traumas. Debt can accrue when people escape abuse, leave a relationship, are made redundant, become very unwell, have an accident, become a victim of fraud and scams, do not get paid on time, work zero hours contracts and so on.

Despite this, there is significant social shame and stigma attached to financial debts, and many systems rely on people having clear credit ratings and no debt in order to access financial support such as credit cards, loans, mortgages, insurances and store accounts.

People who are in debt may experience a range of intense and overwhelming emotions, such as fear, shame, guilt, and a sense of hopelessness.

Being in debt can also create a sense of social isolation and stigma, particularly if people feel they are unable to meet their financial obligations or if they are judged by others for being in debt. This can contribute to feelings of shame and a sense of worthlessness, which can be difficult to overcome.

Deceit

Deceit can be a traumatic experience for people because it involves the betrayal of trust and can create a sense of emotional harm, loss, and a violation of personal boundaries. It is common for people to feel a sense of shock when they realise that they have been lied to, especially if they have been lied to by a loved one.

People who have experienced deceit from others may experience a range of intense and overwhelming emotions, such as anger, sadness, disappointment, confusion, and a sense of betrayal.

Deceit can also create a sense of social isolation and mistrust, particularly if people feel like they are unable to trust others or if they are judged by others for their experience. Sometimes, when a person has been lied to or successfully deceived, they can be judged for not 'spotting the signs' or being 'stupid' or 'naïve'. This can in turn, result in significant self-blame and shame, especially if the person feels they believed the lies and deceit for a very long time, or had ignored warnings from others because they trusted the person who was deceiving them. This can contribute to feelings of shame, self-loathing, regret, anger, injustice, and a sense of worthlessness.

Deported

Being deported can lead to a loss of personal identity and a sense of belonging. People who are deported may feel traumatised by being forced to leave behind their family, friends, culture, language, and social connections, leading to feelings of isolation and loneliness.

Being deported can lead to a loss of control over the person's life and circumstances. People who are deported may feel that their future is suddenly very uncertain, and may struggle to make any plans or set any goals for themselves. This loss of control can lead to feelings of injustice, hopelessness, helplessness, and despair.

It is worth remembering that along with the significant psychological impact of being deported, there are practical, legal and financial complications that can add to the trauma and distress.

Diagnostic tests

Going for medical tests and diagnostic tests can be a traumatic experience for people , as it can create a sense of fear and uncertainty about health and well-being. When attending for diagnostic tests, the root fear is whether the tests will reveal something that will be fatal, or life-changing.

It is important to remember that the diagnostic tests (along with being psychologically traumatic) can be physically painful, invasive, embarrassing, and frightening. If the health issue is also connected to social issues and stigma (HIV, STDs, cervical cancer, liver damage), there can be added trauma and distress arising from fear of judgement and blaming.

Some diagnostic processes can be difficult, and can take long periods of time (weeks, months, years), in which period, the person may have no closure and no further information about whether they have a serious health problem or not. This can cause further distress, worry, uncertainty, and exhaustion.

Disabled (being/from birth)

Having chronic disabilities can lead to a loss of physical ability and independence. People who have chronic disabilities may struggle with everyday tasks such as dressing, bathing, or feeding themselves, which can be psychologically distressing.
Some chronic disabilities can lead to ongoing pain, medical complications, distressing symptoms, and discomfort, which may cause the person to feel frightened, low, angry, sad, and exhausted.

Social isolation and discrimination can also be an issue for people with disabilities. Whilst some people may have supportive networks and families, others may be frequently isolated, excluded, ignored and marginalised.

It is also important to consider the financial implications of being disabled, as having chronic disabilities can lead to distressing and frustrating financial difficulties. People with chronic disabilities may face ongoing medical complications and needs, which can be expensive, invasive, traumatic and stressful.

Disabled (becoming)

Becoming disabled can be a sudden and unexpected life-changing event. Shock, anger, disbelief, and confusion are all common and normal.

Becoming disabled can lead to a sudden loss of independence and a sense of identity. People who become disabled may experience a sense of loss, grief, and a feeling of being disconnected from their former life. They may also experience a loss of income and financial stability, which can lead to additional distress and ongoing worry and fear.
The disability or injury itself can cause physical pain and discomfort, which can be both physically and psychologically difficult to cope with.

For professionals, it is also worth considering how much a person's social life and social circles may change when they become disabled. Whilst some people will be supported and included by friends, family communities, others may be marginalised, ignored, isolated or excluded from their existing social lives, social circles and communities.

Discrimination

Discrimination can be a traumatic experience for people because it involves the unfair, harmful, and unequal treatment of people based on their personal characteristics, such as their race, age, sex, gender identity, sexual orientation, religion, or disability. Discrimination can create a deep sense of emotional harm, loss, distress, anger, injustice, a violation of human rights and personal boundaries.

Discrimination can also create a sense of social isolation and mistrust, particularly if people are made to feel like they are unable to trust others, or if they are judged by others for their personal characteristics. This can contribute to feelings of self-blame, shame, fear, danger, self-loathing, humiliation, exhaustion and marginalisation.

It is important for professionals to understand that discrimination exists on a spectrum, and what may look like harmless comments or misunderstandings can often be embedded, institutional and powerful aggressions and biases which lead to the person being relentlessly targeted and mistreated, attacked, harmed, or even killed.
Due to discrimination being so common for some marginalised groups, it is likely that being subjected to racism, for example, would become a daily, consistent, unending trauma that the person is not being protected from by employers, communities, governments or societies. It is unlikely that most people subjected to discrimination will experience justice or compensation for being denied opportunities, accommodation, resources, safety, rights, and protection.

It is also important to consider that professionals who are not commonly discriminated against (such as white, middle class, healthy, able, English speaking, heterosexual men) may discount or ignore the traumas of marginalised and oppressed groups due to not being able to understanding, relate, or validate their experiences. Similarly, it is important to recognise when systems, companies, organisations, governments and services work in ways that systemically discriminate against marginalised groups.

Displacement

Displacement can be a traumatic experience for people because it involves being forced to leave the home, community, or country due to conflict, persecution, or other reasons beyond their control.

People who have experienced displacement may experience a range of intense and overwhelming emotions, such as fear, uncertainty, anger, confusion, marginalisation, betrayal, resentment, terror, sadness, hopelessness, helplessness, and a deep sense of loss.

Displacement can also create a sense of social isolation and mistrust, particularly if people are made to feel like they are unable to trust others or if they are judged by others for their status as a displaced person. This can contribute to additional feelings of shame and a sense of worthlessness.

Divorce

Divorce can be a traumatic experience for people because it involves the dissolution of a significant relationship or partnership that was once thought to be a lifelong commitment. For many people, divorce is not something they ever thought they would face, and so it often feels like loss, bereavement, or the end of something significant.

For some people though, divorce feels liberatory, exciting, validating, relieving, and freeing. Despite these feelings, there are often still complicated and drawn-out processes that can last months or years. This is particularly true if the divorce proceedings include financial agreements, the selling of the marital home, child custody and splits in finances. These processes can be traumatic on their own (moving house, for example) but they can be more complicated and distressing when caused by the breakdown of a marriage.

It is important to consider two further issues; the reason for the divorce and who brought proceedings against the other, and the cultural and religious implications of divorce. Both of these additional issues may cause significant trauma for one of both parties, and can mean that people become socially isolated, outcast, punished, stigmatised and harmed for wanting to, or being forced to divorce (to be the party forced to stay in a marriage due to religious or cultural expectations and beliefs that divorce is unlawful or sinful).

Domestic abuse

Domestic abuse is a traumatic experience for people because it involves the consistent and harmful use of power and control by one person over another within an intimate or family relationship. Domestic abuse often includes emotional, psychological, sexual, financial, economic, and physical abuse. For those who have been subjected to domestic abuse for many years, this experience could include hundreds of independent traumas (such as verbal abuse, assaults, rapes, sexual assaults, threats, manipulation etc.)

People subjected to domestic abuse often experience profound trauma responses and coping mechanisms, and may feel shamed, angry, hopelessness, helplessness, saddened, confused, frightened, violated, controlled, manipulated, belittled, humiliated, blamed, minimised, and gaslit.

Due to social responses to domestic abuse, there are additional traumas for most people who disclose or have been subjected to domestic abuse such as judgment from others, disbelief from others, victim blaming, mocking, shaming, pathologisation and isolation from family and friendship circles.

Doxing

Doxing is the slang term for publishing other people's private information online. Normally it is done with malicious intent. Typically, the information obtained by a 'doxer' will be anything from name, address, phone numbers, photographs, email addresses, social networking accounts, passwords, and credit details. However, some doxers will steal and obtain as much information about the person's personal life as they can. This can include information on children, family, friends, employers, and associates.

There are several reasons for doxing. Mainly it is to punish, publicly shame, harass, take revenge, or coerce a person into doing something they don't want to. Doxing can also take place for criminal purposes such as extortion. Doxing has become a way of publicly shaming high-profile figures and celebrities. The results can lead to vigilantism, with the victim being subject to both online and offline harassment. Examples of doxing include being publicly falsely accused of wrongdoing, accused of being a member of a hate group, or of having extremist ideologies.

Often, doxing will include publishing or sharing contact details of employers, colleagues, friends, family, children, partners, exes, and associates in order to intimidate or blackmail the victim.

For some people, being doxed may cause embarrassment, whereas in others it may have a significant effect on their emotional wellbeing, employment, lifestyle, relationships, and personal safety. Being publicly shamed can lead to job loss, potential issues when seeking future employment, or having to move home. Doxing is a form of harassment, stalking and cyberbullying, and so it is likely to cause significant distress and trauma responses.

Drowning

Drowning can be a traumatic experience for people because it is a life-threatening situation that involves a sudden loss of control and the fear of imminent death. It is common for people who have almost drowned, or have drowned and then been revived or rescued, to have significant trauma responses and reactions to their experience.
People who have experienced drowning may have a range of intense and long-lasting emotions, such as fear, panic, and a sense of helplessness. They may question why and how they survived, or they may have been traumatised by the

circumstances of the drowning (especially if it was caused deliberately, or there were other circumstances surrounding how and why they were in difficulty in water).

It is common for people to become very frightened and avoidant of water, swimming, or even bathing. For some people, they may also have lifelong injuries from the drowning, such as brain damage, or damage to their lungs.

Economic abuse

Economic abuse can be a traumatic experience for people because it involves the use of financial control and manipulation by one person over another, typically within an intimate or family relationship. Economic abuse can create a sense of emotional harm, loss, and a violation of rights and personal boundaries.

People who have been subjected to economic abuse may experience a range of intense and overwhelming emotions, such as fear, frustration, shame, hopelessness, worthlessness, self-blame, and a sense of helplessness.

Economic abuse can include:

Controlling finances: This involves controlling someone's access to money or resources, such as limiting their access to bank accounts, credit cards, or other financial resources. This can also involve restricting someone's ability to work or earn their own income.
Stealing or misusing money: This involves taking someone's money or resources without their permission, or using it for personal gain. This can include stealing money from a joint account, using someone's credit card without their permission, or refusing to pay bills or debts.

Coercing someone into financial decisions: This involves pressuring or forcing someone to make financial decisions that benefit the abuser, such as signing over property or assets or taking out loans.

Sabotaging someone's credit or financial stability: This involves intentionally damaging someone's credit or financial stability, such as running up debts in their name or refusing to pay bills or debts.

Withholding financial support: This involves withholding financial support from someone who is dependent on it, such as refusing to provide child support or towards joint bills or debts.

Economic abuse often leaves people in debt, or without access to any financial resources. They may have their salaries or benefit payments controlled or stolen, and they may have no access to bank accounts, savings, debit cards, or credit.

Economic abuse can also create a sense of social isolation and mistrust, particularly if people feel like they are unable to trust others or if they are judged by others for their financial status or dependency.

Emotional abuse

Emotional abuse can be a traumatic experience for people because it involves the use of power and control by one person over another, typically within an intimate or family relationship. Emotional abuse can cause significant emotional harm, loss, fear, shame, and a sense of isolation.

Emotional abuse includes:

Verbal abuse: This involves the use of hurtful or degrading words to belittle, humiliate, or control someone. Examples include name-calling, insults, threats, and yelling.

Gaslighting: This involves manipulating someone to question their own thoughts, feelings, and perceptions. For example, someone might tell their partner that they're crazy or mentally ill for thinking a certain way, or deny that something happened even though the other person knows it did.

Intimidation: This involves the use of threats or fear to control someone. For example, someone might threaten their partner with physical harm, or threaten to harm themselves if the other person doesn't do what they want.

Manipulation: This involves using tactics to control or influence someone's thoughts, feelings, or behaviours. For example, someone might manipulate their partner by making them feel guilty or responsible for their own behaviour.

Eviction

Eviction can be a traumatic experience for people because it involves the sudden and forced loss of a home, which can create a sense of sudden insecurity, vulnerability, and loss.

People who have experienced eviction may experience a range of intense and overwhelming emotions, such as fear, and a sense of hopelessness.

Eviction often leaves people in precarious positions including homelessness, sofa-surfing, in temporary accommodation, or living in cars, friends' houses or hostels. A lack of safe accommodation is often traumatic, and violates the basic human need for somewhere to live.

Due to the social stigma and assumptions that come along with eviction and homelessness, it is common for people to have additional traumas to cope with including being blamed, judged, ignored, marginalised, humiliated, mocked, shamed and let down by others.

Failing to resuscitate or rescue someone

Failing to resuscitate someone can be a traumatic experience for the person attempting to provide the resuscitation as well as for witnesses and family members. It can create a range of negative emotions, such as guilt, grief, and a sense of powerlessness.

For medical professionals, failing to resuscitate a patient can create feelings of professional failure, questioning of their own medical skills, and ethical concerns. They may also experience significant and repetitive post trauma responses and flashbacks.

For family members and witnesses, failing to resuscitate a loved one can create a range of intense emotions, such as shock, disbelief, and grief. They may also experience feelings of guilt, regret, and a sense of powerlessness, particularly if they were unable to help or provide support during the resuscitation.

Failure

Failure can be traumatic for people because it can trigger feelings of shame, guilt, regret, and a sense of worthlessness. When people experience failure, they may feel like they have let themselves or others down, which can create intense negative emotions.

For some people, repeated experiences of failure can create a pattern of negative thinking and self-doubt. This can be particularly true for people who have experienced trauma in their past, as they may have difficulty coping with the added distress and pressure of failure.

In addition, societal pressure to succeed can also contribute to the traumatic impact of failure, as people may feel like their failure reflects their personal worth and value. This can create a sense of shame and isolation, as people may feel like they cannot share their struggles with others without being judged or criticised.

It is important for professionals to understand the way this trauma links to capitalism and other systems which rely on the pressure to produce and succeed. Failure is a common and normal part of life, but is usually frowned upon, mocked, or denied.

False allegations

False allegations can be traumatic for people who are accused of a crime or wrongdoing that they did not commit. It can create a range of negative emotions, such as shock, disbelief, anger, and a sense of powerlessness.

People who are falsely accused may experience a range of consequences, such as damage to their reputation, loss of employment, social isolation, and legal consequences.

Some people who are falsely accused of crime or wrongdoing will be subjected to trials, investigations, processes, and tribunals which are often publicly reported. Due to this, being falsely accused can often play out in public, or even in the national and international media.

False or malicious reports or allegations can create a lasting impact on psychological wellbeing, and cause people to feel hopeless, despair, shamed, targeted, confused, exhausted, isolated, abused and bullied.

Family breakdown

Family breakdowns can be traumatic for people because they can create a sense of loss, uncertainty, and instability. When families break down, people may experience a range of negative emotions, such as grief, anger, resentment, fear, sadness and loss.

Family breakdowns can also create practical challenges for people, such as financial difficulties, changes in living arrangements, and disruptions to daily routines. This can contribute to feelings of distress and overwhelm, particularly for people who may be dealing with other challenges or responsibilities in their lives.

Favouritism

Favouritism, particularly in a family or workplace setting, can be traumatic for people who are not the favoured person. When people feel that they are not receiving the same level of attention, care, love, validation, or resources as others, it can create a range of negative emotions, such as jealousy, anger, isolation, humiliation, and sadness.

Favouritism can also create a sense of powerlessness, as people may feel like they are unable to change the situation or receive the recognition and support that they need. This can contribute to feelings of low self-esteem, social isolation, and a sense of injustice.

Fear of dying

The fear of dying, first and foremost, is natural, normal and a part of life. All animals and humans are afraid of death, it is what motivates them to stay safe, avoid illness, and live as long as possible.

The fear of dying can be traumatic for people because it represents a fundamental threat to their sense of safety and security. Death is an unknown and unpredictable event, and the fear of dying can create a sense of powerlessness, vulnerability, and terror.

The fear of dying can also be associated with a range of negative emotions, such as sadness, anger, and despair. People may worry that they have not had the chance to fully experience life or achieve their goals, and they may worry about the impact that their death will have on their loved ones.

Death is inevitable, but we know very little about what it feels like to die. People develop beliefs and theories about afterlife, spirits, angels, judgement, heavens, hells, and other symbolic experiences to understand and process the enormity of death as final.

Additionally, it is worth remembering that death is a common and normal fear, especially in children. Children will often go through several stages of realising that people die, what death means, that their own loved ones will die, and then that they too will die. This is normal, but children can sometimes become very frightened around times of psychological development and realisation of death and dying.

This does not mean that adults are comfortable with dying, or do not fear death, but they tend to develop their own coping mechanisms for it as they grow, which range from totally ignoring the inevitability of death ('no point worrying about it, I'll be dead, I won't know about it') through to believing in elaborate and detailed processes and places where they will go after human life ends.

Female genital mutilation

Female genital mutilation (FGM) is a traumatic experience for women and girls who are subjected to this practice. FGM involves the partial or total removal of external female genitalia for non-medical reasons, and it can have serious physical, emotional, and psychological consequences.

Firstly, FGM can cause physical harm and pain during the dangerous procedure, as well as long-term health problems such as infections, urinary problems, sexual problems, and complications during childbirth. The procedure can also have a lasting impact on the woman's sexual health and functioning.

Secondly, FGM can have significant emotional and psychological effects on women and girls. It can create powerful feelings of shame, guilt, and anger, as well as contribute to a sense of powerlessness and violation. Women and girls who have been subjected to FGM may also experience social isolation and stigma, as the practice is often associated with cultural or religious traditions that are not accepted or understood by others.

Due to the strong social and cultural norms around FGM, it is often women who support and condone this violence against young girls and women. Often, it is women who will manipulate, encourage, or conduct the procedure on their own daughters, sisters and female family members. This is usually as they have been socialised to think this process is required or normal, or know that the girl will be isolated, outcast, abused, or killed if she is not 'cut'.

Thirdly, FGM is a violation of human rights, as it involves the non-consensual removal/damage of female genitals, a woman's bodily autonomy, and integrity. It is often carried out on young girls who are not able to give informed consent, and it can have lasting consequences on their physical and mental health.

Forced forgiveness

Being forced to forgive someone can be traumatic for people because it involves a violation of their personal boundaries and autonomy. Forgiveness is a complex emotional process that involves acknowledging and working through feelings of anger, hurt, and betrayal, and it cannot and should not be imposed or forced upon someone.

When people are forced to forgive someone, they may feel like their emotions and experiences are being invalidated or dismissed, and they may feel pressured to suppress or deny their true feelings. This can create a sense of confusion, fear, and powerlessness, as well as contribute to feelings of guilt, shame, and self-blame.

For people who have experienced trauma or abuse, being forced to forgive someone can also be re-traumatising. It may trigger memories or emotions related to the original traumatic event, and it can undermine their sense of safety and trust in others.

It is important for professionals to consider and understand the way forgiveness is often linked to religion, redemption, judgement, and sin. For millions of religious people, they may feel (or be directed) that they must forgiver someone who has harmed them if they ever want to be forgiven for their own sins or wrongdoings. In this way, some people feel they are not a good enough person, or not a faithful person, if they cannot forgive.

Forced marriage

Forced marriage is traumatic because it involves a violation of an individual's fundamental human rights and can have significant physical, emotional, and psychological consequences. Usually, most victims of forced marriage are women and girls. Sometimes, the girls can be infants or very young. Forced marriage is not the same as arranged marriage.
Firstly, forced marriage involves the coercion or pressure of an individual to enter into a marriage without their free and informed consent. This can lead to feelings of powerlessness, loss of agency, and a sense of betrayal. Forced marriage can also result in the loss of an individual's personal freedoms and autonomy, as they are forced to conform to the expectations and demands of their families or communities.

Secondly, forced marriage can have significant physical consequences for people, particularly for women and girls who may be subjected to sexual and reproductive violence, including forced pregnancy, forced sterilisation, and female genital mutilation. Forced marriage is often related to domestic abuse, economic abuse, rape, and family abuse.

Forced marriage can have significant social and economic consequences for people, particularly for women and girls who may be forced to drop out of school or lose their access to education and employment opportunities. This can perpetuate cycles of poverty and sex inequality, as well as limit women and girls' ability to make choices about their own lives and futures.

Forced restorative justice

Being forced to engage in restorative justice with your perpetrator can be traumatic for people who have been subjected to trauma or abuse, as it involves confronting their perpetrator and reliving traumatic experiences. Restorative justice is a process that aims to bring together those affected by a crime or harm, including victims and offenders, to address the harm and work towards repairing relationships.

However, for people who have been subjected to trauma or abuse, the idea of engaging in a restorative justice process can be triggering and re-traumatising. Confronting their perpetrator may bring up painful memories and emotions, and the power dynamics of the situation may leave them feeling vulnerable and unsafe.

It is important to remember that restorative justice programmes often convey a benefit to the perpetrator, too. This means that some abusers and perpetrators want to engage in restorative justice with their victims in order to get lesser sentences, parole, or access to opportunities. Arguably, this means that the victim is faced with reliving their traumas with someone who is only engaging in order to gain something for themselves.

Additionally, for people who have experienced trauma or abuse, the idea of repairing relationships with their perpetrator may not be feasible or desirable. They may feel a strong sense of anger, resentment, and betrayal towards their perpetrator, and the process of restorative justice may not be able to address or resolve these complex emotions.

Forced therapy or counselling

Being forced to have therapy can lead to a traumatic loss of control over the person's life, privacy, autonomy, and circumstances. People who are forced to have therapy (either by loved ones, or by professionals) may feel that their personal choices and agency are being disregarded, which can lead to feelings of injustice, helplessness, and despair.

Secondly, being forced to have therapy can lead to a sense of mistrust or betrayal. People who are forced to have therapy by someone else may feel that their trust has been violated, or that they are being coerced or manipulated into seeking treatment.

Arguably, being forced to have therapy undermines the therapeutic relationship and the concept of free and informed consent. People who are forced to have therapy may not want to engage in the therapeutic process or trust the relationship with the therapist, which can limit the effectiveness and ethics of the therapy.

Forcibly medicated

Being forcibly medicated can be traumatic for people who have experienced trauma or have concerns about their mental health treatment. It involves being given medication against their will, often by medical professionals or authorities who are seeking to manage symptoms or behaviours that are perceived as problematic.

For people who have experienced trauma or been subjected to violence and abuse, being forcibly medicated may trigger feelings of powerlessness, violation, and loss of control. It can be a reminder of past experiences where their autonomy and agency were taken away from them. The process of being restrained and injected or given medication against their will can be painful, frightening, violating, distressing and overwhelming, and may exacerbate feelings of fear, or helplessness.

When forcibly medicated, the person may feel that their wishes and preferences are not being taken into account, or that their treatment is being imposed on them without their consent. They may also have concerns about the potential side effects and long-term impacts of the medication, and feel that they are not being given adequate information or support to make informed decisions about their care.

Foster care

Foster care can be traumatic for children who have experienced trauma or have been removed from their families due to abuse, neglect, or other reasons. It involves being placed in the care of strangers, often in unfamiliar settings, and can disrupt their sense of stability, security, and attachment.

For children who have experienced trauma or been subjected to abuse, being placed in foster care can trigger feelings of abandonment, rejection, and loss. It may exacerbate developmental delays in very young children, as they are often separated from their families and support systems.

Foster care can also be traumatic due to the potential for abuse or neglect within the foster care system. While there are many dedicated and caring foster parents, there have also been cases of children being subjected to prolific abuse, neglect, or exploitation while in foster care. This can compound feelings of distrust, helplessness, and powerlessness among those in foster care, and can create long-lasting psychological and emotional impacts.

Fraud

Being a victim of fraud can be traumatic for several reasons. It can cause financial losses and can have significant impacts on a person's sense of trust, safety, and security. Victims of fraud may feel violated, vulnerable, and powerless. Some of the ways in which fraud can be traumatic are:

Loss of financial stability: Fraud can result in significant financial losses, leaving victims in a state of financial instability. This can lead to stress, fear, and feelings of helplessness.

Violation of trust: People who commit fraud often take advantage of victims' trust, generosity, vulnerability, needs, desires, or crises in order to commit their crimes. When this trust is violated, victims may feel a sense of betrayal or disappointment, which can have a significant impact on their relationships with others.

Emotional distress: Victims of fraud may experience a range of emotions, such as anger, frustration, betrayal, sadness, self-blame, shame, regret, and fear.

Sense of vulnerability: Fraud can make victims feel vulnerable and exposed. This can lead to a loss of confidence, self-esteem, and a sense of control over their lives. It is also common for victims of fraud to become hypervigilant in order to attempt to protect themselves from further fraud or deception.

Frightening imagery

Seeing graphic imagery can be traumatic for a variety of reasons, depending on the nature of the imagery. Here are some potential reasons:

Exposure to violence: Graphic imagery often involves depictions of violence, such as in photos or videos of war, terrorism, rape, murder, abuse, accidents, or crime scenes. Exposure to such violence can trigger strong emotional responses and cause traumatic distress reactions, especially in people who have previously been subjected to or witnessed violence.

Shock and disgust: Graphic imagery can be shocking and disturbing and can evoke feelings of disgust and horror. This can cause a person to feel overwhelmed, helpless, and traumatised, particularly if they are not prepared for or expecting the content.

Physical harm: Graphic imagery may involve depictions of physical harm or injury, such as in medical procedures or accidents. For people who have experienced physical trauma or have a history of medical issues, seeing such imagery can be particularly distressing.

Triggers: Graphic imagery can act as a trigger for people who have experienced traumatic events in the past, such as being subjected to sexual assault, being impacted, or involved in war, or natural disasters. The imagery may bring back memories or feelings associated with the trauma and cause re-traumatisation.

Vicarious trauma: People who work in professions that involve exposure to graphic imagery, such as first responders, medical professionals, or journalists, may develop vicarious trauma from repeated exposure to trauma-related content.

Genetic testing

Going for genetic testing can be traumatic for a variety of reasons, depending on the personal history and circumstances of the person. It is a complicated and distressing time for a number of possible reasons, including:

Fear of disease or illness: Genetic testing can reveal the presence of genetic mutations or conditions that increase the risk of developing certain diseases or illnesses. The fear of receiving such a diagnosis or of passing it on to children can be traumatic and cause distress and fear.

Family history: For people with a family history of genetic disorders, genetic testing can bring up painful memories and feelings of loss or guilt. It may also cause conflict within families if some members do not want to know their genetic status.

Privacy concerns: Genetic testing involves the sharing of sensitive personal information, including genetic makeup, paternity, and family medical history. This can cause concerns about privacy and the potential for discrimination in employment, insurance, or other areas.

Decision-making: Genetic testing results can impact important life decisions, such as whether to have children or undergo medical treatment. This can cause distress, confusion and fear about making the 'right' decision.

Stigma: Certain genetic disorders may be stigmatised or misunderstood by society, which can cause shame, guilt, and social isolation for people and families affected by them.

Grief

Grief is a natural response to the loss of someone or something important to us. Here are some potential reasons why grief can be traumatic:

Sudden or unexpected loss: Grief can be traumatic when the loss is sudden, unexpected, or violent. This can lead to feelings of shock, confusion, and disbelief.

Multiple losses: If someone experiences multiple losses in a short period of time, such as the death of multiple loved ones or a series of significant life changes, this can be overwhelming and traumatic.

Unresolved trauma: Grief can also be traumatic when it triggers unresolved trauma from the past, such as childhood abuse or neglect, leading to a more complex grief experience.

Lack of support: Grief can be traumatic when the person is unable to access or receive adequate support from family, friends, or professionals. This can lead to feelings of isolation, loneliness, and despair.

Cultural and societal factors: Cultural and societal factors can also impact the experience of grief, including social stigmas surrounding death and mourning, and cultural expectations around how grief should be expressed and processed.

For professionals, it is vital to understand that the grief process is unique to each person, and whilst some people may appear to have processed much of their trauma around the grief in a few months, others will still be processing that trauma many years later. Further, it is important to consider that whilst the presenting trauma may be grief or loss, it is often related to many other traumas that arise from the death of the person.

Groomed online

Being groomed online is not confined to children and sexual grooming. The act of grooming online can be employed to anyone of any age of background. Further, grooming can be in pursuit of many different forms of harm, including sexual violence, exploitation, blackmail, criminal exploitation, radicalisation, terrorism, extremism, manipulation, and fraud.

Being groomed online can be a deeply traumatic experience for several reasons:
Loss of control: The person being groomed may feel that they have lost control of their own life, as the groomer is often in a position of power or authority.

Emotional manipulation: Groomers often use emotional manipulation tactics to gain the trust of their victims. This can include flattery, sympathy, and promises of love or attention. Conversely, it may include violence, threat, blackmail, shame, blame, and verbal abuse.

Exploitation: Groomers may exploit their victims for sexual, financial, or other purposes. This can lead to feelings of shame, guilt, and violation.

Harassment

Harassment refers to a pattern of behaviour that is unwanted, offensive, or intimidating, and is directed towards an individual or a group. Harassment can take many forms, including verbal, physical, or psychological, and can occur in various contexts such as the workplace, schools, public spaces, or online.

Examples of harassment include verbal harassment, physical harassment, psychological harassment, cyberbullying, sexual harassment, discrimination, and online harassment.

Harassment can be traumatic for several reasons. Harassment can cause danger, and loss of safety, a feeling of powerlessness, and helplessness. Further, harassment often means repeated exposure to traumatic and distressing content and behaviour, and is better understood as many traumas than one singular trauma of 'harassment'.

Harassment can lead to social isolation, as the person may feel ashamed or embarrassed to discuss the experience with others. This is particularly true if the perpetrator has deliberately contacted and threatened or harassed people around the victim, including their friends and family, in order to successfully isolate them from any support.

Hating your body

Hating your body can be traumatic because it can lead to a negative self-image, low self-esteem, and feelings of shame and guilt. This can cause significant emotional distress and can lead to a range of trauma and distress responses

When someone hates their body, they may engage in harmful behaviours, such as excessive dieting, over-exercising, or even self-harm. These behaviours can further exacerbate their negative feelings about their body, creating a cycle of self-loathing.

Hating your body can also impact your relationships with others. It can cause social isolation, as people may feel ashamed or embarrassed to be seen in public or to engage in social activities. It can also lead to difficulties in intimate relationships, as people may feel uncomfortable with their bodies or struggle with their sex lives, relationships, and intimacy.

Heart attack

Having a heart attack can be traumatic for several reasons. First, it can be a sudden and unexpected event, which can be frightening and overwhelming. The person may have thought that they were in good health, only to find out that they have a serious, life-threatening medical condition.

Second, a heart attack can be very painful and cause significant physical discomfort. The person may experience chest pain, shortness of breath, loss of consciousness and other symptoms, which can be distressing and frightening.

Third, a heart attack can lead to a range of complications and long-term health problems. The person may need to make significant lifestyle changes, such as changing their diet and exercise habits, taking medication, and managing their distress levels. These changes can be difficult to adjust to and can have a significant impact on their quality of life.

Finally, a heart attack can cause a psychological, spiritual, or religious epiphany or wake-up call for many people, causing them to confront their own mortality and the fragility of life. This can be a deeply emotional experience and may lead to feelings of fear, distress, trauma, uncertainty, regret and loss.

Homelessness

Homelessness is often very traumatic.

People who are homeless often lack access to basic necessities such as food, shelter, and medical care, which can cause physical harm and illness. They may also be exposed to harsh weather conditions, violence, abuse, and other dangers while living on the streets. This can cause fear, distress, and make it difficult for them to feel safe and secure.

Secondly, homelessness can lead to social isolation and loneliness, as people may be cut off from their support networks and struggle to connect with others. This can exacerbate feelings of hopelessness and despair.

Thirdly, people who are homeless may face discrimination and stigma, which can affect their self-esteem and make it difficult for them to access housing, employment, and other resources.

Homophobia

Homophobia can be very traumatic for people who identify as LGBTQ+ (lesbian, gay, bisexual, transgender, queer/questioning) for several reasons.

Firstly, homophobia can lead to social isolation and rejection, as LGBTQ+ people may face discrimination, bullying, and harassment from their families, peers, and communities. This can cause feelings of shame, low self-esteem, self-hatred, and internalised homophobia, and can make it difficult for them to form positive relationships and connect with others.

Secondly, homophobia can cause significant justified fear, as LGBTQ+ people may be at risk of violence, hate crimes, and discrimination in various areas of their lives, including employment, education, travel, and healthcare. This can make it difficult for them to feel safe and secure, and can cause ongoing distress and trauma.

Finally, homophobia can affect the mental health and wellbeing of LGBTQ+ people, leading to higher rates of psychiatric disorder diagnoses and suicide attempts.

Honour based abuse

Honour-based abuse is a form of violence that is motivated by a perceived dishonour or shame that has been brought upon a family or community.

It can include physical, emotional, or sexual abuse, forced marriage, and even murder. Honour-based abuse can be traumatic for several reasons. Firstly, it often involves a betrayal of trust, as the victim is usually abused by someone they know and trust, such as a family member or community leader. This can create feelings of confusion, self-blame, and guilt, and can make it difficult for victims to seek help or report the abuse.

Secondly, honour-based abuse can cause significant physical and psychological harm, including injuries, and ongoing fear and distress. Victims may also face social isolation and ostracism from their families and communities, leading to feelings of loneliness and despair. Honour-based abuse can lead to long-term impacts on the victim's life, such as difficulty forming positive relationships, finding employment, or accessing healthcare.

House fire

Being in a house fire can be traumatic due to the potential for injury or death, loss of possessions and home, and the sudden and unexpected nature of the event.
People who have experienced a house fire may feel a range of emotions, including fear, shock, grief, sadness, anger, guilt, and

worries. They may also experience physical symptoms such as respiratory problems, burns, or injuries. Additionally, they may have to deal with the aftermath of the fire, such as rebuilding their lives and coping with the trauma.

Identifying a body

Identifying a dead body can be traumatic due to the shock and grief that comes with the realisation that someone has died. It can also be a distressing experience to see someone you know in such a different state than you are used to seeing them in.

Additionally, identifying a dead body may involve viewing the body, which can be distressing for some people. The experience may also evoke feelings of guilt or regret, particularly if the person was a loved one and the individual was not able to say goodbye or resolve any outstanding issues.

The trauma of identifying a dead body may have long-lasting effects, including flashbacks, nightmares and intrusive thoughts.

Illness (acute)

Acute illness can be traumatic for a number of reasons. The sudden onset of an illness can be unexpected and overwhelming, causing fear and uncertainty about the future. The severity of the illness, the pain, and the potential for complications or long-term effects can also be distressing.

Acute illness may require hospitalisation or other medical interventions, which can be frightening or uncomfortable. In addition, acute illness can disrupt daily life and activities, causing distress and worries about work, school, or other responsibilities. The trauma of acute illness may also be compounded by social and economic factors, such as lack of access to healthcare or financial strain related to medical bills.

Illness (chronic)

Chronic illness can be traumatic for many people. It can be a life-altering experience that can change a person's sense of identity, self-worth, and future goals.

The physical and emotional toll of living with a chronic illness can be exhausting, leading to feelings of frustration, hopelessness, and isolation.
Chronic illness can also affect a person's relationships with others, including family, friends, and co-workers, and may lead to social isolation and a sense of being misunderstood.

Additionally, the financial burden of managing a chronic illness can be overwhelming and lead to worries and stress. All of these factors can contribute to trauma and impact a person's mental health and overall well-being.

Illness (life limiting)

Life limiting illness can be traumatic because it poses an ongoing threat to a person's life and can lead to physical and emotional suffering. The diagnosis of a life limiting illness can shatter a person's sense of safety, security, and stability, and can bring up a range of difficult emotions such as fear, grief, despair and low mood. The illness can also cause significant changes in a person's life, such as a loss of independence, limitations in mobility and daily activities, and changes in relationships and social roles.

Treatment for the illness can also be invasive, painful, and emotionally challenging. The uncertainty and unpredictability of the illness and its progression can make it difficult for people to plan for the future, leading to further distress and trauma.

Illness (terminal)

Terminal illness can be traumatic because it involves facing the inevitability of death and the potential loss of life and future plans. A diagnosis of terminal illness can trigger a range of intense emotions, such as fear, sadness, anger, and hopelessness. It can also lead to significant changes in one's physical and emotional wellbeing, including pain, fatigue, and reduced quality of life.

Additionally, the diagnosis may impact not only the person with the illness but also their loved ones and caregivers, who may experience significant emotional distress and a sense of loss.

Imprisoned

Being in prison ultimately means the loss of personal freedom and autonomy. People who are in prison may feel that their ability to make free choices and decisions about their lives has been taken away, which can lead to feelings of helplessness, hopelessness, and despair.

Second, being in prison can cause ongoing distress and trauma. The prison environment is often dangerous, violent, hostile, risky and hierarchical. People in prison may experience ongoing feelings of fear, anger, worry, sadness, hypervigilance, danger, threat, isolation, and panic. They may also experience ongoing fears related to the threat from other inmates, such as the fear of being physically or sexually assaulted.

Being in prison leads to a range of practical difficulties which can be distressing or traumatic, including being homeless on release, losing friends and family, being ostracised, not being able to gain employment or access meaningful activities or education, and struggling with the aftermath of their crimes.

Injury

Suffering an injury can be traumatic for several reasons. Injuries can cause physical pain and discomfort, which can be distressing and unsettling. In addition, injuries can limit mobility and daily activities, leading to a loss of independence and a sense of helplessness. Injuries can impact the sense of self and identity, particularly if the injury results in scarring or disfigurement. Finally, injuries can be a reminder of mortality and vulnerability, leading to feelings of anxiety and fear. Recovering from an injury can be a long and difficult process, requiring physical therapy and rehabilitation, which can be emotionally and mentally exhausting.

Jury duty

Jury duty itself is not inherently traumatic, but for some people, the experience of serving on a jury can be stressful or even traumatic. This may be due to a variety of factors, including being exposed to graphic or disturbing evidence, being required to make difficult decisions that could have serious consequences for the defendant, or feeling pressured to conform to the opinions of other jurors. Additionally, for people who have experienced trauma in the past, the experience of serving on a jury could potentially trigger memories or emotions associated with their prior trauma.

Living in a hostel or refuge

Living in a hostel or refuge can be traumatic for many reasons. People who live in hostels or refuges may have been forced to leave their homes due to domestic abuse, human trafficking, or other forms of violence, and may feel isolated, vulnerable, and unsafe. They may also be dealing with the trauma of their experiences whilst adjusting to living in a refuge with other traumatised people.

In addition, living in a hostel or refuge can be stressful and challenging, as residents often have to share living spaces and may have limited privacy and control over their surroundings. They may also be dealing with financial and practical difficulties, such as finding employment or housing, which can add to their distress and anxiety. Overall, the experience of living in a hostel or refuge can be traumatic due to the combination of past trauma, ongoing stress, and the loss of familiar and safe environments.

Loneliness

Feeling lonely can compound a sense of personal and social isolation. People who are lonely may feel disconnected, ignored, marginalised, and therefore lack the emotional and practical support that is needed as we move through life.

Second, being lonely is known to cause trauma and distress. The world is complicated and at times, very hard. Most people feel they need the support of friends, family, and connections when life gets tough. Social connections often provide people with a sense of identity and purpose, and being lonely can leave them feeling lost and unsure of their place in the world.

Losing a sense

Losing one of your senses can be traumatic for several reasons. Our senses provide us with a way to experience the world around us, so losing one of them can be disorienting and distressing. For example, losing sight or hearing can make it challenging to navigate the world and communicate with others. The loss of a sense can also affect a person's identity and self-esteem, leading to feelings of isolation and despair. Additionally, adjusting to a loss of a sense may require significant lifestyle changes and adaptations, which can be stressful and overwhelming.

Losing money, wealth, or status

Losing wealth and status can be traumatic for several reasons. Many people's sense of identity and self-worth is tied to their financial and social status, so losing that can result in a crisis of identity and a feeling of worthlessness. The loss of wealth and status can mean losing access to important social networks, resources, and opportunities, which can lead to a sense of isolation and uncertainty about the future.

Additionally, the sudden loss of financial security can lead to practical problems such as struggling to pay bills or provide for self and family, which can cause significant distress and anxiety. Finally, the loss of wealth and status can also be accompanied by shame and embarrassment, as people may feel that they have failed or are being judged by others.

Losing your faith or religion

Losing your religion can be traumatic for a number of reasons. For some people, their religion is a central part of their identity, community, and way of life. Losing this can lead to a sense of disorientation, isolation, and a loss of purpose or meaning. For others, leaving a religion may result in conflict with family or social circles, leading to feelings of rejection, guilt, or shame. Additionally, some religious communities may use fear and threats of punishment to discourage members from leaving, leading to fear or trauma associated with these beliefs. Finally, some may experience trauma due to negative experiences within a religious community, such as abuse or exploitation.

Loss

Loss can be traumatic because it involves the experience of separation or the end of something significant and valuable. This can include the loss of a loved one, a relationship, a job, a home, a sense of identity, or any other major life change that is deeply impactful. The experience of loss can trigger a range of difficult emotions, including grief, sadness, anger, guilt, and fear. These emotions can be overwhelming and can lead to feelings of powerlessness, disorientation, and a loss of control. The traumatic impact of loss can be influenced by various factors, including the individual's coping resources, support system, and the circumstances surrounding the loss.

Medical abuse, malpractice, or medical negligence

Medical abuse and negligence can be traumatic for several reasons. When someone goes to a healthcare provider seeking help, they expect to receive competent and compassionate care. However, medical abuse and negligence can involve a betrayal of trust by those who are supposed to be helping. It can also result in physical harm, psychological trauma, or even death.

Victims of medical abuse and negligence may experience feelings of powerlessness, helplessness, and anger. They may also experience a sense of betrayal, as their health care providers failed to meet their basic duty of care. These experiences can be particularly traumatic if the victim feels as if they have no recourse to hold the responsible parties accountable. Additionally, medical abuse and negligence can leave victims with long-term physical and emotional harm, which can impact their quality of life and sense of self.

Medical procedures

Medical procedures can be traumatic for several reasons. Firstly, the procedure itself may be painful, invasive, or uncomfortable, causing distress to the patient.

Additionally, patients may experience worry and fear due to the unknown outcome or potential risks of the procedure. The fear of complications or negative outcomes, such as infection or adverse reactions to anaesthesia, can also be traumatic.

Furthermore, medical procedures can trigger memories of past traumas or medical experiences, leading to increased distress and trauma. Patients may also feel a lack of control or powerlessness during the procedure, which can exacerbate feelings of trauma. Finally, medical procedures can be associated with significant costs, both financial and emotional, which can also contribute to traumatic experiences.

Menopause

Menopause is when a woman's periods stop naturally due to lower hormone levels. This usually happens between the ages of 45 and 55. It can sometimes happen earlier. Sometimes, menopause can be caused due to surgery to remove the ovaries (oophorectomy) or the uterus (hysterectomy), cancer treatments like chemotherapy, or a genetic reason. Sometimes the reason for early menopause is unknown.

Perimenopause is a term used to describe the years or months when women experience symptoms before periods have fully stopped. A woman reaches menopause when she has not had a period for 12 months.

Menopause and perimenopause can cause distressing, embarrassing, annoying, confusing, and concerning symptoms like fear, mood swings, 'brain fog', hot flushes, vaginal dryness, low mood, and irregular periods. This process also causes difficulty sleeping, night sweats, palpitations, headaches and migraines, muscle aches and joint pains, changes in body shape and weight gain, skin changes, reduced sex drive, itching or discomfort during sex and recurrent urinary tract infections (UTIs).

For many women, these symptoms will shift and change, and may last several years. This can therefore be a very distressing time for women. Furthermore, menopause is either mocked, or totally ignored in society due to layers of misogyny and ageism. This means that older women going through the menopause are likely to be ignored, pathologised, stereotyped, or minimised by those around them, furthering the distress.

Military service

Serving in the military can be traumatic due to exposure to violence, combat, and other high-stress situations that can cause physical and emotional harm. This can include death of colleagues and friends, direct physical injury, exposure to traumatic events, exposure to poverty, oppression, illness, infection, and the development of significant trauma responses and coping mechanisms.

Military personnel may also be subjected to trauma related to sexual assault, abuse, or harassment, discrimination, or social isolation. The experience of being away from family and loved ones, living in difficult and sometimes dangerous conditions, and the pressure to perform at a high level can also contribute to the traumatic effects of serving in the military.

Miscarriage

Miscarriage can be traumatic due to the sudden loss of a pregnancy, which can be emotionally distressing for the woman and her partner. It can lead to feelings of sadness, grief, guilt, and a sense of loss. For some women, miscarriage can also lead to physical pain and discomfort. Additionally, the experience may be further complicated by the stigma surrounding pregnancy loss and feelings of isolation or inadequacy. All of these factors can contribute to the trauma of miscarriage.

Misogyny

Misogyny can be traumatic because it involves the hatred, contempt, or prejudice against women and girls, and can result in discrimination, harassment, violence, and other forms of mistreatment. Those who experience misogyny may feel devalued, objectified, and unsafe in their own bodies and the world around them. They may feel that they are not taken seriously, that their voices are not heard, and that their experiences are not validated. This can lead to a range of negative psychological and emotional effects, including fear, low mood, low self-esteem, and trauma responses. Additionally, being subjected to misogyny can reinforce systemic inequality and oppression, and can contribute to a culture of violence and abuse against women and girls.

Natural disaster

Natural disasters can be traumatic for a variety of reasons. First and foremost, they can cause physical harm or injury, as well as significant damage to property and infrastructure. They can also disrupt social networks and support systems, leading to a loss of community and a sense of isolation. In addition, natural disasters can trigger feelings of fear, helplessness, and vulnerability, particularly when they are unexpected and sudden. They may also be accompanied by the loss of loved ones, which can exacerbate feelings of grief and trauma. Finally, the aftermath of a natural disaster can be chaotic and overwhelming, with people forced to navigate complex bureaucratic systems and navigate a new and uncertain reality.

Near death experience (NDE)

Near-death experiences can be traumatic due to the sudden and unexpected threat to one's life. When people face life-threatening situations, they may experience intense fear, panic, and a sense of helplessness or loss of control. The experience of being near death, whether due to an accident, illness, or other circumstances, can also lead to feelings of dissociation, depersonalization, and derealization.

The sense of being detached from reality or one's own body can be disorienting and overwhelming, contributing to the traumatic impact of the experience. Additionally, the memory of the event can linger and cause ongoing distress and trauma.

Neglect

Neglect can be traumatic because it involves a failure to provide necessary care, attention, or affection, and can result in physical, emotional, or psychological harm. When basic needs such as food, shelter, and safety are not met, it can lead to physical and developmental problems. Emotional neglect, such as failing to provide love, support, or validation, can result in low self-esteem, difficulty with relationships, and emotional distress. Neglect can also be a form of abuse, and experiencing neglect can leave lasting psychological scars that affect a person's ability to form healthy relationships and cope with distress in the future.

Nursing a dying relative

Nursing a dying relative can be a traumatic experience for several reasons. Firstly, witnessing the physical and emotional deterioration of a loved one can be distressing and emotionally draining. Secondly, it can be challenging to balance the demands of caring for a dying person with other responsibilities such as work and family life, which can lead to feelings of guilt and helplessness. Thirdly, the process of grieving can begin before the person actually passes away, which can be emotionally overwhelming. Finally, the experience of caring for a dying person can bring up unresolved emotions and past traumas, which can further contribute to the traumatic impact of the experience.

Orphaned

Being orphaned is a significant trauma. Losing parents or caregivers can mean that a child (or adult) may feel disconnected from others and may lack the emotional and practical support that is needed in life.

Parents and caregivers can be one of our most influential and important relationships in life. We not only rely on our parents and caregivers for safety, support, guidance and protection for many years, but we derive our sense of identity from our parents. It is therefore a life-changing trauma to lose both parents or caregivers, who provided continuity and heritage.

Outcast from your family

Being outcast from a family can lead to a loss of social support and a sense of isolation. Family members often provide a sense of continuity, identity, belonging and connection, and so being outcast from a family can leave a person feeling alone and disconnected from others.

For some people, being outcast from their family is due to their own behaviour, however for others, it is a form of abuse in which the person has become the family scapegoat, or the family target. This complicates the trauma and distress of being outcast and isolated, as it is done deliberately with the intention of causing harm.

For many people, relationships with parents and siblings are described and perceived to be bonds that cannot be broken. Socially, we are brought up to believe that nothing comes above or before our families. The family also frequently depicted as the centre of important dates and events such as summer, Christmas, Eid, new year, meal times, graduations, celebrations, birthdays, weddings, births of children, Mother's Day, Father's Day, crises, advice-seeking, parenting, babysitting and so on.

To be outcast from a family is therefore a personally and socially traumatic experience, which changes the way the person interacts and connects with people throughout life, including on family-oriented dates and events.

Outed (being outed as gay, lesbian, bisexual, or trans before the person is ready, or without their permission)

'Outing' is when someone discloses the sexual orientation or gender identity of an LGBTQ+ person without their consent. Outing creates issues of privacy, choice, abuse, risk, and harm. In addition, outing can sometimes be publicised on social media to deliberately force someone to come out before they are ready, or in order to shame/humiliate them.

Sometimes, 'outing' can be accidental, but usually, it is a deliberate act of violating someone's privacy in order to harm them publicly. For some people, they are threatened with being outed, so they feel they must publicly come out as LGBTQ+ before someone else does it to harm them.

Being outed is a traumatic, dangerous, and frightening experience that may leave the person at risk of harm, abuse or death. They may be deliberately targeted, harassed, stalked and abused due to being outed on social media or in mass media. These experiences can trigger feelings of shame, fear, anger, confusion, helplessness, self-blame, self-loathing, embarrassment, loss, violation, sadness and despair.

Parental divorce

Divorce can be a traumatic event for children because it often represents a major loss and a significant change in their lives. Children may feel a sense of uncertainty and fear about the future, and they may feel that their world is changing in ways that they do not understand or have control over. Additionally, children may feel a sense of guilt, responsibility, or blame for the divorce, which can lead to feelings of shame, isolation, and low self-esteem. Children may also experience feelings of sadness, anger, or confusion, as they struggle to make sense of their parents' decision to separate. Finally, divorce can disrupt the child's sense of security, and it can affect their relationships with their parents, siblings, and peers. All of these factors can contribute to the traumatic impact of divorce on children.

Paternity questions

Not knowing who your biological dad is can be traumatic for various reasons. It can cause a sense of confusion and insecurity about one's identity and place in the world. It may also lead to feelings of abandonment or rejection, especially if the absence of a father figure is accompanied by a lack of support and connection with other family members. Children may feel a sense of loss and longing to know more about their father and their family history. Additionally, not knowing one's genetic history can impact one's health and may create anxiety around potential health risks or genetic conditions. Overall, the trauma associated with not knowing one's biological father can vary depending on the individual's circumstances and personal experiences.

Pathologisation

Being pathologised can lead to a significant trauma. People who are pathologised feel that their experiences and traumas are being reduced to a psychiatric diagnosis or label, which can lead to feelings of hopelessness, shame, self-doubt, self-loathing, helplessness, self-blame, and frustration. Often, people describe feelings of being gaslit, going crazy, losing their minds, not being believed, and not being listened to.

Pathologisation is the act of positioning a person as disordered, abnormal or problematic. Pathologisation is a common tactic to discredit, silence, control and minimise people, and their experiences. The most common impacts of pathologisation include stereotyping, stigma, biases, discrimination, and social isolation.

Finally, being pathologised as mentally disordered and unstable can have long term practical consequences such as not being able to easily or equally to access education, employment, accommodation, health insurance, mortgages, and life insurance.

Periods (starting and having)

For girls, beginning their period is surrounded by emotional, physical, cultural, religious, and societal context. In some cultures and families, it may be celebrated as a part of the girl becoming a woman, whereas in other cultures and families, periods seen as are shameful, dirty, and disgusting. For this reason, we include periods as a trauma or distress here. Periods can begin for girls aged anywhere between 8 and 17. There are average ages (usually around 12 years old), but this can differ significantly. This means that some girls may be very young and distressed by their period starting, whereas other girls may be impatiently waiting for their period to start, and feeling 'left out' or 'weird' if their friends have all started their period. If girls have not been taught what periods are, or they have not been normalised and destigmatised effectively, they may be distressed and disgusted by their period or their vagina when they have their period.

Starting and having periods can be difficult for many girls, who dislike the experience of bleeding every month. However, for some girls and women, their periods are painful, heavy, difficult and distressing. For some women and girls, there may be restrictions about what they are and are not allowed to do during their periods, including sleeping with their partner, sleeping in the same bed, going to religious events or buildings, praying, touching sacred items, or other activities where the woman or girl is perceived to be 'unclean'.

Menstrual taboos can lead to the abuse, harm, bullying, mocking, and isolation of women and girls, causing them further trauma, distress, self-loathing, shame, blame, and embarrassment.

Police brutality

Police brutality can be traumatic because it involves the excessive use of force, aggression, and violence by law enforcement officers against civilians. It often results in physical injuries, emotional distress, and even death. The traumatic effects of police brutality can be compounded by factors such as racial profiling, discrimination, and a lack of accountability and justice for the victims. The experience of being subjected to or witnessing police brutality can lead to feelings of fear, helplessness, and mistrust towards law enforcement and the justice system, which can have long-term consequences on an individual's mental and emotional well-being.

Police searches

Being searched by police can be a traumatic experience for some people because it can involve a loss of personal autonomy and control, feelings of humiliation or violation, fear of violence, and a sense of injustice or unfair treatment. The power dynamic involved in a police search can be very intimidating and disempowering, especially if the individual being searched is a member of a marginalised or stigmatised group. In some cases, past experiences of trauma or abuse can be triggered by the search, leading to heightened levels of fear, or distress. Additionally, the search may be perceived as a threat to personal safety, privacy, or dignity, which can have long-lasting emotional and psychological effects.

Poverty

Living in poverty can be traumatic for a variety of reasons. People living in poverty often experience chronic stress, which can have negative effects on their physical and mental health. Poverty can also limit access to basic necessities, such as food, healthcare, and education, which can further compound the distress and trauma. In addition, poverty can create a sense of hopelessness and powerlessness, which can contribute to feelings of low mood, and fear.

Pregnancy complications

Pregnancy complications can be traumatic for many reasons. Firstly, there is the potential for harm to the mother and baby. Complications such as pre-eclampsia, gestational diabetes, and placenta previa can lead to serious health problems or even death for both the mother and baby. Secondly, complications can cause significant emotional distress and fear for the mother and family. The uncertainty and fear about the outcome of the pregnancy, as well as the potential for a traumatic birth experience, can take a toll on mental health. Finally, dealing with the financial costs of pregnancy complications can add additional distress and trauma, particularly for those who may not have access to adequate healthcare or insurance coverage.

Pregnancy from rape

Pregnancy resulting from rape can be traumatic for many reasons. First, the woman may have had no choice in whether or not to become pregnant, which can lead to feelings of powerlessness and lack of control over her own body. Additionally, the pregnancy may serve as a constant reminder of the trauma she experienced during the rape, leading to ongoing emotional distress and trauma. The woman may also experience a range of physical and psychological symptoms, such as fear, resentment, regret, anger, sadness, and difficulty bonding with the child. Finally, the woman may face stigma and judgment from others, which can compound the trauma she has already experienced.

Premature baby

Having a premature baby can be a traumatic experience for parents for several reasons. The birth of a premature baby is often unexpected and can be a shock to parents who were not prepared for delivery or the significant emotional distress and feelings of fear.

Premature babies are often very small and may require intensive medical care, such as being placed in a neonatal intensive care unit (NICU). This can be overwhelming and stressful for parents who may be worried about their baby's health and well-being. This can be a huge shock for parents, who had been excitedly awaiting the arrival of their baby, and who had planned everything to fit around a birth that was supposed to happen much later.

Premature babies may have a range of health complications and long-term health problems. They may require medical interventions such as oxygen support, feeding tubes, and medications. This can be traumatic for parents to witness and may cause feelings of helplessness, distress, and guilt.

Pressure to succeed

The pressure to succeed can be traumatic for several reasons. First, it can create an overwhelming sense of responsibility, causing people to feel as though their entire worth is tied to their success. This can result in feelings of low mood, fear, and low self-esteem, especially if they fail to meet their own or others' expectations. Second, the pressure to succeed can lead to burnout and exhaustion, as people may feel that they need to work excessively hard to achieve their goals. This can result in physical and mental health problems, including chronic distress and fatigue. Finally, the pressure to succeed can also lead to feelings of isolation and loneliness, as people may feel that they cannot share their struggles with others for fear of appearing weak or inadequate. All of these factors can contribute to the trauma of the pressure to succeed.

Private images and videos shared

Having your private images and videos shared without your consent is traumatic because it can cause intense emotional distress, fear, and feelings of shame, guilt, and violation. It can also lead to social isolation, damage to personal relationships, and reputational harm. The violation of privacy and control can be deeply traumatic, especially when it is done with malicious intent or for the purpose of shaming or harassing the individual. It can also be traumatic for people who have experienced past trauma or abuse, as it can trigger feelings of powerlessness and a loss of control over their own body and identity. Additionally, the fear and uncertainty of who may have seen the images and videos, as well as potential legal consequences, can be overwhelming and traumatic.

Prostitution (sex work)

Prostitution is defined as the engagement in sexual activity for payment. This can include, but is not limited to, street prostitution, sexual escort, online sexual content creation, online sex chat. It's important to note that some prefer to describe themselves as a 'sex worker' rather than 'prostitute'. However, other people who have been forced into prostitution, or harmed by prostitution, reject the description of prostitution as a form of 'work'. This is a highly contested point, that will not be covered in this resource. However, this experience is included as a trauma, whichever description is preferred by the person, or by the professional, due to the overwhelming evidence of danger, risk, trauma, harm, injury, poverty, addiction, dependency, stigma, isolation, dehumanisation, and violation.

People in prostitution or sex work are often subjected to myriad of trauma due to the several layers of adversity, abuse, stigmatisation, and violence they face globally. Research shows that the majority of people in prostitution or sex work report a history of sexual abuse in childhood, many of which include intrafamilial sexual abuse (Farley & Butler, 2012).

People who engage in in-person sexual activity are at high risk of being subjected to physical assault, rape, and murder. Due to the nature of many of these crimes already being largely unprosecuted, those in prostitution and sex work face the added layer of victim blaming and stigmatisation leading to even lower conviction rates for these victims. It's important to note that men and trans people in prostitution and sex work are also likely to be subjected to violent homophobia due to the majority of sex buyers being male which may further add to abuse, psychological trauma, and victim blaming.

People in prostitution or sex work are also at risk of contracting sexually transmitted diseases and infections, which can lead to chronic health problems.

Many people in prostitution or sex work enter due to financial difficulties or lack of economic opportunities. They may be forced to continue working in prostitution or sex work to support themselves or their families, leading to feelings of powerlessness and hopelessness.

People in prostitution or sex work are also likely to have been coerced, manipulated, or exploited by pimps, traffickers, partners, exes, or clients. This can lead to feelings of being trapped, violated, and degraded.

In a study across 5 different countries across America, Africa, and Asia, 92% of prostituted people reported that they wanted to escape prostitution immediately (Farley et al., 1998).

Puberty

Puberty is a natural and normal process of sexual maturation of humans. All humans go through the process of puberty, and whilst it is vital to transitioning from childhood to adulthood, it can be a highly distressing experience for many children.

Bodily changes can be sudden, frightening, confusing, and embarrassing for all children. They may feel unable to ask for advice or support, and may not know what is normal, what is healthy, and what might be a problem to seek support for.

In addition to the physical changes, puberty is surrounded by societal, cultural, and religious norms, myths, beliefs, narratives and expectations. Children going through puberty are often either treated as small adults, or big children, which leads to much confusion and conflict about their roles, responsibilities and accountability in the world, and in the family.

Puberty of girls is widely sexualised in society, and so it is common for girls to be subjected to sexual assault, harassment, catcalling, sexualised comments, and inappropriate comments about their bodies and sexuality around this age.

For boys, the experience of their voices cracking and dropping, and involuntary erections can be distressing and embarrassing.

Public humiliation

Public humiliation can be traumatic as it involves being publicly shamed or ridiculed, often in front of others. Public humiliation may occur in domestic abuse, when being bullied, or when the victim and/ or the perpetrator is in the public eye. It may be in person, through media, or online.

This can lead to feelings of embarrassment, shame, and humiliation, and can damage one's self-esteem and sense of worth. Being publicly humiliated can also lead to social isolation, as the victim may feel ashamed to be around others or fear further humiliation. If the victim is in a situation wherein there is a power imbalance, they may be unable to defend themselves which may lead to further feelings, and transference, of feelings of powerlessness.

Racism

Racism is a form of prejudice, antagonism, discrimination, or abuse that targets particular racial or ethnic groups, typically one that is a minority or marginalised. Racism can present in overt, systemic, institutional ways, as well as unconscious bias and micro-aggressions. This often limits opportunities and resources for people of certain races and ethnicities, as well as resulting in individual acts of prejudice, discrimination, and violence.

Those subjected to racism often report being told that they're 'being oversensitive' or 'overreacting' along with their experience being minimised, trivialised, and/ or denied when they try to disclose or report to friends, colleagues, or authorities.

In the year ending March 2022, The Home Office reported 109,843 racially aggravated hate crimes occurred in The UK alone (GOV.UK, 2022), similarly, in 2021 The United States department of Justice reported 64.8% of recorded hate crimes were racially aggravated (FBI, 2023). The subjection to, or fear of being subjected to hate crimes due to one's race or ethnicity is likely to be very traumatic and distressing.
Racism can create feelings of shame, anger, fear, and helplessness, which can have long-lasting effects on people and communities.

Racism is often overlooked as a daily trauma for marginalised groups, and as such many coping mechanisms and trauma responses to this type of oppression (and intersecting oppression within) are misunderstood, or pathologised. Professionals must consider and acknowledge institutional racism within mental health provisions, psychology, and psychiatry practice in relation to malpractice, mistreatment, and misunderstanding of such marginalised groups.

Radicalisation

Radicalisation can be traumatic for people and their families due to the extreme changes it brings in beliefs, values, and behaviours. It can cause a loss of sense of identity, cultural alienation, and a deep feeling of being disconnected from one's previous community. In addition, the process of radicalisation can be accompanied by social isolation, conflict with loved ones, and the threat of violence or harm. The individual may also experience a sense of guilt or shame, and the fear of being persecuted by authorities or society at large. All of these factors can cause significant emotional distress and trauma.

Rape

Rape is a highly traumatic experience to be subjected to. Despite this crime being taboo for many people, rape is surprisingly common. Rape is defined as being forced to have sex without consent, this can include oral sex, anal sex, and vaginal sex. In the UK Sexual Offences Act (2003), only males can commit rape because rape must be committed with a penis being inserted into another person's body (male or female). In other countries, rape is more loosely defined as forced sexual contact or forced sexual intercourse without consent, and so this can mean than females can also commit the act of rape, if they have forced someone to engage in sexual intercourse. In the UK, females can be convicted of 'sexual assault by penetration' which carries the same sentence as rape, but acknowledges that this act did not involve penetrating someone with a penis.

It is important to consider that in other countries and cultures, rape may not be acknowledged at all, especially where women are deemed property of men, and must submit to sexual acts even if they do not want to. For example, there are still over 20 countries in the world in which men can have their rape convictions or investigations stopped or overturned, if they marry the woman or girl they raped. This is due to marital rape laws, in which it is impossible to rape a woman or girl who is deemed 'property' by marriage.

Being raped can include being beaten, restrained, physically forced, grabbed, pushed, held down, threatened and seriously injured. However, being raped doesn't always involve overt physical violence.

Rape can still occur where the perpetrator did not use physical force, and may have instead emotionally manipulated the person, coerced them, blackmailed them, verbally threatened them, made them feel bad, told them they would end the relationship if they didn't have sex with them, accused them of being gay (corrective rape), or told them they need to have sex with them to prove they are faithful or in love with them.

Rape is most often committed by males, and usually those males are known to the victim. Victims are predominantly females. Rape most often occurs in domestic abuse, coercive control, families, relationships, teen relationships, and casual dating. Stranger rape is much less common, accounting for around 3% of rape.

However, it is important to note that rape can be used as a tool of warfare, and much international research has shown that women and girls are more likely to be subjected to rape and sexual violence during times of conflict, crises and disaster.

Rape can be a life-changing trauma for children and adults alike, due to the sensitive nature of the violation, the injuries, and the trauma it can cause. Sexual violence can cause people to feel fear, shame, self-blame, sadness, anger, guilt, confusion, despair, helplessness, injustice, hopelessness, embarrassed, and targeted.

In addition, there are complex social and family responses to being raped, and it is common for the person to have been victim blamed, shamed, mocked, outcast, isolated, humiliated, accused of lying and accused of making false allegations.

Rape threat

Receiving a rape threat can be traumatic because it can trigger justified and significant fear and shock related to a potential threatened sexual assault. Some people are threatened with rape as a form of emotional abuse and intimidation, where the perpetrator will not follow through with their threat. However, some people who are threatened with rape will be raped by the perpetrator, seriously injured, or killed, and so it is important that professionals take rape threats seriously, and do not assume that the threats are empty.

For those who have already been raped, a rape threat can trigger their original traumas related to the sexual violence. However, for those with no prior experience of being subjected to sexual violence, there can still be a significant fear and trauma response to a sexual threat.

Realising mortality of others

Realising the mortality of others can evoke feelings of fear, grief, despair, sadness, and helplessness. The thought of losing someone we love, or care about can make us feel distressed. It can also remind us of our own mortality and the fragility of life, which can be difficult to process and come to terms with. The realisation that our loved ones are not invincible, and that we will eventually face their death can be a challenging and emotional experience.
Children often go through several stages of realising the mortality of their parents and loved ones. Most children begin with very little concept of death and dying, and slowly make the transition towards common milestones such as realising that some people die, that their pets will die, that their parents will die, and eventually that they too, will die.

This process can be harder for some people than others and will depend on what cultural and religious meaning they make of life and death. Cultural and religious meaning will often direct the coping mechanism used to understand and process death and finality.

For example, a child who is taught to believe that their dying family member will go to a beautiful, peaceful, loving place called 'heaven' may be less traumatised by mortality than a child that is taught that when humans die, that is the end of their life, and it is very sad, but it is a normal part of life for everyone. Similarly, in some communities and cultures, funerals and mourning are about the celebration of life, and giving thanks for life. In others, funerals and mourning are solemn, quiet, distressing, oppressive environments that can be frightening for adults and children.

There is of course no right or wrong way to address this, and religious beliefs are often only suitable for those who hold the beliefs in the first place and want to use those beliefs to understand the world, life, and death. For others, religious beliefs about afterlife, heaven and hell, only complicate or distract from the reality of the end of biological life, and so they prefer to process death in those terms, despite it providing little to no comfort.

Realising your own mortality

As with realising that others will die, all children and adults eventually realising they will die too. This can be a traumatic experience, and cause a range of trauma responses in the person (whether they are a child or adult at the time).

The realisation that death is inevitable and there is no cure, delay or fix for it can be extremely overwhelming and frightening for people. They may become distressed and even experience significant threat responses in their body (breathing changes, becoming clammy, becoming dizzy, heart racing) when they think about dying and their own death.

For some, this is due to the finality and sadness of death, and for others it is the uncertainty and the unknown of what happens at death, at the moment of death, and after death.

Whilst some people will develop a range of coping mechanisms for this feeling ranging from complete denial and ignorance through to detailed beliefs about death, life, and afterlife, it is still common for people to fear death throughout life. This fear may be exacerbated during illness, crises, violence, trauma, suicidal thoughts, age milestones, and towards the end of life.

Refugees

Before being forced to flee, refugees may experience many significant traumas including imprisonment, torture, loss of property, malnutrition, physical assault, extreme fear, rape and loss of livelihood. The flight process can last days, months, or years.

During flight, refugees are frequently separated from family members, robbed, forced to inflict pain or kill, witness torture or killing, and/or lose close family members or friends and endure extremely harsh conditions. Perhaps the most significant effect from all of the experiences refugees endure is having been betrayed, either by their own people, by enemy forces, or by the politics of their world (Refugee Health TA, 2023).

Even once people seeking refuge have arrived somewhere where they feel safer, they may face significant discrimination, persecution, racism, abuse, violence, social isolation, poverty, lack of human rights, lack of support and services, lack of access to healthcare, housing, and education and being forced to communicate complicated circumstances and experiences in a language that is not their mother tongue.

It is important for professionals to consider the hostile media and social environment towards those seeking refuge and safety from other countries. There is increasing contempt and deliberate misinformation towards people who need safety from serious danger and violence, often caused by media coverage and fake news that can cause people to feel apathy, or to attack and harm those who seek refuge. This level of contempt and harm must be considered a significant trauma for all refugees.

Removal of citizenship

Whilst removal of citizenship is rare, it is a possible trauma that some people may experience. Usually, the removal of citizenship is illegal, but can happen in circumstances in which countries or governments allege that the person is a danger to national security.

Losing citizenship ultimately removes basic rights, access to services, healthcare, education, employment, resources, protection, safety, and accommodation. Psychologically, this experience is likely to be highly traumatic, resulting in feelings such as loss, grief, isolation, uncertainty, powerlessness, hopelessness, statelessness and despair. For some people, being stateless will mean that they have no legal status in any country, leaving them vulnerable to many forms of abuse, exploitation, and violence.

Repatriation

Being repatriated can be traumatic for various reasons, such as leaving behind loved ones, losing a sense of stability and familiarity, having to adjust to a new culture and language, and experiencing discrimination or stigma from the receiving community.

In addition, the experience of repatriation may be linked to previous traumatic experiences, such as forced displacement, persecution, or human rights violations. The trauma of repatriation can also be compounded by the challenges of accessing basic resources and services, including housing, healthcare, and employment.

Limited studies have explored the experiences of people who have been repatriated either forcibly or under voluntary programmes. However, those studies that have explored this usually find significant trauma and sizeable increases in trauma responses, distress and coping mechanisms of people who have been repatriated (Lersner et al., 2008).

Reporting to police

Reporting a crime to the police can often be so distressing or traumatic that some victims will describe the reporting process as worse than the crime itself.

Most people never report crimes committed against them to the police. It can be a difficult, triggering, frightening and emotional experience to recount the details of a traumatic event to a stranger, especially if the event involved violence, abuse, personal details, or sexual assault. This process can also be re-traumatising, as it requires the individual to relive the experience in significant detail, answer questions, respond to the judgement and practice of the officer, and confront the emotions associated with it.

Secondly, some people may feel hesitant to report a crime due to fear of retaliation or not being believed by police. This fear can be heightened for marginalised communities, such as those who are frequently subjected to systemic abuse and discrimination, as they may have experienced distrust or mistreatment from the police in the past (or be well aware of the stereotyping and profiling of themselves).

The criminal justice system can be a lengthy and confusing process that may take years, with multiple stages and bureaucratic hurdles to navigate. This can lead to feelings of frustration, helplessness, despair, exhaustion, hopelessness, worthlessness, injustice and a sense of being re-traumatised by the system itself.

Repossession (of a home)

Repossession of a home can be traumatic because it involves losing a place that a person may have lived in for a significant period of time, and where they may have built a life, created safety, and created memories. The process of repossession can be humiliating, embarrassing, distressing, saddening, angering, and overwhelming, often involving court proceedings and the possibility of being evicted from the property. Losing a home can also lead to financial, personal and social instability, which can cause a great deal of emotional distress.

Usually repossession is associated with financial difficulty, poverty, arrears and debt, which as discussed in other sections, is traumatic in itself. Often those experiences are connected to, or caused by other traumas and forms of distress such as divorce, illness, injury, redundancy and addiction.

Repossession of a home is a serious financial consequence which may affect the credit rating of the person, meaning they may find it very difficult to find new accommodation, even if that accommodation is rented. This can leave the person in a significant unstable position regarding safety, security, accommodation, employment, education and personal relationships.

Restraints

Being physically restrained is often a distressing and traumatic experience. Adults and children can be restrained by police, carers, doctors, support workers, other law enforcement professionals, security guards, and prison guards. Despite restraints being technically legal in some circumstances, being restrained can be traumatic and painful.
Being restrained involves a sudden physical loss of control where physical force and pressure is applied to keep someone still, or stop them from doing something. It is fairly common for restraints to cause injury to the person.

Just like any other assault, being restrained (especially as it is often done by two or more people) can feel like being physically assaulted and harmed. It can be distressing, frightening, triggering, painful, angering, humiliating, embarrassing, and feel like a violation of human rights, boundaries and bodily autonomy.

Restraints can often become 'part of the job' for some professionals who use them frequently, and so it is important that they either consider alternatives, or acknowledge that the restraint procedure is likely to be traumatic, painful and harmful.

Ritual abuse

Ritual abuse is a form of abuse that involves the use of rituals, ceremonies, or practices that inflict physical, sexual, or emotional harm on an individual. It is traumatic because it involves a repeated and systematic pattern of abuse that can cause significant psychological and emotional harm to the child or adult.

People subjected to ritual abuse may experience feelings of helplessness, shame, blame, anger, sadness, resentment, and guilt, and may develop flashbacks, intrusive thoughts, hypervigilance, and other responses and coping mechanisms.

Additionally, ritual abuse may involve cult-like groups, which can create a sense of betrayal and mistrust in the person's relationship with others and the world around them. The trauma of ritual abuse can also impact the victim's ability to form healthy relationships, maintain employment, and pursue a fulfilling life.

Due to the collective and powerful nature of cults, they can cause a loss of identity and a sense of isolation. People who are abused in a cult may be separated from their families and friends, and may be subjected to a strict set of rules and beliefs that can contradict or compromise their own values and beliefs. This loss of identity and isolation can lead to feelings of confusion, loneliness, and a loss of authenticity.

Cult leaders may use techniques such as brainwashing, gaslighting, threats, rewards, promises, or other psychological manipulation to control their members.

Much like leaving abuse, leaving a cult can be difficult, dangerous, and traumatic. People who have been abused in a cult may face barriers to leaving, such as fear of reprisal, financial dependency, or a lack of support from family and friends. Sometimes, people who leave cults find themselves totally isolated and outcast.

It is also worth considering the way they might need to re-evaluate and reprocess their understanding of the world, religions, politics, sexuality, and many other personal and social issues once they have left the cult. This can be both liberating and terrifying.

For professionals working in abuse and violence, it is important to remain aware that ritual abuse is socially and culturally denied. There have been multiple studies and theories which suggest that disclosures and reports of ritual abuse have been fabricated, or the result of 'mental disorders' or 'mass panic'. Currently, there is still significant denial of ritual abuse and abuse within cults which causes further trauma for people subjected to abuse and violence in these contexts.

Robbery

Robbery can be traumatic for many reasons. The experience of being robbed can leave a person feeling violated, vulnerable, harmed, hypervigilant, and powerless. It can also lead to a sense of ongoing fear, particularly if the robbery involved the threat or use of violence. In addition to the emotional trauma, a person may also experience financial loss if valuable or uninsured items were stolen. The traumatic effects of a robbery can last long after the incident itself, and may impact a person's sense of safety and security in their daily life.

Sectioned (involuntary commitment)

Being sectioned can lead to a significant loss of personal autonomy, freedom, rights, and control over a person's experiences, body, and wider life. Being sectioned is a complex experience, but is often experienced as traumatic, frightening, worrying, sad, isolating, strange, unpredictable, unwanted, stigmatising and complicated.

Whilst people might think that sectioning people is for their own good, and will ultimately lead to them feeling safer and being safer, this is often not the reality for many people. Being sectioned involves being involuntarily placed in a secure facility, forced to accept diagnoses, medications, therapies, and treatments for days, weeks or months. Often the facility is miles from home, family and friends.

The ward environment can be dangerous, violent, hostile, risky and frightening. People in wards may experience ongoing feelings of fear, anger, worry, sadness, hypervigilance, danger, threat, isolation, and panic. They may also experience ongoing fears related to the threat from other patients, such as the fear of being physically or sexually assaulted.

Being sectioned also leads to a range of practical difficulties which can be distressing or traumatic, including being homeless on release, losing friends and family, being ostracised, being judged, not being able to gain employment or access meaningful activities or education, and struggling with way people perceive and treat them.

Seeking asylum

People who seek asylum are often fleeing from war, persecution, or extreme poverty, and the journey to safety can be dangerous and traumatising. Additionally, the process of seeking asylum can be lengthy and complex, requiring people to share traumatic personal experiences and provide evidence to support their claims. The uncertainty of the outcome can also create fear and stress, especially if an individual is separated from their family or support system during the process.

Even once people seeking asylum have arrived somewhere where they feel safer, they may face significant discrimination, persecution, racism, abuse, violence, social isolation, poverty, lack of human rights, lack of support and services, lack of access to healthcare, housing, and education and being forced to communicate complicated circumstances and experiences in a language that is not their mother tongue.

It is important for professionals to consider the hostile media and social environment towards those seeking asylum and safety from other countries. There is increasing contempt and deliberate misinformation towards people who need safety from danger and violence, often caused by media coverage and fake news that can cause people to feel apathy, or to attack and harm those who seek asylum. This level of contempt and harm must be considered a significant trauma for all those who seek asylum.

Seizures

Having seizures can be traumatic for several reasons. Firstly, seizures can be unpredictable, and people who experience them may worry about when the next one will occur. They may feel that they have little control over their body, which can be frightening and disorienting.
Additionally, seizures can sometimes cause minor to serious injury, particularly if the person falls, is on a staircase, hard floor, driving, walking on a busy footpath, or is operating heavy

machinery when the seizure occurs. This can cause physical pain and lead to fears about engaging in many day-to-day activities. Finally, the stigma associated with having seizures can be traumatic as well. Some people may feel embarrassed or ashamed about their seizures, particularly if they have occurred in public or caused them to lose control of their bodily functions. They may worry about being judged or discriminated against because of their condition.

Self-harm (cutting)

Cutting self-harm is a type of intentional self-injury that involves cutting or scratching your own skin with a sharp object, such as a razor blade, knife, or piece of glass. The injuries caused by cutting can range from superficial scratches to deep cuts that require medical attention. Cutting self-harm is often associated with trauma and significant emotional distress. It can sometimes be a developed coping mechanism that can provide a temporary sense of relief from emotional pain, but can also lead to physical harm and further emotional distress and trauma. This will be considered more fully in 'trauma responses and coping mechanisms'.

Self-harm (picking skin)

Skin picking, also known as 'dermatillomania' or excoriation, is a form of self-harm in which people repeatedly pick, scratch, or dig at their skin, causing damage and sometimes scarring. It is often done in response to stress, fear, or boredom and can be a coping mechanism for dealing with intense emotions. However, it can become a compulsive behaviour and lead to serious physical and psychological harm.

Self-harm (poisoning)

Self-harm by poisoning is a type of deliberate self-harm where an individual intentionally ingests a substance in order to harm themselves. This can include taking an overdose of medication, consuming household chemicals, or intentionally eating or drinking poisonous substances. Self-harm by poisoning can have serious physical consequences and may be life-threatening in some cases.

Self-harm (pulling eyelashes)

Pulling out eyelashes or other body hair is a type of self-harm behaviour known as 'trichotillomania'. It involves recurrent urges to pull out hair from various parts of the body, including the eyelashes, eyebrows, scalp, and pubic area. It can result in noticeable hair loss and can be distressing and disruptive to a person's life.

Self-harm (situations)

Self-harm by putting oneself in dangerous situations is a form of self-harm where the individual purposely engages in risky behaviours that may result in harm or injury. Examples of this type of self-harm include reckless driving, drug use, excessive drinking, causing fights, and engaging in extreme sports without proper safety measures. The individual may engage in these behaviours to feel a sense of control, to cope with emotional pain or trauma, or to numb themselves from difficult feelings. However, these behaviours can have serious consequences and can lead to physical harm, injury, or even death.

Self-sabotage

Self-sabotage refers to behaviours or thoughts that undermine or damage our own goals or well-being. It can manifest in different ways, such as procrastination, self-doubt, self-destructive behaviours, or negative self-talk.

Self-sabotage can be traumatic because it often leads to feelings of helplessness, shame, and self-blame. It can reinforce negative beliefs about ourselves and create a vicious cycle of self-destructive behaviours that can be difficult to break. Moreover, self-sabotage can prevent people from achieving their goals and fulfilling their potential, which can lead to feelings of regret and disappointment.

In some cases, it may be a way of coping with difficult emotions or traumas. For some people, sabotaging the self, and the progress or happiness they have is a form of self-punishment or self-hatred, in which they may destroy their own potential for happiness and success as they do not feel worthy of positive experiences and peace.

Sex trafficking

Being trafficked, bought, and sold for sex is highly traumatic and dangerous. People subjected to sex trafficking (usually women and girls) are often subjected to physical and sexual violence, threat of death and rape, torture and abuse which can cause physical injuries and psychological trauma. It is common for women and girls who are trafficked for sex to contract STDs and other life-threatening illnesses, and to become pregnant. It is unlikely that women who are being trafficked will have access to healthcare, as their abusers will isolate them from authorities and support services. Due to this, they may suffer with illnesses, infections, miscarriages, diseases and injuries for months or years without support.

Miscarriage, forced miscarriage through being abused and beaten, and repeated terminations are common. Women and girls are typically held against their will and subjected to forced labour, criminal exploitation, rape, abuse, and sexual exploitation, which can cause feelings of distress, despair, helplessness, shame, blame, confusion, and loss of control. Women and girls may be separated from their families and support networks, leaving them isolated, missing, and vulnerable. Finally, the stigma associated with being subjected to sex trafficking can cause additional emotional distress and trauma, including feelings of shame, guilt, and social isolation.

Sexual assault

Sexual assault refers to any form of unwanted sexual contact or activity that occurs without the explicit consent of one or more of the individuals involved.

Sexual assault can include:

- Kissing or forcing someone to kiss
- Attempted rape
- Touching someone's breasts or genitals – including through clothing
- Grabbing or groping someone's body – including over clothing
- Touching any other part of the body for sexual pleasure or in a sexual manner – for example, stroking someone's thigh or rubbing their back
- Pressing up against another person for sexual pleasure
- Touching someone's clothing if done for sexual pleasure or in a sexual manner – for example, lifting up someone's skirt

Sexual assault is often highly traumatic. However, it is also common for the trauma of sexual assault to present much later (months or years later) due to the person not realising they were sexually assaulted at the time. Sexual assault is a common experience in society, with the majority victims being women and girls. The trauma can stem from the feeling of powerlessness and violation of boundaries that comes with the experience or being sexually assaulted by someone. Sexual assault can also lead to feelings of shame, guilt, and self-blame, as victims may question if they did something to provoke the assault.

Sexual harassment

Sexual harassment is defined as carrying out unwanted sexual behaviour towards another person that makes them feel upset, scared, offended or humiliated.

Sexual harassment can include:

- Unwanted sexual advances or flirting
- Sexual requests or asking for sexual favours
- Sending emails or texts with sexual content
- Intrusive questions about a person's sex life
- Commenting on someone's body, appearance, or clothing
- Spreading sexual rumours
- Showing images of a sexual nature
- Showing someone pornography
- Unwanted physical contact of a sexual nature – for example, brushing up against someone or hugging, kissing or massaging them
- Sexual posts or contact on social media
- Sexual comments or noises
- Catcalling or wolf-whistling
- Sexual gestures
- Leering, staring or suggestive looks
- Sexual jokes and 'banter'
- Sexual innuendos or suggestive comments

The trauma from sexual harassment can include feelings of shame, guilt, fear, sadness, disappointment, disgust, betrayal, self-blame, shock, anger, hypervigilance, and a loss of self-worth.

Sexually violent imagery

Viewing or being shown sexually violent materials can be traumatic as the content can be extremely disturbing and violent. For some people, the content (photographs, videos, or illustrations) may cause feelings of shock, disgust, violation, retraumatisation, horror, disbelief and confusion.

For those who view this material (whether voluntary or forced) it can lead to a distorted view of sex, intimacy, violence and relationships. Watching or looking at sexually violent materials can result in feelings of shame and guilt, as the individual may feel complicit in the harm being done to others by consuming this type of content.

It is important for professionals to consider that this may have formed part of broader experiences of abuse, such as child sexual abuse, sex trafficking, grooming, child abuse, domestic abuse and coercive control. This is especially true for those who have been forced to watch and replicate violent porn by perpetrators.

Slavery (being bought/sold into)

Being sold into slavery can be extremely traumatic for several reasons.

First, being sold into slavery involves a complete loss of personal autonomy and control over the person's own life. People who are sold into slavery are forced to work against their will and are often subjected to physical, sexual, and emotional abuse. People who are sold into slavery may be subjected to forced labour, organ harvesting, criminal exploitation, or sexual exploitation, which can result in death, physical injuries, lifelong illnesses, and sexually transmitted diseases.

Being trafficked and sold is a human rights abuse and violation. It is traumatic to be commodified and used as a product, whether that is for physical labour, drug running, or sex trafficking. This often results in people feeling dehumanised and depersonalised.

The risk to life whilst being trafficked is significant, and so people become frightened for their lives, their future, their body, their freedom, their rights, their well-being, their children (and if they become pregnant, their unborn babies).

Many people attempt to plan how to escape, but often realise that they risk being harmed or killed.

Smear campaigns

Smear campaigns can be traumatic because they involve targeted and malicious attacks on an individual's reputation, character, and credibility. Such campaigns can be carried out through various means, including social media, the press, or by word of mouth. The trauma can arise from feelings of shame, blame, injustice, fear, anger, hopelessness, humiliation, and isolation caused by the false and often hurtful allegations made against the individual. Smear campaigns can also have long-lasting effects on a person's mental health, personal relationships, and professional prospects.

Smuggling (people)

The smuggling of migrants, as defined in Article 3(a) of the Smuggling of Migrants Protocol, involves the facilitation of a person's illegal entry into a State, for a financial or other material benefit. Although it is a crime against a State, smugglers can also violate the human rights of those they smuggle, ranging from physical abuse to withholding food and water (UNHCR, 2023).

Being smuggled into a country can be traumatic for several reasons. Firstly, the journey itself can be dangerous and life-threatening, as people are often crammed into small, dangerous, and unsanitary spaces without access to basic needs such as food, water, and sanitation. Additionally, people may be subject to physical or sexual abuse by smugglers or other people during the journey.

Furthermore, upon arrival in the destination country, people who have been smuggled may face a range of challenges and traumas, including the fear of being caught and deported, the risk of exploitation or abuse by perpetrators, the difficulty of finding safe housing and employment, and the trauma of being separated from family and loved ones. Additionally, people who have been smuggled may face stigma, discrimination, and marginalisation within their new communities, which can exacerbate existing trauma and create new sources of distress and injustice.

Sofa surfing

'Sofa surfing' refers to the practice of temporarily staying with friends or acquaintances on their couch or spare room, when someone is unable to afford a permanent home of their own.

This situation can be traumatic due to:

Instability: Living with others temporarily can create a sense of instability and uncertainty, which causes further distress and fear.

Lack of privacy: Living in someone else's space, without a private area, can feel intrusive and uncomfortable, leading to a sense of loss of control over the person's life.

Lack of control: Being dependent on the goodwill of others can make someone feel powerless and vulnerable, which can be a traumatic experience.

Exposure to unsafe environments: People who are sofa surfing may not always know or trust the people with whom they are staying, which can put them at risk of exposure to unsafe, exploitative, or abusive situations.

Overall, sofa surfing can be a challenging and stressful experience, particularly for people who are experiencing financial difficulties and struggling to find a stable and secure place to call home.

Spiked

Being spiked or drugged can lead to a range of trauma responses and coping mechanisms. People who have been spiked or drugged may feel violated, abused, poisoned, tricked, manipulated and frightened about the impact the drug might have on their brain and body.

For some people, being spiked or drugged can be a terrifying experience, which caused near-fatal side effects. For others, they were rendered completely unconscious and have no memory or understanding of what happened to them. Some people (especially women) are spiked and drugged by men in order to rape and sexually assault them whilst they are unconscious or unable to fight off their attacker. This often means that there is an extra layer of the trauma: either that the person realises they were almost raped or assaulted, or coming to terms with the fact that they were raped or assaulted whilst helpless or unconscious.

People who have been spiked or drugged often face social stigma, judgement, victim blaming and even total disbelief. It is common for people to be ignored or not taken seriously, meaning they do not get the right tests to ascertain what they have been drugged with. Due to many crimes of spiking and drugging happening in bars and clubs, there is often a lack of interest or sympathy for victims, as they are deemed to be putting themselves at risk. There is also the common belief that they haven't been spiked at all, and have simply drank too much alcohol and regretted it.

Taken together, this experience is highly traumatic, and often leaves people with little to no closure or justice.

Stalking

Stalking is when someone repeatedly behaves in a way that makes someone else feel scared, distressed, or threatened. Stalking may include:

- cyber stalking (using the internet to harass someone)
- antisocial behaviour
- sending abusive text messages
- sending unwanted gifts
- unwanted phone calls, letters, emails, or visits
- being followed
- being monitored
- being watched
- threats to harm or kill
- sitting outside someone's house or workplace
- contacting family and friends of the victim

Being stalked can be traumatic for several reasons. Stalking involves repeated and unwanted attention, harassment, or contact that causes fear, alarm, and distress for the victim. The constant feeling of being watched or followed can lead to a sense of vulnerability and loss of control, which can be very traumatic. Stalking can also involve threats or actual physical harm, which can escalate over time and lead to serious physical and psychological trauma.

It is common for people who have been stalked to struggle with ongoing fear, hypervigilance, nightmares, anger, sadness, despair, hopelessness, helplessness, uncertainty, and exhaustion.

Starving or becoming malnourished

Experiencing starvation or becoming malnourished can be painful, physically harmful, distressing, and traumatic, causing significant weakness, fatigue, and lethargy. Starvation and malnutrition can lead to cognitive and psychological changes, such as difficulty concentrating, memory problems, guilt, fear, shame, self-blame, disgust, shock, self-loathing, and despair. These changes can exacerbate feelings of helplessness, hopelessness, and worthlessness, which can in turn lead to feelings of trauma. Additionally, experiencing starvation or malnutrition can be a result of larger systemic issues such as poverty, inequality, sexual and domestic abuse, torture, violence, child abuse, and political instability, which can further compound the traumatic experience.

Stealthing

'Stealthing' is the act of removing, piercing, or sabotaging a condom deliberately and then having perceived 'protected' sex with a woman, in order to impregnate her, humiliate her, trick her, control her, rape her, or abuse her.

Stealthing can technically be considered a form of rape, as the consent is conditional on the agreement of informed, protected sex. If the man removes or damages the condom during or just before penetrative sex, he may be committing a crime in some states and countries.

For those who have been subjected to stealthing, the impact on them varies from anger, distrust, betrayal, distress and trauma through to pregnancy, STIs, and having to seek an abortion.

STIs/STDs (sexually transmitted infections/diseases)

STIs and STDs are illnesses, infections, and diseases that are passed to each other through sexual contact with the mouth, anus, vagina, penis, or other infected areas of skin.

Types of STI include Chlamydia, Gonorrhoea, Trichomoniasis, Genital warts, Genital herpes, Pubic lice, Scabies, Syphilis, Human papillomavirus (HPV), HIV, Hepatitis B, and pelvic inflammatory disease.

Contracting an STI or STD can be distressing for many people, as it may cause feelings of embarrassment, shame, fear, anger, and self-blame.

Stillbirth

Having a stillbirth can be traumatic due to the sudden and unexpected loss of an expected baby. It can also cause significant physical and emotional pain for the mother, as well as feelings of guilt, shame, self-blame, confusion, injustice, and failure. In addition, the experience of stillbirth can have long-term effects on the parents and their relationships, leading to relationship breakdown, social isolation, withdrawal, change in world-view, a sense of injustice and the questioning of faiths and religions.

It is often considered good practice to allow the parents to hold their baby after a still birth, or allow them to see the baby/dress the baby or spend time with them before their body is taken away. Whilst this can provide some closure for parents, it is often a deeply traumatising experience that can cause long term flashbacks, nightmares, fear responses and trauma coping mechanisms.
The loss of a child can be a significant and life-changing event that can leave women with injuries, illnesses and health problems, including future fertility concerns and difficulties.

Stroke or TIA

Having a stroke or TIA (trans-ischaemic attack) can be a traumatic experience for several reasons. A stroke occurs when there is a disruption of blood flow to the brain, which can cause brain damage and long-term health problems. The physical and emotional impact of a stroke can be significant, leading to a range of challenges for the person and their loved ones.

The physical symptoms of a stroke can be severe and life-changing. These symptoms can include paralysis, difficulty speaking or understanding language, loss of coordination, and vision problems. These symptoms can be overwhelming and may require significant changes in the individual's daily routine, including rehabilitation and physical therapy.

People who have experienced a stroke may feel overwhelmed by the changes in their physical and mental health, which can lead to feelings of despair, confusion, exhaustion, sadness, hopelessness and helplessness.

For many people, a stroke is an unexpected and shocking medical event, and causes profound lifestyle changes. Some people become housebound, isolated, disabled, and dependent on others. This can make them feel guilty and ashamed that they feel such a 'burden' on others.

Suicide threats

When an abusive partner threatens suicide to control their victim, it can be incredibly traumatic for the victim for several reasons:

Emotional manipulation: The abuser is using emotional manipulation to control their victim by making them feel responsible for their life or their death. This can lead to the victim feeling guilty, blamed, shamed, and trapped in the relationship.

Fear: The victim may fear that their abuser will harm themselves if they leave or try to get help, which can lead to extreme distress and guilt.

Trauma bonding: The victim may feel a strong emotional attachment to their abuser due to the abuse and may feel responsible for their well-being, even when it is not their responsibility, and even though their abuser causes them significant harm.

Trauma from suicide: If the abuser does follow through with their threat and takes their own life, the victim may experience severe trauma and guilt, questioning whether they could have prevented the suicide, or whether they did indeed cause someone to kill themselves. Some abusers attempt suicide or do not complete suicide, or deliberately self-harm whilst telling the victim (and family and friends) that it was their fault, which causes further trauma and guilt that can be used to control the victim.

Supporting someone who is abusive

Supporting someone who is abusive can be very traumatic. Examples of where this can happen include:

- Mothers looking after children and teenagers who become abusive and violent
- Partners looking after their abuser during illness or injury
- Children looking after their elderly abusive parents or family members
- Professionals looking after an abusive, violent, or dangerous person

These situations are not uncommon, but can be distressing and confusing. Supporting someone who is abusive can take an emotional toll on the supporter, as they may be constantly worried about the safety of themselves and any possible victims.

If the supporter has a close relationship with the abuser, such as a family member or friend, they may feel a sense of betrayal when they learn about the abuse, as they may have previously trusted and cared for the abuser. If the person they are caring for is their own abuser, they may feel resentment, anger, injustice, exploited and further abused by having to care for someone who harmed them.

Surrogacy

Surrogacy can be a complex and emotionally charged experience for all parties involved, including, and especially, the surrogate mother. There are several reasons why surrogacy can be traumatic for surrogate mothers:

Emotional attachment: During pregnancy, the surrogate mother may form a strong emotional bond with the baby. However, the surrogate mother knows that the child will not be hers at the end of the pregnancy, which can cause confusion, sadness, fear, and distress.

Physical toll: Pregnancy and childbirth are physically demanding and risky, and the surrogate mother is taking on this responsibility for someone else. This will often take a toll on her body and her wellbeing.

Legal issues: The legalities surrounding surrogacy can be complex, and surrogate mothers may face legal challenges or disputes regarding custody of the child.

Surrogacy for family or friends: Some surrogacy arrangements are consensual, safe, informed, free decisions by a sister, female friend or relative who wants to voluntarily carry a baby for their family or friend who cannot carry a baby themselves. This experience can still be emotionally complex, and can become difficult if relationships break down or become strained during or after the pregnancy.

Paid and exploitative surrogacy: Some surrogacy arrangements are done via agencies and companies as a paid service, which can raise significant ethical issues for the surrogate mother. Mothers are usually paid very little sums of money for the use of her body and for the pain and risks of childbirth, and can be forced to sign contracts, stay in certain monitored accommodation, only eat the food stipulated by the purchasing parents/clients, only engage in activity stipulated by the purchasing parents/clients etc. Many surrogacy agencies deliberately use women in low-income areas or countries, who are already being exploited and oppressed in order to make significant profits from abusing women to sell their services. For reference, some surrogacy services charge £100,000 to £300,000, whilst the mother carrying and birthing the baby may only receive £10,000-£20,000 for being pregnant for 9 months, giving birth and then parting with the baby (inclusive of all risks, illnesses, health issues, injuries, and complications). The rest of the profit goes to the service.

For some women who are surrogates, the experience can be traumatic, as it may make them feel like a commodity or service to others. She may find that her own choices and rights are violated, such as not being allowed to terminate the pregnancy if she no longer consents, or becomes extremely ill during the pregnancy. This may leave women feeling dehumanised, trapped, scared and angry.

Terrorism

Terrorist acts often involve deliberate fear, violence, destruction, and the loss of life, which can cause immediate and long-lasting psychological trauma to those who are directly affected as well as to those who witness or hear about the events.

Terrorist attacks can also create a sense of social fear and insecurity in people and communities, particularly if they are repeated or ongoing. This fear and insecurity can lead to feelings of hypervigilance, lack of safety, uncertainty, nightmares, and flashbacks.

Additionally, terrorist acts can cause disruptions to daily life, such as increased security measures and changes in routine, which can also be stressful and traumatic. The aftermath of terrorist attacks, including media coverage and public discourse, can also be triggering and exacerbate trauma responses.
It is also worth remembering that acts of terrorism often target specific groups, such as religious or ethnic minorities, which can lead to feelings of targeted discrimination, lack of protection, targeted violence and abuse, and marginalisation, further adding to the trauma of the event.

Theft

Theft can make a person feel violated as it involves someone else invading their personal space and taking something that belongs to them without their permission. It can also affect their sense of security, making them feel vulnerable and exposed.

Theft can result in the loss of valuable or sentimental possessions, which can be difficult to replace. This can lead to feelings of anger, frustration, and grief. It can also result in financial loss, particularly if the stolen item was expensive or essential. This can lead to financial hardship and stress.

The experience of being a victim of theft can also have an emotional impact, leading to feelings of fear, shock, betrayal, and mistrust towards others.

Torture

Being tortured can be traumatic for many reasons.

Torture involves extreme physical and emotional pain and suffering, which can lead to long-lasting physical and psychological trauma. People who are tortured may experience ongoing physical pain, disabilities, or disfigurement. People who are subjected to torture are forced to endure extreme conditions and often have no control over what will happen to them. This extreme form of abuse and violence causes deep distrust of others due to betrayal. Guilt and shame about humiliation during torture, and about the person's perceived inability to withstand it, as well as guilt for surviving when others might have died or suffered much more, are common problems which discourage disclosure and acceptance. Additional fear and distress may be added due to uncertainty about the future, lack of power, lack of support network, and any possibility of being sent back to the place, family, or cult in which they were tortured.

Transphobia

Transphobia refers to the prejudice, discrimination, or hatred directed towards transgender people, those who do not conform to traditional gender norms, or those who identify as a gender different from their assigned sex at birth.

Experiencing transphobia can be traumatic for several reasons. It can lead to feelings of rejection, shame, self-blame, and self-hatred, and can create a hostile and unsafe environment for transgender people. It can also lead to social and economic marginalisation, loss of relationships, and limited access to resources, employment, education, healthcare, and services.

Transphobia can also lead to physical and sexual violence, which can be traumatic and life-changing for transgender people.

Trapped

Being trapped can be a traumatic experience because it can trigger feelings of helplessness, fear, and panic. When a person is trapped, they may feel like they are unable to escape or get away from a situation that is dangerous or threatening, and this can cause a sense of loss of control.

The feeling of being trapped can also be associated with a sense of being enclosed or confined, which can lead to feelings of claustrophobia or suffocation. Being trapped in a situation where there is a risk of physical harm or injury can also lead to feelings of trauma, as the person may experience a threat to their safety or survival. Overall, being trapped can be a highly distressing experience that can have a lasting impact on a person's mental and emotional well-being.

Vicarious trauma

Vicarious trauma, also known as secondary trauma or compassion fatigue, is a form of trauma that results from repeated exposure to the traumatic experiences of others. It can occur when a person is exposed to the trauma of another person, often through hearing their stories, witnessing their experiences, or providing care or support to them. This repeated exposure can cause emotional, psychological, and physical symptoms similar to those experienced by the person who was subjected to the primary trauma.

Vicarious trauma can be particularly challenging for healthcare professionals, social workers, police officers, paramedics, firefighters, first responders, therapists, and others who regularly work with trauma, distress, abuse, violence, death, and oppression. They may experience feelings of helplessness, hopelessness, guilt, and shame, and may struggle with their own sense of safety and security. It can also affect their ability to provide effective care and support to those they are working with, leading to burnout and other negative outcomes.

Victim blamed

Being blamed can be a traumatic experience because it can trigger feelings of shame, guilt, and self-doubt. When a person is blamed for something, they may feel like they are responsible for a negative outcome or situation, even if they are not at fault.

This can cause feelings of self-blame, and can lead to a loss of self-esteem or self-worth. Being blamed can also be associated with a sense of betrayal, as the person may feel like they have been unfairly accused or singled out for criticism or punishment.

If a person has a history of trauma or abuse, being blamed for being targeted by a perpetrator can be particularly triggering, as it can cause deep feelings of shame, self-doubt, self-loathing, powerlessness and secondary victimisation.

Victim in a trial

Being a victim in a trial can be very traumatic. Some people describe the trial as more traumatic than the crime committed against them. One of the major sources of trauma includes the way the victim must relive the traumatic event in order to testify in court. This can be emotionally exhausting, frightening, and triggering. It is common for victims to be cross-examined by the defence barristers or lawyers, who are acting on behalf of the perpetrator of the crime. This often means that victims are criticised, and evidence is presented for why they are not telling the truth, may be mistaken, not know the truth, cannot convince a jury, or can be discredited. This is particularly traumatic for victims who do not expect to be questioned in this way.

Additionally, the trial process can be lengthy and stressful, involving multiple court appearances and the need to provide details of the trauma repeatedly. The victim may also feel exposed and vulnerable during the trial, with personal information being discussed in a public setting. There may be fear of retaliation or repercussions from the perpetrator or their families and friends. The victim may also feel a sense of powerlessness in the face of the legal system and the outcome of the trial.

This is particularly important for marginalised and oppressed groups of people, who are aware that their ethnicity, sexuality, identity, religion, or other characteristics may mean that judges and juries do not listen to them, take them seriously or believe them as a victim of crime.

Violent sex

Violent sex is defined here as a form of sexual violence. However, it is being discussed in this context to mean sex in which one partner encourages, expects or wants to introduce violence, aggression, pain, humiliation, threats or harm into the sex for pleasure. This may involve acts such as choking, strangulation, burning, slapping, spitting, hitting, restraining, hurting and scaring the person as part of the sex act.

Professionals need to be aware that due to the rise of violent pornography which normalises violence against women and girls in what is portrayed as consensual sex, there is increasing levels of normalised violence in sex lives among couples and groups.

Some people may feel that they wanted to try aggression and violence during sex, or may have been forced, coerced or manipulated into trying it. Others may have thought they would enjoy it, and then realise that their partner was enjoying harming them, or that the power dynamic was abusive. Some people may normalise violent sex due to their own trauma histories and experiences of rape and sexual abuse.

War

War is traumatic because it involves violence, destruction, and loss of life, and can result in physical and emotional harm to people, families, and communities. During war, people may be exposed to intense and prolonged stress, danger, and trauma, including witnessing, or experiencing violence, injury, or death.

War may also result in displacement from home and community, loss of family members and friends, and economic devastation. Additionally, the ongoing effects of war, including social and political instability, can create ongoing distress and trauma for those affected by it.

It is also important to consider the social division that is created before, during and after wartime, using propaganda, fake news, misinformation and misdirection. This often increases hatred and contempt for particular groups of people in order to justify violence, death, invasion and military intervention. This is best understood as a social grooming process which uses fear and manipulation to control millions of people to the desired effect (supporting war).

Witnessing a crime

Witnessing a crime can leave a person feeling helpless, vulnerable, shocked, traumatised, and exposed to danger. It can also trigger feelings of guilt, self-blame or shame, particularly if the witness believes they could have done something to prevent the crime. Additionally, the criminal justice process can be lengthy and stressful, with witnesses often required to relive the traumatic event during interviews, and court proceedings. All of these factors can contribute to the traumatic impact of being a witness to a crime.

Working in a slaughterhouse

Working in a slaughterhouse involves taking the lives of animals, which can be emotionally challenging and traumatic for many people. Witnessing and causing animals to be killed and processed can cause lifelong psychological trauma. The work environment can also be physically demanding and dangerous, with workers at risk of serious injuries and death from machinery and sharp objects. Long hours and repetitive work in addition to dehumanisation and desensitisation to the sounds, sights and smells of killing animals can also lead to significant distress, burnout, exhaustion, guilt, and despair.

Wrongful conviction

Wrongful conviction refers to the situation where an innocent person is found guilty of a crime they did not commit. It is a traumatic experience because the person is punished for something they did not do, and they must go through the criminal justice system, which can be intimidating, humiliating, and stressful. The trauma can be compounded by the loss of freedom, stigma, and the impact on relationships and employment opportunities. The person may also experience feelings of anger, frustration, and injustice.

Xenophobia

Xenophobia, which refers to a fear or dislike of people from other countries or cultures, can be traumatic for those who are subjected to it because it can lead to discrimination, abuse, isolation, harassment, and violence. Xenophobic attitudes and behaviours can make people feel excluded, unwelcome, and unsafe, leading to trauma and distress.
Additionally, xenophobia can cause people to feel isolated and alone, especially if they are living in a foreign country and do not have a support system. The trauma of xenophobia can have long-lasting effects on well-being.

CHAPTER 4

Trauma responses and coping mechanisms

This section includes an A-Z of responses to trauma and coping mechanisms. It is not an exhaustive list. Throughout the descriptions of coping mechanisms, it is important to remember that coping strategies and mechanisms are often deemed either 'healthy' or 'unhealthy' by professionals and society, despite this being an unhelpful distinction. Many coping mechanisms can be harmful and unhealthy, but be deemed socially acceptable, or even socially desirable (overworking, and perfectionism are good examples of this).

Abusive (becoming)

During and after trauma, neglect, abuse, oppression and chronic distress, some people may use control, violence, abuse, and manipulation of others. Psychological theories of how people become abusive are multi-faceted and integrative, and usually include a mixture of personal experience, societal norms, environmental reinforcement, developmental experiences, entitlement, a need for power and control and personal distress.

Whilst trauma and distress may be a factor for someone who is abusive and harmful to others, it is not causal, and adversity, trauma and distress do not 'lead to' abuse. Many people who have been subjected to trauma and abuse never externalise their suffering, or subject others to the same experiences. To inflict abuse and harm on another person is an active choice, usually by someone with mental capacity to understand consequence and their actions. Their active choice-making to be abusive can usually be demonstrated by the common behaviour of targeting certain victims, presenting as kind and caring to others, and being able to control their abusive behaviours around people they respect, need, like, or fear.

Acceptance

For some people, acceptance will be key to whether, how, and when they are able to process their traumas and distress. Acceptance is the process of fully acknowledging the facts of a situation of experience without judging or denying any part of it, or ourselves.

Traumas are often complicated and multi-faceted in nature, and so too is our journey to understanding what happened and why it happened. Even this first step can be one of the hardest to overcome, as it is natural and common for people to struggle to accept the reality of their trauma or distress. It may be easier, and more protective for themselves to temporarily deny or refuse to accept the truth about a person or a situation.

Activism

Being subjected to trauma, distress, abuse, neglect, and oppression can be a life-changing experience. It often causes feelings of injustice, and a change in world-view, which compels the person to question and criticise institutions, systems, beliefs, religions, policies, governments, political beliefs, traditions, gender role norms, and discrimination. For some people, one way of processing their feelings of injustice and their lack of closure, is to engage in social issue activism. Whether it is campaigning against laws, or raising money for domestic abuse charities, activism can help people to feel useful and purposeful, when trauma has made them feel hopeless and helpless.

Activism, and striving for social change, is a coping mechanism for many people who go on to specialise or work in areas that have impacted them personally. Whilst it is generally considered to be a positive coping mechanism based on growth, action, and development, it can also regularly retraumatise, trigger, and exhaust the people involved. This is especially true for those who begin to suffer burnout after months or years of campaigning or working in difficult settings, whilst very little changes. It is also worth considering that for some, even successful activism can be a poor coping mechanism, if it is merely a distraction from the original trauma, or if the activism was held as the 'solution' to what happened to them and others.

Alters

Research with people subjected to abuse and trauma find that some can develop alternative versions of themselves or 'alters' that they developed in early childhood, usually to cope with extreme distress. For some people, their alter is not clearly apparent to them, and only becomes known when someone points it out. For others, they are aware of a different part of themselves, or a different version, personality, or identity that 'takes over' or 'takes control' when triggered, scared, stressed or traumatised.
It is safe to say that everyone has different parts, personalities or identities. We may present as very different people at work, at home, with our parents, with our partner, and with our friends. However, the presence of 'alters' is usually characterised by memory loss or a lack of awareness between alters.

A trauma-informed approach to understanding alters could argue that when a child is extremely distressed, they may create other 'parts' of themselves to cope with what is being done to them. For example, instead of waiting to be rescued, they might develop a part of themselves that comes to rescue them. When girls have been raped or abused, they may develop male alters that have never been abused, and would never be abused in the same way. In this way then, the alters are not 'split personalities' or 'mental disorders' but are a purposeful, useful, and essential coping mechanism for trauma.

Anger

Anger is a natural and normal response to trauma, distress and injustice. It is more likely to be pathologised in females than in males, due to socially constructed gender roles. Whilst masculinity prizes and normalises anger and even aggression, femininity prizes peace, submission, calm and kindness. Despite this, anger is a universal emotion experienced by all humans, and is theorised to have developed in order to react to danger, distress, or in order to defend ourselves from harm.

Anti-climax of achievements

In some people who have been subjected to trauma, abuse, distress and control, they might seek out achievements, projects, goals and accolades that they feel will fulfil them. During the process of striving for these positive rewards for hard work, they may imagine that when they come to the end, they will feel accomplished, complete, whole, fixed, satisfied, validated, or content.

Instead, people report feeling anti-climactic, disappointed, unfulfilled, empty and confused – even when they have reached their full potential, and achieved great things. When a person has been subjected to such trauma that has harmed their sense of self, esteem, identity and purpose, they can search for the 'missing piece', or seek approval by working towards a positive achievement.

When the achievement does not fulfil them, they can feel very confused as to why their long-awaited success does not bring them joy or contentment. This is usually because the underlying traumas have not been addressed, resolved or supported by the journey towards the achievement, and the achievement was merely a distraction or a temporary fix for a much deeper or more complex feeling of inadequacy, sadness, or emptiness.

It is also vital to remember that society often encourages people in distress or oppression to seek out positive, enriching and rewarding experiences as a way to find self-worth and confidence. This may be why so many people feel confused when they feel the anti-climax.

Anxious/Anxiety

To be anxious is to be scared. The emotion that underlies 'anxiety' is simply fear. Fear is natural, normal, common, and purposeful. Feelings of fear can range from mild worries to severe horror and panic. Rather than framing the fears, worries or anxieties as a disorder, it is important to understand that they are linked to legitimate concerns and fears that can be based around, caused by, or related to distress and trauma (either personal, or societal).

'Anxiety' is often used as a colloquialism for psychiatric diagnosis 'generalised anxiety disorder', which suggests that feelings of general and persistent fear or worry are a mental disorder.

A trauma informed approach refutes this suggestion, and instead would argue that the fears and worries have developed over time, in response to an event or experience, due to distress or trauma. It is most important to explore and understand the core fears of the person, which in most cases boil down to the fear of being killed, the fear of dying, fear of being hurt, fear of loved ones being hurt, killed or dying, and the fear of being harmed.

Anxiety Attacks

A common response to trauma, distress and chronic stress. 'Anxiety attacks' are intense feelings of fear and worry, which cause physiological symptoms in the body. They are often experienced as a racing or pounding heartbeat, sweating or becoming clammy, body temperature changes, feeling dizzy, feeling a sense of doom or terror, chest pains or tightness, throat tightness, tingling/numbness in extremities, muscle spasms, changes in breathing, palpitations, blurred vision, echoey or distorted hearing, and weakness.

The experiences of an anxiety attack can vary from mild to debilitating, but all are related to the way the brain and body naturally responds to threat and risk. When the distress or threat response is triggered in the brain, epinephrine and cortisol is released into the bloodstream, and the body responds by constricting blood vessels, preparing for fight or flight, opening airways, tensing muscles, dilates pupils, and changes heart rate.

Usually, an anxiety attack will be triggered by a stimulus in the environment (a smell), in the mind of the person (a memory or worry), a sensation (suddenly feeling their heartbeat rise due to running or rushing), a person (the abuser) or something else that is linked to the original distress or trauma. Sometimes the trigger of an anxiety attack is obvious, and other times it is tenuous or vaguely related.

It may also be useful to consider that an anxiety attack is traumatic in itself, and so people learn to fear having another one. This inadvertently fuels the cycle of fear and adrenaline release, and also means that when people begin to feel anxious, they can suddenly become fearful of having an anxiety attack, which fuels the anxiety attack further. The same can be said for those who do not realise their symptoms are related to trauma and distress, and those who believe they are instead having a heart attack or are dying of an unknown physical illness. The natural and innate fear of suddenly dying of a heart attack also fuels the anxiety and adrenaline release which causes the physiological symptoms to escalate or repeat.

Apologising

After trauma and distress, especially where the person was blamed, shamed or encouraged to take responsibility for what happened, it is common to develop a trauma response of repeatedly apologising to others. It could be apologising before speaking, apologising before asking a question, apologising when walking into a room, apologising when someone else bumps into them, apologising for having a different perspective, apologising for feeling 'in the way', apologising to keep the peace, or apologising even when they know they have nothing to apologise for.

This behaviour may be both a trauma response, and a coping mechanism. Both are related to feelings of self-doubt, self-blame, shame, and self-worth. Further, it might be that the person apologises in advance because they are used to being attacked, blamed or criticised.

Ashamed

Feeling ashamed during or after trauma, abuse or assault is common and normal. It is a common trauma response that can be linked to feelings of blame, shame, self-worth, self-esteem, and desert. Often, when people feel ashamed, they feel they deserved what happened to them, or what was done to them. Further, for some people, feeling ashamed is linked to feeling embarrassed about the trauma or distress (this could be the act itself, their perceived role in the trauma, the way others responded, the experience of people finding out, the experience of disclosing and describing, or explaining the trauma to others).

Attachment issues

Trauma can interfere with a person's ability to form healthy attachments with others, leading to a variety of attachment issues. Some examples of attachment issues that may arise after trauma include:

Avoidant attachment: After experiencing trauma, people may avoid forming close relationships with others. This can stem from a fear of being hurt or a belief that they are not worthy of love or care. People with avoidant attachments may avoid intimacy and may prefer to be alone for their own safety. This is not disordered or abnormal, and instead should be seen as justified and rational after abuse, neglect, or trauma. Research shows that 20% of children are 'insecurely attached – avoidant' (Moulin et al. 2014).

Ambivalent attachment: People with ambivalent attachment may have difficulty trusting others and may oscillate between seeking out close relationships and then pushing others away. This can stem from a fear of abandonment and a belief that others cannot be relied upon. This is not disordered or abnormal, and instead should be seen as justified and rational after abuse, neglect or trauma. Research shows that 25% of children are 'insecurely attached- ambivalent/anxious' (Moulin et al. 2014).

Disorganised attachment: Trauma can also lead to disorganized attachment, which can involve contradictory behaviours such as seeking out closeness while also exhibiting avoidance. This can stem from a sense of confusion and a lack of trust in oneself and others. This is not disordered or abnormal, and instead should be seen as justified and rational after abuse, neglect or trauma – especially where the abuse has included significant confusion, and changes in grooming tactics and manipulation from abusers. Research shows that 5% of children are 'insecurely attached – disorganised' (Moulin et al. 2014).

Instead of pathologising children and adults with attachment disorders, it may be worth considering how their experiences of attachments have taught them how to protect themselves from abuse and harm.

More recent research has rejected the notion of fixed attachment styles that are static over the lifetime, arguing that children (and adults) can have many different attachment 'patterns' with many different people in their lives. A child can have a very unhealthy attachment to an abuser, but a very secure attachment to their grandparents, for example.

Meins (2017) argued that attachment was being overrated and overused to 'predict' outcomes of children or to pathologise them as disordered. Meins (2017) also argued that the most recent research clearly showed that attachment was fluid, changeable, and individual to each person in the life of the child.

For professionals, it is pertinent to reflect on the different attachments the person has in their life. They may have dynamic and varied attachments, for example. They might be securely attached to their partner, but have attachment issues with their parents. They may have secure attachments to their family, but not to partners. They may have many different experiences of attachment caused by betrayal, abuse, harm, neglect and gaslighting. It is therefore unlikely that they have one blueprint attachment style that is applied to every person they meet.

Avoidance of certain people or situations

Choosing or feeling compelled to avoid certain people or certain situations is a common coping mechanism for people who have been subjected to trauma or distress.

One of the simplest and most obvious ways to cope, is to ensure that the person does not have to face a person or situation that is likely to make them uncomfortable or distress them further. It may be that the person is not ready, or does not feel able to face them, and this could last days or decades. It may also be that the person has an awareness of their own trauma triggers, and knows that certain people and situations trigger them to recall or re-experience traumatic events.

Avoidance of social events

The avoidance of social events is a common and normal response to trauma and ongoing distress, especially as social events and environments often require the person to play a social role, engage in conversation, observe social etiquette, engage in pro-social behaviours, and conform to a social dress code. Whilst struggling with trauma or distress, a social event demands an unreasonable and unmanageable amount of concentration, energy, commitment, engagement and conversation, which may not be achievable. It is therefore understandable that some people choose, or feel compelled, to avoid social events and environments as much as possible.

Social events also go hand in hand with social judgement and scrutiny, and so if the person has traumas or has been subjected to distress that relates to being criticised, publicly humiliated, mocked, bullied, judged, or socially isolated – a social environment may be a difficult, triggering, and scary place to be.

Belief in a Just World

A just world belief can be a response to trauma in some people. A just world belief is the belief that people get what they deserve in life, and that good things happen to good people, while bad things happen to bad people. This belief can provide a sense of order and control in the world, and can help people make sense of their experiences.

Some common signs of a just world belief as a response to trauma may include:

Blaming the victim: People may attribute the cause of the trauma to the victim's actions or choices, and may believe that the victim brought the trauma upon themselves.

Denial: People may deny the reality of the trauma, or may minimise its impact, in order to preserve their belief in a just world.

Moral judgement: People may judge others based on their actions or choices, and may view those who have experienced trauma as being less deserving of empathy or support. They may believe that bad things happen to bad people, or that there is a reason why bad things have happened to themselves or others.

Theories suggest that there is a difference between 'just world belief to others' and 'just world belief to self'. This means that whilst some people may hold the belief in a just world about themselves (blaming themselves for being abused or raped for example), they will not then apply that belief to others. The same can be found in reverse.

Betrayal

Feeling betrayed is a common trauma response, especially when the trauma is interpersonal, deliberate, abusive, or negligent in nature. The person may feel strongly let down, lied to, deceived, or tricked.

Feelings of betrayal can be a common response to trauma. After experiencing trauma, people may feel betrayed by people or institutions that they trusted. Some people may also experience feelings of self-betrayal, such as feeling like they should have done more to prevent the trauma or blaming themselves for what happened. Feelings of betrayal can have a significant impact on a person's ability to trust others and to form healthy relationships.

Binge drinking

Binge drinking is defined as heavy drinking (often defined as 4-5 or more alcoholic drinks in one sitting). Most people who 'binge drink' are not dependent on alcohol. Binge drinking is best described as a possible coping mechanism for distress or trauma. For some people, it is a way to relax, to have fun, to distract themselves, to escape, to get to sleep, to socialise, to disinhibition themselves, or to punish themselves.

It is worth paying attention to issues of classism and stereotyping in binge drinking behaviours too. It is commonly accepted for busy white-collar professionals to openly talk about drinking a bottle of wine after work, or to feel they need a few drinks to relax after a complicated day – but that same behaviour can be framed as disordered or problematic in working class or marginalised groups of people. Despite this, international research has confirmed that binge drinking is most common in higher income households than in households with lower incomes (CDC, 2023).

Binge eating

Binge eating is usually defined as the frequent consumption of large amounts of food in one sitting. People who binge eat can be all different weights, shapes and sizes. Binge eating is not always accompanied by any kind of 'purging' behaviour such as the use of laxatives, or vomiting. Binge eating is best described as a possible coping mechanism for distress or trauma. For some people, binge eating could be a way to comfort or reward themselves, a way to distract themselves, a way to relax, to socialise, or to punish themselves. Binge eating is often described as including a feeling of loss of control or lack of control over eating portions or eating behaviours.

It is important to consider the social context of eating large amounts of food. First of all, there is a celebratory culture around eating, sociable dining with friends and family, eating competitions, bulk buying deals, and discounts on fast food. For some people, eating becomes associated with reward, and doing something nice to 'treat' themselves.

This is particularly relevant if the person started binge eating during or after a period of distress or trauma. It may be that the preparing, presenting and eating of the food is an enjoyable activity that makes the person feel temporarily good about themselves. It may also be that this behaviour has become the main coping mechanism, which socially, is much less undesirable than other coping mechanisms such as drinking, smoking, or taking drugs. As the behaviour is not connected with as much stigma or social consequences, it is easy to see why someone may not recognise eating to be a coping mechanism for them.

Further, it may be important to consider the background and historic relationship with food, and whether the binge eating has any connection to a previous lack of food, experiences of poverty, or long periods of hunger or lack of consistent access to food.

Breaking promises to others

There can be a variety of reasons why some people break promises to others. These reasons may include:

External factors: Sometimes, unexpected events or circumstances can arise that prevent someone from keeping their promise. For example, a sudden illness or emergency may make it impossible to follow through on a commitment.

Lack of commitment: In some cases, people may make promises without truly intending to keep them. This may be due to a desire to please others or avoid conflict in the moment, without considering the long-term implications of the promise.

Difficulty with follow-through: Some people may struggle with completing tasks or following through on commitments due to issues with motivation, organisation, or time management.

Trauma or stress: People who have been subjected to trauma or are under significant distress may find it difficult to keep promises due to the impact on their psychological and emotional state. This can lead to difficulty with memory, decision-making, and follow-through.

It is important to note that breaking promises can be hurtful and damaging to relationships, which can then compound or complicate the distress the person is feeling.

Catastrophic thinking

A common form of thinking that is best described as a trauma response, which may sometimes present as a coping mechanism for intense fear and lack of control.

Catastrophic thinking is defined as intrusive thoughts about possible catastrophes and 'worst case scenarios' in any given situation. These thoughts may present as common fears of car crashes, aeroplane crashes, falling into deep water, being attacked by a stranger, or witnessing the injury or death of a loved one.

For some people, catastrophic thoughts are much more imaginative and detailed, and may include extreme graphic imagery such as suddenly imagining their loving family dog turns on their baby and violently kills the baby in front of them. Some people describe catastrophic thoughts which last for a couple of seconds, whereas some people feel trapped in the thought whilst the while scenario plays out, such as having to drag the dog off the baby, the blood, trying to call an ambulance, the ambulance crew arriving, the medics saying that they cannot save their baby, the weeks afterwards, the funeral of their baby, who would attend, how they would cope and so on.

A common form of catastrophic thinking is a fear that the person will suddenly kill themselves by doing something unexpected and spontaneous. Some people will report going about their normal day, and then thinking, "I hope I don't jump in front of that train", or "what would happen if I just threw myself off this cliff edge?" even then they are not at all suicidal at the time (and may never have been).

As a trauma response, it is possible that imagining catastrophes relates to the experience of suddenly being thrust into previous real life catastrophes such as their own traumas (being attacked, being raped, being in a car crash, or having an unexpected illness or accident). In these cases, the person has lived through a real-life catastrophe, and so knows that they can and do happen. If the experience was sufficiently traumatic as to cause fear that it might happen again, catastrophic thoughts could be ways to pre-empt possible tragedies in order to mentally prepare for them.

Trauma also causes a change in world view, and it is common for people to report feeling like the world has become an inherently dangerous place, with risk and threat around every corner. For some people, especially those subjected to repeated and chronic traumas, this world view has been confirmed many times, and so catastrophic thinking may only reflect the person's perception of an unpredictable, dangerous, uncontrollable, and risk-filled world.

Causing conflict with others or between others

Some people may deliberately cause conflict as a response to their own trauma as a way to cope with their emotional distress. Trauma can leave people feeling powerless, out of control, and overwhelmed, and causing conflict can be a way for people to regain a sense of power and control in their lives.

Some people who have experienced trauma may seek attention through causing conflict, as a way to validate their existence and gain recognition or validation from others. Causing conflict can provide a sense of control over the environment, as people can manipulate and dominate others to meet their needs and desires. Causing conflict can also provide a temporary release of emotional tension, as people may feel a sense of relief or pleasure from the act of causing conflict between others.

Change in personal goals

Trauma and distress can considerably change the life goals, short-term goals, and long-term goals of a person. The change in personal goals may be temporary or permanent. Whilst for some, it may negative changes (abandoning important and positive personal goals, talents, plans or experiences), for others, it may mean positive changes (exploring and engaging in new personal goals, plans, experiences, or hobbies that were not present before the trauma).

A change in personal goals may be caused by a feeling that nothing is worth accomplishing, that life is not worth living, or that the goals suddenly feel meaningless or empty in comparison to the enormity of the trauma or distress they have been feeling. However, a change in personal goals could also be a response to physical illness, injury, social constraints, financial and economic issues, discrimination or marginalisation related to the trauma or distress.

Conversely, some people may become motivated by hardship, trauma and distress, which causes them to set solution-focussed or empowering goals to work towards such as getting a job, taking a course, starting a new hobby, engaging in activism, inventing something new, or seeking out new friendships or relationships.

It is common for these goals to change shape and size, especially if they are being set as a coping mechanism, distraction, or a way to process the trauma and distress. For some people, they may be small, manageable goals – but for others, the goals may be life-changing, difficult, and extremely challenging to attain. Neither should be written off, but focus should remain on why the goals are changing, what that feels like, how it might be related to the trauma, and whether the journey to the goal change is harming or helping the person.

Change in speech

A commonly reported experience during or after trauma responses is a change in speech. Usually, the change is noticeable by others, and can range from speech becoming slow, quiet, meandering, circular, hesitant, and stunted,

through to speech becoming rapid, detailed, pressured, loud, and dominant.
It may be that the change in speech ultimately reflects a change in mental life for the person, or it may be that it is only the way the person is communicating which is subject to change. It is also worth considering when the change happened, who the change happens around, when the speech tends to return to their own normal, and whether it is really the 'speech' that has changed.

Change in world view

A common trauma response for many people is a complete change in world view.

Where once, they may have had beliefs and perceptions of the world being a generally positive place, or that people are generally good with a few bad, trauma may initiate a significant change in which the person views the world as generally bad, or people as generally bad, with only a few decent people left.

The change in world view may also include common themes such as safety (the world is generally unsafe), danger (the world is dangerous), risk (there is risk around every corner), harm (you are very likely to be harmed), death (frequent and imminent risk of death), luck (feelings of being generally unlucky, or becoming convinced that the world revolves on luck and chance), reward (feelings about who is rewarded in society and who isn't) , justice (views on formal and more conceptual forms of justice and judgement), authority (a rejection of authority, or a change in belief or trust in authority), and control (a change in the view of who or what is in control of the world, the government, community, or your personal life).
Trauma is likely to be unexpected, harmful, and commonly related to emotionally charged themes such as fairness, justice, reward, punishment, desert, control, and consequences. For some people, being subjected to trauma

or distress challenges core beliefs and values that were guiding and framing their understanding of the world, and the human experience. Therefore, it is a common and normal response to trauma, to consciously or unconsciously shift the understanding of 'how the world works', especially when the trauma has revealed new knowledge of the way institutions, laws, support networks and society responds to traumatic incidents and people in need of support.

Changing physical appearance

A common coping mechanism after trauma, particularly abuse trauma, is a desire or need to significantly change appearance. This could include a new hair style, new fashion choices, dieting, weightlifting, having/removing tattoos, having/removing piercings, growing/removing facial hair, growing/removing body hair, changing jewellery, changing make-up, seeking cosmetic surgery, choosing to cover the body or expose the body more often, waxing, shaving, or fake tanning.

For some people, the trauma represents a part of their life that they seek to disassociate from, or escape from. By changing their appearance, they can disconnect from the person they 'used' to be. For example, a woman who was raped who believes her body and her clothing led to the rapist attacking her may decide to wear baggy clothing and change the way she presents herself. A woman whose husband left her for a much younger woman may feel under pressure to lose weight, appear younger, change her hair, and fashion sense in order to protect herself from this happening to her again. In both examples, there is an element of unreasonable self-blame (where the actions of the person who caused harm become eclipsed by other reasons for their choices, such as the appearance of the woman). It is common for those subjected to abuse to be told, to read and hear from others that their partner cheated on them, or abused them, because they were not attractive or desirable enough, or ironically, were too attractive and too desirable. This leads many women and girls to change their appearance after trauma.

For some, the change in appearance is protective, and can be seen as a self-preservation mechanism. For example, a teenage boy who was abused by his father realised that none of his four sisters were abused, and so he begins to appear and dress more feminine, and more like his sisters, in the belief that it will protect him from his father. Similarly, it is common to see young and teen girls significantly change their appearance, and refuse to engage in conformist femininity, grooming, make-up and self-care of appearance when they feel, or are told, that they were abused because they were so 'pretty'.

There may also be specific changes, such as removing tattoos of ex-partners, or becoming free enough to wear the clothes they prefer, or have a hairstyle they love, without the control or negative comments of abusive or oppressive people and environments.

For others, a change in appearance represents a new chapter of themselves, their life, and their presentation to the world. This is common in many different forms of trauma, and not specific to abuse. A makeover or transformation in appearance may be a way to regain control of their lives, and the way they are perceived by others. Some people also report feeling more confident, and report higher self-esteem and motivation after they changed their appearance.

Co-dependency

Co-dependency is defined as a learned behaviour which can develop during or after trauma, distress, or whilst living in a toxic or dysfunctional family. Co-dependency can be either a trauma response or a coping mechanism for trauma. Someone who is co-dependent may report that they are in relationships where they become the caregiver, the rescuer, or the person who excuses, covers for, supports, protects or enables someone else who is behaving in harmful ways. They might also report feeling that they sacrifice much of themselves for others, in order to put everyone else's welfare, health, safety, and happiness above their own. For some, they may eventually develop a feeling of reward or satisfaction at being needed or wanted by those who are struggling, as the role they play gives them a sense of purpose and value.

Research spanning over a decade has found that people who become co-dependent are often the spouse, sibling, child, parent or loved one of someone who is living with addiction or dependency.

Compulsions to a behaviour

A compulsion is defined as an irresistible urge to behave in a certain way. It has a secondary definition, which means being forced, or feeling forced to do something. A compulsion is best understood as a coping mechanism for trauma or distress, where the behaviour or action reduces, limits, soothes, or prevents distress in some way.

Usually, the compulsion to act or behave in a certain way may be attached to a specific fear or to avoid a specific outcome. From a trauma-informed perspective then, it may be important to consider what the underlying fear is, that is motivating the compulsive behaviour – and how the compulsive behaviour relates to the fear and the original trauma(s).

Some behaviour may appear to be closely related to the underlying fear and traumas (compulsively hand-washing and disinfecting the house several times per day due to the fear of becoming ill and dying, after the pandemic and losing family members to COVID-19). In these cases, the route to the compulsions is logical, rational, and expected.

However, other behaviours may initially appear to be unrelated or vaguely related, such as compulsively checking door handles and plug sockets at least four times before leaving the house, even though the original trauma was being subjected to sexual and domestic violence. In these cases, it is important to consider what the behaviour means, and why/when it developed. For example, the door handles are being checked four times to ensure security and safety. The plug sockets are also being checked four times to ensure safety. Therefore, it is possible that the underlying fear is related to the theme of 'safety' and a fear of being unsafe again, which may relate to feelings of lack of safety in domestic and sexual violence. The number of times may be related to a ritual required to make the person feel safe or may be borne out of the fear that they will forget to check, or only thought/imagined they checked, so by counting, the action is confirmed and makes the person feel safe again.

Counterfactual thinking

Counterfactual thinking can be a response to trauma in some people. Counterfactual thinking involves imagining alternative scenarios or outcomes to a traumatic event, and can be a way for people to make sense of their experience or cope with their emotions.

Some common signs and symptoms of counterfactual thinking as a response to trauma may include regret. People may imagine how the traumatic event could have been prevented or avoided, and may feel regret or guilt for not taking different actions. Some people may dwell on the 'what-ifs' of the traumatic event, and may have persistent and intrusive thoughts about alternative scenarios or outcomes.

For some people, they cope with or process the trauma by trying to imagine alternative scenarios or outcomes as a way to cope with their emotions or escape from the reality of the traumatic event.

It is important to note that counterfactual thinking as a response to trauma is a normal and natural response to an overwhelming experience. Many people engage in counterfactual thinking, despite it contributing to self-blame and shame. However, it is important to be aware that excessive counterfactual thinking can interfere with the healing process and prevent people from accepting and processing the reality of their experience.

Covering body parts or body shape

Best described as a coping mechanism for trauma or distress, a person may begin to cover their body parts or their entire body shape with baggy clothes, long garments, and styles of clothing which conceal their frame and silhouette. This response is commonly reported by women and girls who have been subjected to child abuse, rape, domestic abuse, sexual harassment, and sexual assault. This coping mechanism has strong links to societal norms, rape myths and victim blaming narratives in which victims of these types of crimes will be told that it was their body, or the act of revealing their body in certain garments that 'caused' a perpetrator to target them or attack them.

Whilst some will be directly told that their body shape (large breasts, large bum, small waist, large hips, hourglass figure etc.) were the 'cause' of the abuse, others will arrive at this conclusion themselves, having being exposed to years of media and cultural references to victim blaming and body shaming.

Covering the body is a personal choice, and for some, it will make them feel safer, more empowered, more in control, and less anxious when in public. However, for some, it may be an action they resent or wish they didn't have to do, but feel they must in order to protect themselves from further abuse or violence. It is important therefore, to understand the root motivation and purpose of covering the body, instead of assuming.

Creating rigid rules for safety

Creating rigid rules for staying safe is best described as a coping mechanism for fear and worry. This can be brought on by a one-off trauma or event, or by many years or months of abuse, bullying, harm or distress.

This behaviour is likely to be related to predictability of the world/environment, a need for control, and a need for safety. For some people, being subjected to trauma is a pivotal and life-changing experience, which reframes their world view, and leaves them feeling violated, unsafe, and at risk of serious, unpredictable danger. Therefore, creating a set of rigid rules to follow such as 'never walk home alone, always check your back seats before getting into your car, never wear too much make-up, do not smile at people you do not know' may be clearly related to a set of fears around safety and risk.

Other examples of rigid rules can include much broader thoughts about the world such as 'I should never show any vulnerability' or 'I must respect my parents no matter how they treat me'. In these cases, rigid rules or assumptions about people, the world, or events, may be defensive coping mechanisms, or ways to understand the world – but ultimately, they all come back to fear, protecting the self, and themes of safety.

Criticising yourself

A common response to trauma, is to search for flaws in ourselves to explain why something is happening, or has happened to us. A person may become critical of themselves as a result of growing up in a family where they were heavily criticised. Other people may only begin criticising themselves when they start to question why they were subjected to a trauma or distressing event. Some people conclude that they were stupid, naïve, lazy, submissive, too nice, too calm, a bad person, deserving of trauma, didn't do something well enough, didn't escape quickly enough, didn't protect themselves enough, didn't see the signs, didn't work hard enough, didn't deserve the good things in life, were not worthy of happiness etc.

For some, self-criticism is a habit that develops over a long period of time, borne out of a general feeling of low self-esteem, lack of confidence, self-loathing and feelings of worthlessness. For some people, engaging in frequent self-criticism may be a form of self-punishment for perceived mistakes. Self-criticism may also be a way to stop the self from 'bragging' or 'loving themselves', especially if self-love has been framed as arrogance, undesirable or selfish.

It is worth noting that in addition to experiences of being criticised, and development self-criticism, there is also a global social pressure to self-criticise, and not to indulge in self-love. It is arguably more socially acceptable and desirable to criticise and put yourself down, than it is to affirm and support yourself.

Day dreaming

A globally common experience of mentally disassociating from the current stream of attention, and moving to an imaginative, personal or internal stream of attention. Some large scale studies have found that day dreaming is common to most people around the world, and that we can spend up to 47% of our time each day, in a 'day dream' (Gilbert and Killingsworth, 2021). Day dreaming is generally defined as a mild type of disassociation, which affects most people. It is common for people to 'tune out' other stimuli, and not be able to hear or see external prompts. For some people, it may take a while to shift back to the original stream of consciousness. For some people, they are unaware they have been daydreaming until someone interrupts them and regains their attention.

An interesting response to trauma and distress, some studies have found that daydreaming reduces distress and fear, by disconnecting the person from immediate streams of attention. It has also been found to support problem-solving and enhances creativity (Kam et al, 2021). Daydreaming during or after trauma and distress may take many forms, including positive, future-focussed visions through to anxious, negative, frightening visions.

Deception

Feelings of deception can be a common response to trauma. Trauma can involve situations where an individual was deceived, misled, or betrayed by someone they trusted, such as a caregiver, authority figure, or loved one. This can create a sense of confusion, disbelief, and mistrust in the person. People may feel a sense of betrayal by someone they trusted, such as a family member, friend, or caregiver, who failed to protect them from harm or who actively participated in the traumatic event. They may feel confused and disoriented during the traumatic event, struggling to understand what is happening to them or why it is happening.

Gaslighting is a form of emotional abuse that involves manipulating someone's perceptions of reality, often making them question their own memory or sanity. People may feel a sense of deception and confusion when they are subjected to gaslighting. It is common and likely that some people will experience a general sense of mistrust in people and institutions as a result of their trauma, which can be difficult to overcome even after the trauma has ended.

Decrease in sex drive

A common response to trauma which has a range of roots from physiological through to psychological. If the causes are primarily physical (impotence, vaginal dryness, injury to genitals, physical pain during sex, vaginismus, vaginal mesh, bleeding during sex), please see the physical section of this resource on page 331. However, it is important to remember that many physical causes of a decrease in sex drive are related to psychological distress, discomfort, shame, trauma, embarrassment, and fear.

A decrease in sex drive as a psychological trauma response may be related to high levels of distress which leave the person disinterested in sex. When people are feeling distressed, it is common for them to lose interest in sexual pleasure. For other people, their decrease in sex drive comes from trauma itself (if the trauma was sexual, abusive, interpersonal, shaming, humiliation, embarrassment, intrusive, or violating).

When a person has been subjected to sexual violence, it is common to become triggered during intimacy, foreplay, penetrative sex, and exposure to sexual materials, which leads to the person feeling safer without any form of sexual contact with others.

It may be worth considering social and cultural factors with the person, especially as sexual contact is sensationalised and romanticised so much in society, it is seen as 'abnormal' to not want sexual contact, despite there being no requirement or health need to have sex. Some people may go many years without sexual contact with others, and feel healthy and content. We therefore cannot and should not assume that a low sex drive needs to be solved, or increased, unless the person expresses a desire to address it themselves.

Further, it may be important to consider whether the person is able to masturbate as normal, or whether the decrease in sex drive has also meant a reduction or elimination of masturbation. If masturbation has continued, the reduction in sex drive may be related to interpersonal sexual contact. If masturbation has stopped too, it may be of interest to the person to explore how masturbation makes them feel (whether they have developed a disgust for it, or if it makes them feel weird, dirty, guilty, bad, ashamed, sad, anxious, embarrassed, or whether they no longer feel any physical pleasure at all).

Overall, it is common to experience a decrease in sex drive during and after trauma, whether the trauma is sexual or not. The reduction in sex drive is not as important for some people, as it will be for others.

Delusions

Delusions can be a response to trauma in some people, and can be understood in a trauma-informed way. Trauma can affect a person's perception of reality, and delusions may develop as a way to cope with the overwhelming emotions and experiences associated with trauma.

Delusions can take many forms, but some common examples include those in which a person believes that they are being targeted or persecuted by others, or that they have become someone important or different. In a trauma-informed approach, it is important to recognise that delusions may be linked to the individual's traumatic experiences. The delusions are often linked to the abuse, violence, control, fear, or harm they have been subjected to.

Even some of the most intriguing or extreme delusions can make sense if they are explored and validated. For example, a person who has been neglected, harmed, persecuted and abused for many years may begin to think they are Jesus Christ. Whilst this may be difficult and distressing for people around them, the link between a suffering servant, religious symbolism about suffering and deserving, and Jesus Christ is clear. Similarly, a young man who has been gossiped about and outcast from his family for being gay may develop delusions that he is always been watched and listened to, that then develop into fears that the government watch him through his TV and his phone. Again, it is clear that this delusion is resulting from his feeling of being judged, watched, and feeling exposed.

An important note here: do not assume delusions just because you do not have proof of something. For example, if a person reports that they believe their housemate is going through their things and stealing food, this may well be true. There is no reason for this to be a delusion, and not everything will be delusional, even if other experiences are.

Some people have their disclosures and reports put down to delusions when they are being abused, harmed, neglected, stalked, harassed, and controlled.

Desperation

A common trauma response in which the person feels a sense of helplessness, despair, and hopelessness. It may result in rushed or extreme decision making or actions. Some people describe this common feeling as an urge to do 'anything' to change a situation or an outcome.

Feeling desperate can be traumatic in itself, especially when a person is searching for solutions or answers but cannot find them. It is argued that feelings of desperation therefore worsen with each unsuccessful action that is taken. It can result in feelings of being totally overwhelmed and out of control. It is common to begin feeling desperation during or after long periods of distress, trauma, worry, helplessness, or situations in which there is a significant lack of control over the future or outcomes.

Difficulty making decisions

A common trauma response in which the person feels insecure, or lacks confidence in their own judgement, decision making abilities and predictive abilities. This can be caused by a fear of failure or making mistakes, or a fear that the wrong decision will lead to something terrible happening to them or others. Distress and trauma can leave a person feeling indecisive. Some theories suggest this is because we use our emotions to make decisions, and not just logic and information. When a person is highly distressed or traumatised, and their emotions are affected or exhausted by the situation they are facing, they may find it much harder to think clearly, and then engage their emotions to make decisions.

It is also worth considering whether the indecisiveness is a learned behaviour instead of an internal fear. In cases of domestic abuse for example, it is common for victims to be denied decisions, and all decisions are made for them by the abuser. Everything from what they eat for dinner to what clothes they wear to work are chosen and decided for them, until they doubt their own ability to know what it best for them. If a person seems to have become indecisive during or after suspected domestic or sexual abuse, it may be that their confidence in their decision-making abilities has been significantly harmed by their abusive partner.

Disclosing publicly

A common trauma response and/or coping mechanism, some people disclose their traumas in detail in public. This might be a frequent behaviour in which the person tells strangers, professionals, friends, family and acquaintances significant detail of their traumas and experiences. However, it may also manifest as an urge to tell the truth, or to disclose or report what happened to them. This could be in person, in writing, in therapy, to the police, on social media, or to friends and family.

Whilst there may be social consequences of disclosing details of traumas and distress publicly, this behaviour is not in itself problematic or harmful. For some people, speaking openly about what they have been through is an important part of processing their trauma and distress. For some people, especially where they have felt under pressure to keep secrets or not to speak publicly about what they have lived through, it may be a feeling of injustice or unfairness that they must stay quiet when they wish to be able to talk about their life.

Some people get closure and power from disclosing publicly, despite the possible risks and consequences. Some people disclose to who they need to, and then move on. Other people feel they must write and talk about their experiences to help others in the same situation.

It is worth considering the social and cultural norms around disclosure, and whether the person is being framed as problematic or harmful for simply expressing their human rights to talk about their own life. Speaking publicly about experiences of trauma, abuse, oppression, and distress can sometimes be celebrated and sensationalised in the media and global stage, but the same action can also be vilified, pathologised, and positioned as abnormal, attention seeking and vindictive in other contexts. The priority, therefore, should be the well-being of the person who is disclosing, whether the disclosure is safe, whether it was made freely, whether it was made with capacity and consent, and whether it is harming or helping the person.

Disinhibition

A common trauma response is to become disinhibited, unconstrained and to stop responding to, or caring about, inhibitions. An inhibition is a feeling that makes a person self-conscious, or aware of their restraining their behaviours or thoughts, usually leading to the person not engaging in the behaviour or thought. It is most commonly used when describing impulses and desires.

Many people subjected to trauma or distress will report that they simply stopped caring about the perceptions or judgement of others, and their own inhibitions reduced as a result of being traumatised, abused or distressed. Whilst disinhibition has been framed as abnormal, and a symptom of a mental disorder, a trauma informed approach may suggest that disinhibition comes from the release or discarding of multiple social norms, conformities and layers of control.

Disorganised

Feeling disorganised is a common response to distress and trauma. Some people report a feeling of being out of control, becoming forgetful, not being able to plan ahead or follow through with planning, feeling indecisive and feeling 'scattered'.

For some people, feeling disorganised is an accurate reflection of how much they are processing, juggling and responding to. For example, a busy single parent who has just lost their job, recently left an abusive relationship, needs to move house, needs to apply for benefits and is struggling to remember or organise extracurricular activities and dinnertimes. In these cases, feeling disorganised is likely and expected.

For some people however, feeling disorganised is not related to external pressures, and is instead an internal feeling of lack of control, forgetfulness, and lack of ability to plan. During times of distress and trauma, some people thrive on rigidity, planning, structure and routine, whereas others find it difficult to maintain any plans, structure or routine, which can lead them to feeling disorganised. When a person is feeling overwhelmed with other emotions and responses to trauma and distress, they may not have the energy or focus to plan, organise and remember chores/errands.

Dissociation

Dissociation is a common trauma response and/or coping mechanism in which the person feels disconnected from themselves or the world around them. It is theorised to fall into different types, and is commonly pathologised as a mental disorder or illness. In more severe or prolonged dissociation, the disconnection from self and others can be accompanied by memory loss, changes in identity, perceptions, or consciousness. Despite this, there are other ways of understanding and discussing dissociation as a common, natural and purposeful trauma response or coping mechanism.

As previously discussed, day dreaming is recognised as a mild form of dissociation – and this is experienced by most of the global population.

Other forms of dissociation include:

Depersonalisation – the person may report feeling like they are detached from, or not inside their own body. Some people call these 'out of body experiences'. For some people, they will talk about not recognising themselves in the mirror, or not feeling connected to their appearance or their body.

Derealisation – the person may report feeling that the world is not real. Some people say the world seems faked, far away, or as if seen as an observer looking through a window or a veil. Some people describe the world as if they are watching a movie, as if they are just watching it instead of living in it.

Dissociative amnesia – People may not be able to remember blocks of time, events, abuse, or an incident. This may range from a few minutes through to many years. Most commonly though, they report micro-amnesia, in which they cannot remember a moment, a conversation, a word, an action or an experience.

Identity confusion and identity alteration – identity confusion is described as a sense of confusion about who the person is, or when a person suddenly acts completely out of character. Identity alteration is described as a sense of being a different person, or the person feeling that they have different parts of themselves.

Research has demonstrated that around 75% of everyone subjected to traumatic incidents will experience dissociation in the weeks and months after the trauma (ISST, 2023).

Dissociation is generally considered to be adaptive, because it reduces the distress and trauma the person is trying to cope with. A person may have developed dissociation as a coping mechanism during traumas which helped them to disconnect from reality. Later in life, they may find that they dissociate during similar situations, triggers, or stressful events as a coping mechanism.

Distracting yourself

A common coping mechanism related to avoidance behaviours. Distracting the self from memories, feelings, experiences, and distress is a common way to cope with ongoing situations or trauma.

It is also important to consider that many professional approaches to behavioural and emotional change also include distraction techniques, which means that distraction should not be assumed to be negative or positive without exploring what it means for the person themselves. For some, distraction is an important mechanism that works positively, whereas for others, distraction is a temporary technique that eventually breaks down because the root cause of the distress is not being addressed or solved.

Distrust of others

Distrust of others can be a common response to trauma. Trauma can erode a person's ability to trust others, and survivors may feel hesitant to form new relationships or to rely on others for support. Some may feel a sense of betrayal by someone they trusted, such as a family member, friend, or caregiver, who failed to protect them from harm or who actively participated in the traumatic event. Trauma can leave people feeling afraid and vulnerable. As a result, some people may struggle to trust others out of fear of being hurt again. Trauma can leave people feeling like they have lost control over their lives. As a result, some people may feel like they need to control every aspect of their environment and interactions with others, leading to feelings of mistrust.

Dominance

Dominance can be defined as the state of having power, influence, or authority over others. In social contexts, dominance often refers to the ability to control or direct the behaviour of others, typically through the use of physical, emotional, or social resources.

For some people who have been subjected to trauma which left them feeling helpless, submissive, downtrodden, victimised, powerless and worthless, becoming more dominant over other people may be a way to regain a sense of power. This behaviour change may be deliberate, and driven by anger or fear. A person may feel they are to blame for what happened to them, and so they attempt to protect themselves in future by becoming more dominant in relationships, believing that if they remain in control and in power they cannot be hurt again.

Becoming more dominant might not be harmful on its own, but if the dominance behaviours are targeted towards partners, loved ones, colleagues or friends in a way which seeks to control and retain power, it is likely to harm others.

Dreams

Dreams are a series of thoughts, images, and sensations that occur during sleep. Dreams can be vivid, intense, and often involve surreal or unrealistic experiences that may or may not be related to events or thoughts that occurred during the day.

There are different theories about why we dream. Some theories suggest that dreams serve a biological purpose, such as helping to consolidate memories, processing emotions, or regulating the nervous system. Other theories propose that dreams serve a psychological purpose, such as helping us to work through unresolved issues or providing insight into our unconscious thoughts and desires.

Dreams can take many different forms and may include a range of emotions, from pleasant to unpleasant. Dreams may also include symbolic representations of real-life experiences, people, or emotions, or may be entirely surreal or fantastical. Dreams can be influenced by a variety of factors, including sleep environment, physical health, emotional state, and external stimuli. While the exact purpose of dreams remains unknown, they are a natural and universal experience that occurs during the sleep cycle for most people.

Dreams can be a response to trauma in some people. Trauma can have a significant impact on a person's thoughts, emotions, and behaviours, and can lead to vivid and intense dreams that may be related to the traumatic event. For some people, trauma-related dreams may involve re-experiencing the traumatic event in a way that feels as if the event is happening again. These dreams can be vivid and may cause the individual to feel distressed or anxious upon waking. In other cases, trauma-related dreams may involve symbolic representations of the traumatic event or may be completely unrelated to the trauma but still cause distress for the individual. It is important to note that trauma-related dreams are a normal response to trauma and can be a way for the brain to process and work through the traumatic event.

Drinking alcohol

A common coping mechanism during or after trauma and distress is to drink alcohol. Some people drink large amounts of alcohol in one sitting, which is discussed under 'binge drinking'. For others, drinking alcohol becomes a daily act with a purpose. The purpose of drinking alcohol is often closely related to the impact it has on the brain and body. Alcohol affects the central nervous system (CNS), impacting the way the brain communicates with the nerves in the body. It may produce a calming or relaxant effect, disinhibition, numbness, a feeling of the mind 'slowing down', sleepiness, or a temporary feeling of excitement, happiness, or fun. For some people, alcohol is an easy, quick, accessible, and relatively cheap way to feel differently, both mentally and physically. It is widely available, and it is important to consider the social and cultural norms surrounding alcohol.

Whilst people generally recognise a 'drink problem', they are also bombarded with images and marketing which celebrates, sensationalises, encourages, and supports alcohol consumption. It is connected to sociability, and

spending time with family and friends. Alcohol is suggested or recommended with meals, at celebrations, funerals, events, to relax, to unwind, to commiserate, to drink whilst watching sports, to go camping, to dance, and to party.
It is therefore very likely that people who are subjected to distress or trauma will be encouraged to drink to make themselves feel better, despite the fact that alcohol is toxic, and causes severe health and social problems.

Further, it may be worth considering the added stigma and barriers for those who drink alcohol to cope, when they belong to communities or religions which prohibit the use of alcohol.

Embarrassment

A common response to trauma or distress which is defined as a sense of shame, awkwardness, or self-consciousness. Embarrassment can arise in response to many forms of distress or trauma, especially when the person feels stupid, naïve, ashamed, humiliated, belittled, exposed or guilty.

Feeling embarrassment can be a response to trauma in some people. Trauma can impact an individual's self-esteem and can lead to feelings of shame, guilt, and embarrassment. These feelings can be exacerbated if the individual perceives that they are being judged or scrutinised by others. For example, if the trauma involved a sexual assault or other form of abuse, the individual may feel embarrassed or ashamed of what happened to them, even though they were not responsible for the trauma. This can lead to social isolation, avoidance of certain situations or people, and a general feeling of low self-worth.

It is important to note that feeling embarrassment or shame is a normal response to trauma.

Empathy changes

A noticeable change in empathy (increase or decrease) may occur as a trauma response and/or coping mechanism. For some people, empathy for others may decrease as a result of feeling harmed or betrayed by people, systems, communities, or family. For others, retaining high empathy for other people may become exhausting and overwhelming when also processing significant trauma and distress for themselves. This may lead to a conscious or unconscious decision to stop caring as much about others, in order to protect the self from further burnout or harm. This may be especially true for those who feel they have been exploited, used, or deceived into helping, loving, caring for or supporting someone who then harms them.

Increased empathy may also occur. This can be in relation to the trauma itself (developing higher empathy for others going through cancer treatment because they now have lived experience and insight into the process themselves), or it may be as a broader shift in worldview after being subjected to trauma, distress, marginalisation, or disaster. For some people, trauma or prolonged distress is transformational, and causes a change in world view which may elicit higher empathy for other victims, or a greater understanding of human suffering.

Neither an increase or decrease are inherently good or bad. The change in empathy should be considered in context, and assumptions should not be made that a decrease in empathy creates a bad person, or that an increase in empathy creates a better person. It may also be useful to remember that whilst high empathy is generally considered positive, people with high empathy tend to burnout quickly, experience vicarious trauma, exhaustion and overwhelm from trying to support other people whilst also in a state of distress themselves.

Envy

Envy is defined as a painful or resentful awareness of an advantage or possession enjoyed by another and the desire to possess the same thing.

Envy may develop during or after trauma or distress if the person becomes resentful that other people have lifestyles, possessions, relationships, opportunities, wealth, experiences, adoration, success, or family that they long to have. For some people, envy may be broad and generalised, for example, the person may feel that they have had a terrible and difficult life so far, and then become resentful and envious of someone they perceive to be having an easier or happier life. For other people, envy can be more specific. A person who has had several failed marriages may become angry, envious, and hurt by their best friend having a long happy marriage, for example.

Envy is often borne out of comparing ourselves to others, overstating their happiness or success, and downplaying the reality that their life is probably complex, difficult, and stressful, but in different ways.

Exaggerating

Exaggerating information, anecdotes, facts, and experiences is a possible trauma response or coping mechanism after periods of distress or trauma events. Exaggerating is often perceived to be lying, and therefore, many people do not admit to doing it. Some people who do report exaggerating truths or stories say that they do it when they are scared they won't be believed, won't be supported, or don't feel like they belong.

Research into exaggerating theorises that exaggeration is common, and rather than it being an abnormal or specific behaviour, exaggeration can be found everywhere.

Companies exaggerate the value of their products. The health benefits of certain medical and wellbeing procedures are exaggerated. Politicians exaggerate their commitment to causes or policies. Academics exaggerate the significance of their findings.

People exaggerate frequently when they need to be taken seriously at their doctors' appointments, and so they overstate or exaggerate their health symptoms to ensure the doctor listens. People also exaggerate their inconveniences or grievances when submitting complaints to a company or service, in order to secure a refund or good service. It is common for people to exaggerate their income, social status, popularity, confidence, academic ability, exam scores, and successes.

This arguably points to exaggeration being a behaviour that is engaged in when the person is looking for belonging, acceptance, importance, self-esteem, validation, and support.

Expressive art

Using expressive art as a coping mechanism for trauma can be a helpful way for people to process and work through their emotions and experiences in a safe and creative way. Expressive art can include a variety of mediums, such as painting, drawing, sculpture, writing, music, or dance, and can be used to express feelings that may be difficult to put into words.

Expressive art can be a particularly effective coping mechanism for trauma for several reasons. Firstly, it allows the individual to express their emotions and experiences in a non-verbal way, which can be particularly helpful for people who may struggle to verbalise their thoughts or feelings. Additionally, engaging in creative activities can be a calming and meditative experience, which can help to reduce distress and fear associated with trauma.

Expressive art allows people to express their emotions and experiences in a safe and non-judgmental way, which can help to promote a sense of self-expression and creativity. Engaging in creative activities can help people to gain insight into their emotions and thought processes, which can promote self-awareness and personal growth.
Trauma can leave people feeling powerless and out of control. Engaging in creative activities can provide a sense of control and autonomy, which can be empowering.

Fabricating illness

Some people may fabricate illness as a response to trauma as a way to cope with their emotional distress.

People who fabricate illness may do so in order to receive attention and care from others, which can temporarily alleviate feelings of loneliness or emotional distress. Trauma can leave people feeling powerless and out of control. Fabricating illness may provide a sense of control over their environment, as they are able to manipulate others' perceptions and actions. Fabricating illness may provide a temporary escape from difficult or stressful situations, as people may be able to avoid responsibilities or obligations due to their perceived illness.

Fantasies (sexual)

For some people, their sexual fantasies may change, develop, stop, or begin during or after trauma. Sexual fantasies are usually normal and natural, and most people have them. However, if the person disclosed that their sexual fantasies have changed since or during the trauma, it may be worth discussing this with them if they feel comfortable to do so. Sexual fantasies may stop completely whilst the person is feeling overwhelmed, distressed, traumatised, afraid, angry, anxious or sad.

However, for some people, trauma can influence their sexual fantasies. For example, it is not uncommon for women to report fantasises of being raped, dominated, abused, beaten, choked, harmed or assaulted even though they recognise they have been subjected to it in real life, and it was terrifying and traumatic. Some people develop fantasies that exactly replicate the sexual abuse they were subjected to as children, almost as exact re-enactment. This may arouse some people, but terrify others. There is often some confusion, shame and guilt around sexual fantasies that replicate sexual abuse or violence, too.

Some changes in fantasies may also give some clues to how the trauma has impacted or changed the sexual preferences of the person, which is discussed under 'sexual preferences'. For example, some people may begin fantasising about different kinds of sexual acts, different kinds of people, different sensations, environments, or sexualities.

Fatigue

A common response to trauma is to feel exhausted. Fatigue is defined as a reduction in energy, and a feeling of extreme tiredness that doesn't get better with rest. There is not usually a physical cause (such as an underlying disease or illness), but fatigue can be caused by mental and emotional exhaustion. Feeling exhausted can significantly impact the ability to do things, live a normal day-to-day life, the ability to concentrate or focus, or to take part in usual activities.

It is common for people to assume their fatigue is medical or caused by an underlying undiagnosed illness or health complication, and whilst this should always be ruled out, it is also common for people to report severe fatigue which may last weeks, months or years following acute or chronic trauma and distress. For some, the fatigue may be caused by heightened levels of adrenaline and cortisol, which means the body is becoming tired quickly due to consistently high levels of energy being used up whilst traumatised or scared.

For others, fatigue may be due to hypervigilance and a feeling of lack of safety. If the person is waking up in the night, not able to rest or sleep, doesn't feel safe, and is frequently triggered back into a state of distress, it is likely that they will become fatigued.

Fear of the dark

A fear of the dark can be a response to trauma in some people. Trauma can leave people feeling vulnerable and fearful, and the darkness may represent a sense of danger or the unknown. Some people may avoid being in the dark or may seek out sources of light in order to feel safe and protected. The fear of the dark can lead to heightened levels of fear and distress, as people may feel constantly on guard and hypervigilant. The fear of the dark can make it difficult for people to relax and fall asleep, as they may feel constantly alert and on guard. It is important to note that a fear of the dark as a response to trauma is a normal and natural response to an overwhelming experience.

Feeling empty or meaningless

A response to trauma or distress, a person may begin to feel empty, meaningless, or without purpose. This may arise from a change in their understanding or world view, post-trauma or distress. The trauma itself may have caused significant upheaval in the core beliefs about the world. For example, if a person believed that if they were a good person, they would live a good life and be treated well by others, it may come as a considerable shock to them when they are harmed or abused by someone else. It may cause them to question their understanding of the world, and of other people, ultimately coming to the conclusion that there is no meaning or purpose to anything.

It is worth considering the cultural significance of 'meaning' and 'purpose', too. We often hear influential messages from society about what our life should be, who we should be, and what role we should play in the community and in life. When we feel that we are not achieving or living up to that expectation or goal, it is likely that we may begin to feel empty, or question the meaning or purpose of life itself.

In a capitalist society, the vision of a 'meaningful' life is often wealth, possessions, travel, house purchases, nice car, good job, or even fame and authority. It is therefore important to understand that for some people, being subjected to trauma or distress may make them feel that they will never achieve their goals, or may never have any 'meaning' or 'purpose' in their life.

Feeling lost

Similar to the feelings of emptiness or meaninglessness, feeling lost is a common response to trauma which is caused by significant change. Where once, a person may have had a sure understanding of who they were, where they were headed, who their friends were, and how they felt about things, it is likely that trauma and distress will distort or destroy some of that certainty. The resulting feeling is one of feeling as though the person is lost in a sea of people, or in a large situation.

Feeling of being watched

A common experience for people who have been subjected to trauma or experienced significant distress, especially where there is an element of power, control, threat, stalking or harassment. Whilst it is common for professionals to describe the feeling of being watched as 'paranoia' or 'suspicion' or even 'delusions', it is natural and normal to fear being watched.

Ultimately, the root of the fear of being watched, is a fear of being harmed, betrayed, killed or controlled. However, it is also important to note that there have been many studies into the 'sense of being stared at', and many psychological researchers suggest that humans can feel when they are being watched or monitored by others.

Our brains do spend a lot of time scanning an environment for connection, communication, or risk, and this can increase following trauma or distress. Therefore, it is likely that a person may become aware of being watched or looked at, whereas others who are not scanning the room or the street for threats and harm, may not notice the same people looking at them.

Being subjected to violence and abuse, or experiencing a significant accident or injury may have caused a change in understanding and worldview, in which the person may realise that sometimes, there are people targeting them or planning to harm them that they are not yet aware of. This is technically correct for many victims of violence, abuse or attacks, as they may well have been being watched for some time before being harmed by someone with intent.

Further, it is important to remember that for some people whose trauma arose from being stalked, harassed, watched, monitored, controlled, followed, or threatened, their feeling of being watched may come from a long period of time in which they were indeed being watched. They may also have been told they were wrong, they were making it up, or they were paranoid, only to find out that they were right all along.

Feeling of going crazy

During and after trauma and distress, some people will describe a feeling of 'going crazy'. This is usually a unique mixture of experiences for each person, and so it is worth exploring what that means to the person. Do they feel they are forgetting things? Do they feel as though they are misunderstanding events or information? Are they worried they are misinformed or misremembering events? Are they experiencing changes in the emotional and mental health that are frightening them or making them feel uncomfortable? Are they having panic attacks or flashbacks that are becoming difficult to ground out of? Are they hearing voices or seeing visual hallucinations? Are they suffering from sleep deprivation?

It is worth exploring whether they also have a fear of 'going crazy' which is arguably linked to stigmatising and sensationalised images and films of people becoming incoherent, detached, inconsolable and uncontrollable. For many people, there is a significant fear of 'going crazy', which they may touch upon as a partial joke, or they may disclose as a real fear, as if they will one day become 'crazy' or 'insane' and not be able to participate in their normal lives.

Feeling of losing control

Similar to the feeling of 'going crazy', some people experience a trauma response in which they feel they are losing control. 'Losing control' means different things to different people, and can range from the person feeling they are losing control of their lives, relationships and routines, through to feeling that they are losing control of their minds, thoughts, behaviours, feelings and abilities. The feeling of 'losing control' is closely related to 'going crazy' in language, literature and art.

Losing control has often been portrayed as someone being put under increasing pressure until they become explosive, incoherent, violent, dangerous, suicidal, and even criminal. This frequent depiction of 'losing control' in such extreme terms may fuel the fear some people have that if they allow themselves to feel everything or think about everything they need to, they will simply lose control of their lives and their minds, and commit acts they will regret.

Feelings of purpose and importance

Rather than feeling worthless and meaningless, some people report feeling a sense of purpose, and importance after trauma. For some people, this is a result of deliberately seeking purpose, meaning, and importance in their lives after being subjected to events that made them feel low, insecure and lost. Some describe this as a positive process or a result of 'post-traumatic growth', in which the person finds meaning, purpose and lessons in their experiences.

For others, this is a trauma response that may manifest to combat feelings of meaningless that may arise during and after experiences such as neglect, abuse, and coercive control.

Fight or Flight Response

Our 'fight or flight' response is an accessible term to explain the way our brains and bodies respond to threat. Whilst 'threat' would have originally meant physical, life-threatening danger, we also now understand it to include psychological and emotional harm.

The fight or flight response is a physiological response to distress or danger that prepares the body to either confront the threat (fight) or escape from it (flight). It is a natural and instinctive response that is controlled by the autonomic nervous system, which regulates unconscious bodily functions such as breathing, heart rate, and digestion.

When the body perceives a threat or danger, the sympathetic nervous system activates the fight or flight response. This causes a surge of hormones, including adrenaline and cortisol, to be released into the bloodstream. This triggers several physical changes in the body, including increased heart rate and blood pressure, rapid breathing, dilated pupils, increased blood flow to the muscles, and heightened alertness and awareness.

The fight or flight response is an evolutionary adaptation that has helped humans and other animals to survive in dangerous situations by providing the necessary physical resources to either fight off the threat or flee from it. While the fight or flight response is a normal and natural response to distress or danger, chronic activation of this response can have negative effects on the body and mind, including increased risk of heart disease.

In addition to the fight or flight response, a third response, freeze, is also recognised by some experts. This involves the body becoming immobile and unresponsive as a way to protect oneself from a perceived threat. This response may be more common in situations where the individual feels overwhelmed and unable to effectively fight or flee.

It is important to note that everyone responds differently to distress or danger, and the fight or flight response may not be the only way that people respond to perceived threats.

Finding religion

Religion is defined as a belief in, and the worship of a superhuman power, a God, or a system of Gods. Religions are generally recognised to be a set of global faiths, including but not limited to Buddhism, Judaism, Hinduism, Islam, Christianity, Sikhism, Taoism, Wicca and Jainism. Religion is often an important part of life, as it lends explanation to how and why events and experiences happen to us all, whether they are good or bad. Religion can also shape the worldview of the person, changing the way they see social issues such as crime, punishment, law, control, forgiveness, suffering, poverty, life, and death.

Some people turn to a new belief in religion, or lean into an existing religion as a coping mechanism. Beliefs in a higher power can enforce a better sense of control, meaning, purpose, direction, justice, reward, and punishment.

Often, when a person experiences trauma, loss, or is subjected to violence or oppression, they are left with many unanswered questions. Many of these questions centre around 'why' this happened to them, and what it 'means'. Whilst some people might accept that life is unpredictable and random, others may find more meaning in believing that there is a higher power which plans, controls, watches over, protects, and understands the person and their experiences. Therefore, for some people, believing that there is meaning, learning, direction and purpose in every element of existence may bring comfort.

Finding spirituality

Similar to finding religion, finding spirituality can be understood as a coping mechanism for traumatic experiences. Whereas a religion traditionally has a structure, laws, and heads, spirituality has no specific structure. It is arguably more personal, abstract, and vague than organised religion, too.

Spirituality involves a recognition or belief that there is something greater than humanity, or that humans are only a small part of a greater whole which may include magic, cosmic beliefs, our role in the wider universe, in energy, or in other contexts.

Similar to finding religion then, finding spirituality after trauma may be related to searching for higher purpose, meaning, importance, context or direction. When a person has been subjected to trauma or distress, they may question the reasons or meanings of those experiences. Spirituality may help people feel more in control, or help them to understand their role in the world. Further, some people describe spirituality as a journey towards wisdom, knowledge, love, kindness, authenticity and openness, which might be beneficial to those who are trying to find ways to cope with experiences such as trauma, distress, abuse, violence, oppression, poverty or loss.

Flashbacks and memories

Flashbacks and memories are a normal, natural experience, whether they are related to trauma or not. We access and process thousands of memories every day, from where we left our phone to the last memory we have of our Grandma before she died. Our memories make up our story of who we are.

Flashbacks are described as a memory which is so intense that it can make the person feel as though they are back in that moment of the memory. Whilst most people only discuss or acknowledge trauma flashbacks of frightening, harmful or sad memories, they may also include happy, exciting, and exhilarating memories. They may describe multi-sensory flashbacks, including being able to see, smell, taste, hear and feel things they could at the time of the trauma. Some people explain their flashbacks to feel as though they are reliving the trauma all over again.

For some people, a flashback is like watching a movie from a third-person perspective, as if they are a witness, or a fly on the wall. In that sense, the 'flashback' has been reconstructed, as it is impossible for the person in the trauma to have also been outside of their body, watching themselves suffer the trauma from a distance. However, some people experience flashbacks in first-person perspective, as if they are re-experiencing the exact events again. This can include experiencing pain or sensations that occurred at the time.

Flashback memories are involuntary, and sometimes described as intrusive.

Forcing yourself to be sick

A coping mechanism during or after trauma or distress, some people force themselves to vomit. Whilst being involuntarily sick during trauma or shock is common and normal, a person deliberately and voluntarily making themselves sick is more accurately considered a coping mechanism for distress.

It is important to consider the underlying reason the person has for making themselves sick, which may be related to issues with eating, bingeing and purging – but equally, may not be related to this at all. Some people report making themselves sick as a form of self-punishment, self-harm, self-control, and low self-esteem.

Whilst exploring this behaviour, it is equally important to establish how vomiting makes the person feel (is it making them feel better, or worse? Does it make them feel worried, or does it make them feel more in control? Do they think it's a problem, or do they see it as normal?)

Forgetfulness

A common impact of trauma and distress, especially where it occurs over long periods of time, is forgetfulness. Some people describe this trauma response as being severe, and impacting their daily lives, whereas others describe it as occasional and irritating. Forgetfulness is usually related to short term memory and working memory, due to distress impacting focus, concentration, attention span, and distractibility.

Forgetfulness can be a response to trauma in some people. Trauma can have a significant impact on an individual's cognitive function, including their memory and ability to focus. For some people, forgetfulness is caused by chronic exhaustion and sleep deprivation.

Trauma can also lead to hyperarousal, in which people may feel overly alert and on edge. This can make it difficult to focus or pay attention, leading to forgetfulness or memory lapses. In some cases, people may avoid thinking or talking about the traumatic experience as a way to cope. This can lead to forgetfulness or a lack of clarity around the details of the traumatic event.

It is important to note that forgetfulness as a response to trauma is a normal and natural response to a traumatic experience.

Forgiveness

Forgiveness is a complex issue for many people who have been subjected to trauma or abuse by another person. Forgiveness can also be shown towards the self.

Forgiveness is the act of stopping feelings of anger, resentment, or contempt towards another person, or towards the self. Whilst the act of forgiving is generally positioned as a positive and kind thing to do, which makes people feel better about situations, or helps them to move on – forgiveness is often more complicated in trauma, abuse, violence and oppression.

First, forgiveness does not always make someone feel better about a situation. People can expect than when they forgive the person who has harmed them, they will feel better and be able to move on from their trauma. Second, forgiveness can be expected or pressured by self or others, on the mistaken belief that trauma processing or 'healing' can only begin to occur once everyone has been forgiven. Third, and relatedly, forgiveness can be expected from a religious or moral perspective, based on the belief that the person must learn to forgive others, if they ever wish to be forgiven for their own wrongdoings in life.

In this way, forgiveness can become toxic rather than positive, and some people may describe feeling that they have been forced, coerced or guilt-tripped into forgiving someone who harmed them. They may also discuss feelings of superficial forgiveness, where they originally thought they had forgiven the person who harmed them, but realised later that they simply said or thought that, but are still angry or resentful towards them.

Due to forgiveness being awarded such generous, gracious and kind status as a behaviour, many people will feel obliged or pressured to forgive others in order to be a 'good person'. They may describe feeling like a 'bad person' for not being ready to forgive someone else.

It is important that people know they do not need to forgive others who have abused, violated, oppressed, harmed or controlled them – and this is not required in their own trauma processing journey.

Forgiveness is therefore private and personal, and will have different impacts and meanings for each person. It should not be assumed that forgiveness is positive, helpful or freeing.

Freeze response

The most common trauma response to threat or harm, is to freeze. Whilst most people recognise the 'flight or fight' trauma response, they are much less common than the 'freeze' response. Research has found that over 70% of people who are subjected to rape or sexual assault will freeze during the attack, for example.

Moor et al. (2013) reports the 'freeze response' as a common form of paralysis and behavioural inhibition which prevents the person from any type of response to the sexual trauma – resulting in the person being silent and feeling 'frozen' to the spot, unable to move or respond. This response is so common in fact, that Bucher and Manasse (2011) found that 42% of all women who were raped experienced a complete freeze response during their rape which included being incapable of verbal or physical response. More recent research found that over 70% of women who are raped freeze during the attack (Muller et al., 2017).

Despite this common response, which Moor et al. (2013) argue is an adaptive survival tactic to reduce further damage to the body – it is still viewed as an inadequate victim response and therefore contributes to the social blaming and personal self-blame of women who have been subjected to sexual assault or rape.

The freeze response is a physiological response that can occur during a traumatic experience. It is a natural and instinctive response that is controlled by the autonomic nervous system, which regulates unconscious bodily functions such as breathing, heart rate, and digestion.

During a traumatic experience, the body may perceive a threat that is overwhelming or impossible to fight or flee from. In these cases, the freeze response can occur, in which the body becomes immobilised and unresponsive as a way to protect oneself from the perceived threat. This can involve a range of physical and emotional responses, including numbness, dissociation, and detachment from the situation.

The freeze response can be a helpful survival mechanism in certain situations, such as when an individual is facing a predator or other physical threat. However, when the freeze response occurs during a traumatic experience, it can have negative effects on the individual's mental and emotional wellbeing, including feelings of helplessness, shame, and guilt.

It is important to note that everyone responds differently to traumatic experiences, and the freeze response may not be the only way that people respond to perceived threats. Additionally, some people may experience the freeze response in situations that have triggered them into a threat response.

Frequently moving house

Whilst frequently moving house may be related to practical or financial issues (temporary accommodation, eviction, end of tenancy, moving area, needing to upsize or downsize, debt, divorce, or arrears), sometimes, frequently moving house or area can be a coping mechanism for trauma.

For some people, trauma leaves them feeling disconnected from their town or community, and in search of where they belong, or where they feel safe. They may also move frequently due to feelings of risk, threat and danger (either real or perceived).

It is not uncommon for people who have been impacted by trauma and distress to feel the need for a 'fresh start' or 'new surroundings' in order to move on, and rebuild their lives after significant trauma.

Gambling

Gambling is usually recognised as a coping mechanism for distress and trauma. Some people may begin gambling for a range of reasons. It may start out as something fun and exciting to do, a way to socialise with others, something to distract the person from other difficult experiences, or a temporary escape from reality.

Gambling and winning can provide reward, excitement, positive reinforcement, and fun. However, gambling and losing (which is statistically more common) can cause fear, anger, resentment, self-loathing, financial issues and further distress. Gambling can be a coping mechanism for some people who are dealing with difficult emotions or life circumstances. Gambling may provide a temporary escape from problems, a way to cope with stress, or a source of excitement and stimulation.

However, using gambling as a coping mechanism can have negative consequences. It can lead to financial problems, relationship difficulties, and the development of a gambling addiction. Gambling can also mask underlying emotional issues and prevent people from addressing the root causes of their distress.

Going to the gym (exercising)

In some cases, people report that one of their main coping mechanisms for trauma or distress, is to exercise. In moderation, this is often advised by medical and therapeutic professionals, due to the positive impact in mind and body for many people. However, for some people, excessive exercise or spending hours in the gym can be a coping mechanism for a range of feelings and thoughts.

For some people, exercise is a way to tolerate excessive anxious energy, anger, and aggression. Some people may use exercise to help them to sleep or relax, by engaging in hours of physical exertion until they become extremely tired. For others, exercise is a way to quieten the thoughts and memories they are dealing with as a result of trauma or distress. Exercising can distract the person, and force them to think about something structured, numerical or ritualistic (counting reps, monitoring progress, watching a running programme on a treadmill, increasing weights, or repeating exercises).

In addition to these reasons, excessive exercise may be related to issues around body image, eating, weight gain, weight loss or transforming physical appearance after trauma and during periods of distress.

Guilt

Guilt is a common trauma response for people who have experienced a range of traumas and distress. Some people report feeling guilty due to not being able to cope, feeling like a burden, or feeling as though they have failed in some way. Other people feel intense guilt when they have done something wrong, or when they feel they have done something they regret. Further, guilt is common when people feel that their reaction or inaction to abuse, violence or oppression led to others being harmed or put at risk (for example, a mother who feels intense guilt that her children witnessed her being abused by their father, where she was not at fault in anyway, but still feels accountable and guilty for her children being exposed to years of violence and trauma).

Another form of guilt associated with abuse, disaster and traumatic events is described as 'survivor's guilt'. This type of guilt may occur where a person survives, or is not subjected to traumas that others suffer from. Examples of events which might cause survivor's guilt include surviving an earthquake, flood, eruption, explosion, house fire, or car accident where others did not survive, or were seriously injured. Another common example in child abuse, is guilt of one sibling who was not sexually abused, where they become aware that all other siblings were subjected to years of sexual abuse.

Overall, guilt can be a useful and helpful feeling if it holds us accountable for something genuinely wrong or harmful that we did to another person, but can become toxic and distressing if the guilt is misplaced, coerced, manufactured or inaccurate.

Hatred of particular groups of people

Hatred of particular groups of people can be a response to trauma in some people. Trauma can lead to intense feelings of anger, fear, and resentment, and can result in people projecting these feelings onto certain groups of people. In some cases, people may blame an entire group of people for the traumatic event, even if that group was not directly responsible. This can lead to prejudice, bigotry, and discrimination, and can further perpetuate negative attitudes towards marginalised communities.

It is important to note that hatred towards particular groups of people as a response to trauma is not a healthy or productive way to cope with emotional distress. It can lead to further feelings of isolation, anger, and resentment, and can hinder the healing process. Instead, it is important for people who are struggling with feelings of hatred or prejudice towards particular groups to seek support from qualified professionals, such as a therapist.

Hatred of the body

Developing a hatred of the body, or parts of the body during and after trauma is likely to be a trauma response. For some people, the link from their original trauma or distress to their hatred of their body will be clear and direct (such as hating their body ever since they were sexually abused as a child, in which their body was violated or harmed). However, for some people, the link between their body hatred and the original trauma or source of distress may be less clear.

Controlling or hating our bodies could be related to control, self-punishment, shame, disgust, self-loathing, self-esteem, embarrassment, guilt, fear or anger. Some people develop hatred or resentment for their bodies when they perceive them as 'not working properly', too. This may be true for some people with chronic illnesses, disabilities, terminal illnesses, or fertility issues.

It is worth considering the cultural and social implications of body hatred, and of loving our bodies. We live in a society that encourages to criticise and hate our bodies in order to sell us products and regimes that will 'fix' our bodies. Constant exposure to these messages via magazines, social media and societal messages may cause significant distress for some people. Further, due to the social pressure to remain young and look visibly toned, youthful and small, some people report resenting or hating their bodies as they naturally age, too.

In all cases, it is important to explore why the person hates their body (or specific body part), and what that means to them. Do not make assumptions or employ stereotypes.

Hatred of the self

A common trauma response, some people begin to hate themselves for many reasons. In some cases, the person is aware that they hate themselves, and may even discuss that hatred openly and frankly. In other cases, the person may have behaviours or feelings that are linked to their self-hatred, despite having never understood it.

Hatred of self may come from deeper roots such as shame, guilt, blame, embarrassment, low self-esteem, worthlessness, or hopelessness. Some people report that they began to hate themselves once they started thinking (or someone told them) that there was something wrong with them, or that they were worth less than other people.

It is common for self-hatred to begin as self-criticism, or self-punishment, before developing into a hatred. The person may explain to you that they are highly critical of themselves, or feel that they never live up to certain standards that have been set by themselves, or by others.

Having increased casual sex

After sexual trauma, it is common for some people to seek out increased casual sex. Whilst this is a personal choice, and there is nothing inherently negative about this behaviour (as long as the sex is mutually consensual, enjoyable, safe, and respectful), there are many stigmas and social norms around casual sex which causes people to feel that their response is abnormal.

For some people, they may seek out casual sex in order to control their sexuality on their own terms. If they had been previously sexually abused or raped, they might feel they need sex and pleasure that is initiated and controlled by themselves, as opposed to someone else. For that reason, they may also have no interest in dating or ever speaking again to the person they had sex with.

For others, seeking out casual sex might be about pleasure seeking. When people have been subjected to sexual traumas and violence, they can begin to wonder if they will ever enjoy consensual sex again, especially if they have had flashbacks or have been triggered during sex. It might be that the person is using casual sex to normalise sex again, and seek sexual pleasure that they did not have for many months, years, or even decades.

There is a possibility that this behaviour can be destructive or frightening though, and so it is important to establish the reason for the behaviour. Similarly, it is important to understand how the sex feels, and how they feel after the sex. If they feel ashamed, guilty, dirty, embarrassed, or upset, this might be a destructive coping mechanism.

Some people report attempting to replicate their rape or sexual abuse which is covered under sexual fantasies and having casual sex.

Health anxiety

For many people, their fears will manifest into concerns, worries and anxieties about their health. They might find themselves becoming obsessed with checking their health, their body, symptoms, possible illnesses, diagnoses, and worrying about rare or impossible health issues.

For some people, health anxiety can take over their day-to-day lives. They might find themselves searching every little twinge, ache, bump, and cough, convinced that they have a rare illness or undiagnosed health issue that will kill them.

It is this that needs to be considered most importantly, because ultimately, at the root of all health anxieties, is a fear of dying. Whilst the fear of dying may have manifested as a pre-occupation with health, the underlying motivation is to stay alive. Therefore, it is important to understand that people with health anxiety are chiefly worried about illness, disease, and death.

It might be very clear how this links to the original trauma or period of distress. For example, the person might have had a serious illness as a child, or recently had a cancer scare, both of which would motivate and cultivate a strong fear of death and illness in a person. However, in some people, the link is less clear. For some, the fear of becoming ill and dying is about lack of control, and a lack of being able to predict the future. For others, they might describe their health anxiety peaking not in moments of stress, but in moments of happiness and achievement.

There may be a feeling that when things are going well, there must be something around the corner to upset their progress or happiness. On this basis, some people recognise that they begin to fear they will die of a heart attack, stroke, or suddenly become extremely ill just before, or on the day of something wonderful happening to them (the day they graduate university, their birthday, the first day of their great new job, the day they go on holiday, their wedding day).

If it does seem that their health anxieties peak around happy and important events, it might be that the root is more to do with feeling that they do not deserve happiness, or that they have come to expect terrible things to happen to them when they least expect it.

Whilst supporting someone who struggles with health fears, it is worth remembering that the average person is bombarded with messages about staying healthy, lengthening their lifespan, avoiding diabetes, how to self-check for lumps and cancerous changes, increasing cancer rates, unhealthy choices, and public campaigns about strokes and heart attacks. Many people with health anxieties feel that these public messages trigger them, or worsen their fears of dying or becoming unwell.

Finally, whilst health anxiety and a fear of dying may be very difficult to process and cope with, it is rooted in a logical and rational fear that most humans possess: the fear of death. The fear in itself is not abnormal, or irrational at all – and may be better seen as an extension or magnification of the natural fear of dying that motivates animals and humans to stay alive.

Hearing god

During and after trauma and distress, some people can report that they hear voices or messages. For some, they sound like their own voice, for others, they sound like someone else's voice (their mum, their ex-partner, their boss, or a stranger).

For some people, they recognise or identify the voice or message as coming from God. It might be that this happens as a coping mechanism when feeling helpless and powerless, but it is also worth considering that millions of people strive and worship Gods in order to 'hear' their voice. To understand the latest research about the neuroscience underpinning auditory hallucinations, without pathologisation, please see Marchant & Taylor (2021).

It is worth considering that there is significant stigma and myth around hearing voices, and so people become very worried if they begin to hear their own voice, or the voices of others when they are traumatised.

Hearing voices of other people

During and after trauma, some people report spontaneously hearing the voices of other people in their minds. It might be the voices of their perpetrator, their parents, their siblings, their exes, or the voice of a teacher who used to bully them. For others, it is the voice of a stranger, or a public figure.

Whilst this experience can be very distressing, it is fairly common to hear voices, and people will often describe hearing the voice of their late mother, or the voice of their old driving instructor giving them helpful advice or telling them not to do something dangerous. It is important then, that we seek to explore and understand the voices people hear when they are distressed and traumatised, as the mechanism which underpins this experience is likely to be similar. To understand the latest research about the neuroscience underpinning auditory hallucinations, without pathologisation, please see Marchant & Taylor (2021).

It is worth considering that there is significant stigma and myth around hearing voices, and so people become very worried if they begin to hear their own voice, or the voices of others when they are traumatised.

Hearing your own inner voice

Research shows that a large proportion of people have an internal narrator or monologue. This happens with or without distress and trauma. For some people, they hear their own thoughts, or several streams of thoughts at once. They might also be able to 'have conversations' with the voice in their head, and know it is themselves, or perceive it as their 'brain' voice. Around 60% of people think in an audible voice, whereas others never hear a voice. They think in images, or sensations. They might describe thinking in symbols, too. All of these experiences are normal, and being able to hear a voice in the mind/brain is common and natural.

It is worth considering that there is significant stigma and myth around hearing voices, and so people become very worried if they begin to hear their own voice, or the voices of others when they are traumatised.

Helplessness

A feeling of helplessness is a common response to trauma and distress, especially when the person feels unable to escape or protect themselves from harm. Helplessness can also arise when the person feels there is nothing they could have done, or can do, for someone else they wish to protect.

Feelings of helplessness can be a common response to trauma in some people. Trauma can be overwhelming and can leave people feeling powerless and out of control. These feelings can be exacerbated if the individual perceives that they were unable to prevent or escape the traumatic event.

Some people may avoid situations or people that remind them of the traumatic event, as a way to protect themselves from feelings of helplessness and vulnerability. Feelings of helplessness can lead to heightened levels of fear and stress, as people may feel constantly on guard and hypervigilant. Prolonged feelings of helplessness can also lead to significant trauma, as people may feel hopeless and unable to cope with their emotions and experiences. It is important to note that feeling helpless as a response to trauma is a normal and natural response to an overwhelming experience.

Hoarding

Hoarding is defined as the act of collecting or accumulating something and then feeling the need to keep those items, even though they are not needed. Sometimes, hoarding is defined as including the way the items are stored, such as that so many hundreds of items are collected that they clutter the house, fill entire rooms, make it impossible to move around the house, or the hoarding becomes dangerous.

Hoarding can be a trauma response and a coping mechanism for traumatic events. For some people, they develop intense emotional and sentimental attachments to items, so they can never throw anything away. The feeling or thought of throwing away or giving away their collected items causes them significant distress, fear, anger, or concern. For others, they develop strong connections (even if they are distressing) to particular types of items, and collect hundreds or even thousands of them.

When working with someone who may be 'hoarding' it is important to understand when the behaviour began, what it means to them, how they feel about it, and how it is impacting them. It is best understood as a behaviour that is purposeful and meaningful to the person, as opposed to disordered, lazy, greedy, or abnormal.

Hopelessness

Hopelessness is a common response to trauma, especially where the person feels there is no escape, no solution, or no way of helping or protecting themselves from harm.

Hope is a belief, expectation, or a desire for some outcome, or something. Hope can eventually be extinguished by significant, chronic distress or trauma. This is particularly important when a person loses hope accurately. For example, someone may hold on to the hope that their dying relative will become well again, and not die at all. The hope they have may protect them and motivate them when they are feeling distressed by their illness of their relative, but eventually, they may need to face that their desired outcome will not happen. However, some people lose hope through mental exhaustion, especially in circumstances of ongoing harm.

Humiliation

Feeling humiliated, and being humiliated is a common experience during and after trauma and distress. Feeling humiliated may arise as a trauma response where the trauma, involved shaming, embarrassing, exposing, frightening, or blackmailing the person.

Humiliation often arises from traumas which significantly impact the dignity, pride, privacy, and integrity of the person. Therefore, it should be expected that the person who is feeling humiliated may also carry a lot of related shame and self-blame with their trauma.

Some forms of abuse, control, oppression and discrimination rely on humiliation as a form of power, and so it is important to consider whether this was a poignant factor for the person you are working with.

Hyper-independence

Hyper-independence is a coping mechanism for traumatic events in which the person either consciously or unconsciously feels they are safer if they do not rely on anyone else for support, help, or safety.

Independence is a social behaviour that is celebrated and encouraged in individualistic cultures and communities. Hyper-independence is often defined as the following behaviours and choices:

1. Overachieving and perfectionism
2. Refusing to delegate tasks or work to others
3. Never asking for help or support
4. Mistrust of others
5. Expecting to be let down or betrayed
6. Guarding the self, and not allowing anyone in
7. Dislike of 'needy' or 'clingy' behaviour

8. Not allowing close relationships, in case they get hurt
9. Keeping secrets and protecting private information about themselves

For some people, the trauma or distress they have been through has left them feeling as though they do not deserve support, that people will often let them down or hurt them, that people will pretend to support and help them, or that it is weak to ask for help.
For those who have been neglected, they may have had periods of their lives in which they needed to be totally independent in order to stay alive. Independence therefore becomes a successful and much needed survival strategy, that can continue as a coping mechanism throughout life.

It is also worth considering that hyper-independence is a rational and justified coping mechanism when the person has been let down, neglected, betrayed and isolated. They are arguably taking the learning from past traumas and attempting to protect themselves from further trauma by becoming hyper-independent.

Hyperactivity

Hyperactivity can be a trauma response in which some people engage in significant activity, ranging from small movements such as tapping and fidgeting to repetitive talking, exercising, or body movements. Hyperactivity may be a way to distract the mind, a way to express excess anxious energy, or a coping mechanism for distress. Trauma can lead to intense feelings of fear, and restlessness, and can result in people engaging in hyperactive behaviours as a way to cope with their emotions.

Hyperactivity can manifest in a variety of ways. People may engage in excessive physical activity, such as pacing, fidgeting, or restlessness, as a way to burn off excess energy and cope with feelings of anxiety or restlessness. Trauma can also lead to impulsive behaviour, as people may feel a sense of urgency or a need to take action in response to their feelings of distress. Distress and trauma can impact an individual's ability to focus and concentrate, leading to distractibility and difficulty completing tasks. It is important to note that hyperactivity as a response to trauma is a normal and natural response to an overwhelming experience.

Hypervigilance

Hyper-vigilance is a common trauma response and coping mechanism in which the person constantly assesses and scans situations, environments and people for potential threats, dangers, and risks. During and after trauma, in which the person has been subjected to danger, risk and threat, they will have developed a set of behaviours to attempt to keep themselves safe.

Even after the violence, abuse or trauma has ended, it is very common for people to remain frightened and alert. The root of this coping mechanism is fear of being harmed again, and is therefore a self-protection behaviour.

Hypervigilance from trauma and distress may present as an increased startle response, where people may have an exaggerated startle response to unexpected noises or movements, because of their heightened sense of danger.

Some people may find themselves constantly scanning their environment, looking for potential threats or signs of danger. Hypervigilance can also make it difficult for people to relax and fall asleep, as they may feel constantly alert and on guard. It is common for hypervigilance to lead to irritability and a short temper, as people may feel constantly on edge and easily triggered.

Identity changes

A change of identity can be a trauma response and coping mechanism for traumatic events and experiences. Identity is defined as a unique set of characteristics that makes a person themselves. It includes anything from personality through to appearance. People also report that they identify strongly with political ideologies, religions, roles in society, gender roles, abilities, social classes, and ethnicities (although the experience and meaning of identifying with something is frequently debated and discussed).

For some people, a significant change in identity may be a deliberate choice, in order to break away from the identity they had during the trauma, abuse or distress. It may be that creating a new version of themselves feels safer, or makes them happier. For other people, a significant change in identity can be unconscious, or not fully understood, and the person may not be able to explain why they feel, act, and look so differently. In both circumstances, the change in identity may be conscious and active, or unconscious. In this way, the changing, destroying of, denying of, or creating of a new identity can be a trauma response, or a coping mechanism.

Impatience

Impatience can be a response to trauma and distress, arising from exhaustion, frustration, distraction, and sleep deprivation. Impatience can also be a response to trauma, especially in cases where the trauma has resulted in a loss of control or a sense of powerlessness. Impatience can manifest in a variety of ways, including a lack of tolerance for delays, a need for immediate gratification, and difficulty waiting for things to happen.

In some cases, impatience can be a way to try to regain a sense of control or agency in life. By pushing for things to happen quickly, a person may feel like they are taking charge of their situation and not letting their trauma dictate their life. However, this can also lead to a lack of consideration for the consequences of hasty actions or decisions. Impatience can also be a symptom of trauma-related fear responses. If a person feels constantly on edge or hypervigilant, they may feel the need to rush through tasks or situations in order to alleviate their worries and fears. This can result in a cycle of impatience and distress that can then become a secondary source of trauma and stress.

Imposter syndrome

Imposter syndrome is not a medical 'syndrome'. It is better understood as a colloquial term to mean feelings of inadequacy, or a feeling of being an imposter when a person achieves something positive. Many talented and successful women talk about a feeling of being a fraud, an imposter, or a describe a fear of being found to be a fluke or a fake in their own success.

Imposter syndrome may be a trauma response, particularly if the trauma involved feelings of inadequacy or a loss of self-worth. Imposter syndrome is characterised by persistent feelings of self-doubt and a fear of being exposed as a fraud, despite evidence of accomplishments or competence.

For some people, imposter syndrome can develop as a way to protect themselves from further trauma. If a person has experienced a traumatic event or subjected to abuse that has left them feeling powerless or worthless, they may develop a belief that they are not deserving of their successes or that their accomplishments are the result of luck or external factors, rather than their own abilities. This belief can be a way to avoid the risk of being hurt or rejected again.

However, imposter syndrome can also be a barrier to processing trauma and moving on. If a person is constantly doubting their abilities and feeling like a fraud, they may be less likely to seek out opportunities for growth or to believe that they can make positive changes in their life. Additionally, imposter syndrome can lead to feelings of isolation and a reluctance to seek support from others.

Inability to orgasm, climax or feel sexual pleasure

Some people will retain their sex drive during and after distress and trauma, but will not be able to climax, orgasm or feel pleasure when engaging in sex or masturbation. This is a trauma response. Stress can cause tension in the muscles throughout the body, including those involved in sexual arousal and orgasm. This tension can make it more difficult to achieve orgasm.

Even though someone may want to have sex, the trauma or distress can cause their mind to be preoccupied with worries, memories, or concerns, making it more difficult to focus on sexual sensations and achieve orgasm.

Long periods of distress can cause changes in hormone levels, which can affect sexual desire and arousal. For example, distress can increase levels of cortisol, a hormone that can decrease libido and interfere with sexual function. When someone is struggling with trauma and distress, they may find that it can affect their relationship with their partner, which can impact sexual desire and function. Relationship issues, such as conflict, lack of trust, embarrassment, or lack of emotional intimacy, can make it more difficult to achieve orgasm.

Inadequacy

Feelings of inadequacy are common during and after trauma, particularly if the trauma has involved a loss of control or a threat to sense of self-worth. Inadequacy can manifest in a variety of ways, including a sense of not measuring up to the person's own expectations or those of others, a fear of failure, and a lack of confidence in their own abilities.

For some people, feelings of inadequacy can develop as a way to protect themselves from further trauma. If a person has experienced a traumatic event that has left them feeling powerless or helpless, they may internalise a belief that they are not capable of handling difficult situations or that they are not deserving of positive outcomes. This belief can be a way to avoid the risk of being hurt or rejected again.

Intrusive thoughts

Intrusive thoughts can be a response to trauma, and are understood to be thoughts which feel unpredictable and uncontrollable. Thoughts can include memories, flashbacks, ideas, thoughts, fears, and voices.

Intrusive thoughts can be a common response to trauma, particularly if the trauma involved a threat to life, safety, or well-being. Intrusive thoughts are unwanted and distressing thoughts or images that keep recurring in a person's mind, despite their efforts to suppress or ignore them. Intrusive thoughts can take many forms, including flashbacks, nightmares, and distressing memories of the traumatic event. These thoughts can be triggered by a wide range of stimuli, including sights, sounds, smells, and emotions that are associated with the traumatic experience.

For some people, intrusive thoughts can be a way of trying to make sense of, or process the traumatic event. However, for others, intrusive thoughts can be a source of significant distress and can interfere with their ability to function in their daily life. It's important to note that intrusive thoughts are a normal response to trauma, and many people who have experienced or been subjected trauma will experience them at some point.

Irritability

A common response to trauma and distress, many people describe a feeling of being easily annoyed, irritated, and impatient.

Irritability is characterised by feelings of frustration, annoyance, or anger, and can manifest in a variety of ways, including lashing out at others, feeling easily agitated, and having a short fuse.

For some people, irritability can be a way of coping with the intense emotions that are associated with trauma. If a person has experienced a traumatic event that has left them feeling overwhelmed or helpless, they may use irritability as a way of exerting control over their environment or as a way of protecting themselves from any further harm.

It is important to note that irritability, annoyance, and feeling impatient may also be a sign of mental and physical exhaustion and burnout.

Jealousy

Jealousy is defined as a feeling of feeling of being envious and hostile, especially about situations, possessions or relationships the person feels entitled to, or seeks control of. There is not one root cause of jealousy, but some theories suggest that people may become jealous due to their own insecurities, their own issues with self-esteem and self-worth, and their fear of loss.

Jealousy may be a trauma response, or coping mechanism for people who become insecure during and after their own trauma.

For some people, jealousy can range from feelings of suspicion, envy, entitlement, and ownership through to threats and humiliations, violence, and rage. In relationships, some people begin to feel jealousy when a person perceives a threat to a valued relationship from a third party. For others, jealousy arises from feelings of control, ownership, and entitlement to the personhood, body, time and attention of others.

Losing interest in hobbies or causes

During and after trauma and distress, it is common for people to lose interest in their previous hobbies, interests, causes and talents. When a person is subjected to ongoing trauma and distress, and they spend significant time in survival and coping, their personal interests and hobbies may become less of a priority. Further, due to the common change in world view that can occur when people experience trauma or distress, previously important activities and interests may feel irrelevant, meaningless, or unimportant.

Loss of interest in work or school

During and after trauma and distress, it is common for children and adults to lose interest, or not to be able to cope with a work or school environment. The traditional work day, or school day, demands very specific, submissive, and structured behaviour from people, which may become very difficult to adjust to or conform to during and after trauma.

When a person is subjected to ongoing trauma and distress, and they spend significant time in survival and coping, their occupation may become less of a priority or focus. Further, due to the common change in world view that can occur when people experience trauma or distress, previously passions, vocations, educational goals or occupations may feel irrelevant, meaningless, frivolous, or unimportant.

Loss of sex drive

Some people may lose their sex drive as a response to trauma as a way to cope with their emotional distress. Trauma can have a significant impact on an individual's psychological and emotional well-being, and can affect their ability to engage in healthy sexual relationships. Some common reasons why a person may lose their sex drive as a response to trauma may include:

Fear: Trauma can leave people feeling fearful and vulnerable, and this fear can be triggered in sexual situations, making it difficult for them to feel safe and comfortable.

Guilt and shame: Trauma can leave people feeling guilty or ashamed of their bodies, which can lead to feelings of low self-esteem and a lack of confidence in sexual situations.

Emotional detachment: Trauma can lead to emotional numbness or detachment, which can make it difficult for people to connect emotionally with others, including in sexual relationships.

Triggers: Some people may become triggered during sexual activity or intimacy due to previous abuse and sexual trauma. They may then avoid or prefer not to engage in sex due to the likelihood of being triggered.

Exhaustion: During distress and trauma, it is common for people to feel emotionally and physically exhausted. This may last weeks or years, and can impact on desire to have sex.

It is important to note that losing your sex drive as a response to trauma is a normal and natural response to an overwhelming experience, and it is not acceptable to push or speed up the process of returning to sexual activity (especially where it is being pushed due to a partner feeling 'neglected'). It the professional notices that the person feels under pressure to have sex by someone else, it is important to discuss consent, and to consider if the person is being abused or forced to have sex they are not ready for.

Further, it is important that professionals understand that some people are asexual, or may experience a change in their sexuality, and a loss of sex drive may be a manifestation of no sexual attraction at all, or a change in sexual attraction.

Low confidence

Feelings of low confidence are common during after trauma and distress, especially if the trauma has involved a loss of control or a threat to the person's sense of self-worth. Low confidence is characterised by a lack of belief in the self, and can manifest in a variety of ways, including a lack of assertiveness, a fear of taking risks, and a reluctance to speak up for yourself.

For some people, low confidence can develop as a way to protect themselves from further trauma. If a person has experienced a traumatic event that has left them feeling powerless or helpless, they may internalise a belief that they are not capable of handling difficult situations or that they are not deserving of positive outcomes. This belief can be a way to avoid the risk of being hurt or rejected again.

It is important for professionals to consider that a decrease in confidence, or many years of low confidence (even from childhood) may be a trauma response caused by abuse, humiliation, control, belittling and minimising from a perpetrator. For some perpetrators, destroying the confidence of the person they are targeting is central to their power and control.

Low self esteem

Feelings of low self-esteem are common during after trauma and distress, especially if the trauma or distress involved the harm of the person's self-worth. This can be deliberate (an abuser choosing to damage the self-worth of their victim), or can be a consequence or relation to the trauma (a person feeling low self-worth after they failed at something they had worked hard for). Low self-esteem is characterised by a lack of confidence in the self, and can manifest in a variety of ways, including feelings of worthlessness, a negative self-image, and a lack of belief in abilities or worth.

Lying to others

Lying to others may develop as a coping mechanism for trauma and distress. As trauma and distress significantly impacts the sense of self, self-worth, confidence, identity, abilities, potential, and focus, some people may develop lying behaviours so they appear more competent, happier, more accomplished, or more confident than they truly are.

Lying to others can be a common response to trauma, particularly if the trauma has involved a threat to safety, identity, or well-being. Lying can manifest in a variety of ways, including telling half-truths, exaggerating or minimising details of the traumatic event, or hiding information altogether.

It is important to note that many people who have been subjected to trauma, abuse and violence have lied about it at some point. However, this is usually to minimise it, protect the perpetrator, pretend to be coping, lie about injuries, lie for the abuser, or other lies that are related to the abuse and trauma itself. For example, many women subjected to domestic abuse will lie to others about how they got bruises. This can therefore also be a behaviour that has grown from survival, and protecting the self from further harm.

For some people, lying can be a way of coping with the intense emotions that are associated with trauma. If a person has experienced a traumatic event that has left them feeling overwhelmed or ashamed, they may use lying as a way of avoiding further shame or judgment. Lying can also be a way of exerting control over their environment or protecting themselves from further harm.

However, lying can also be a barrier to healing from trauma. If a person is not honest with themselves or others about the trauma, their own life, their choices, their thoughts and feelings, they may have difficulty processing their emotions and may be less likely to seek out support from others. Additionally, lying can lead to feelings of guilt and shame, which can further exacerbate the negative effects of trauma.

Mood swings

During and after trauma and distress, it is common for people to experience mood swings.

Mood swings can be a common response to trauma, particularly if the trauma has involved a loss of control or a threat to the person's sense of safety. Mood swings can include sudden shifts in emotional state, difficulty regulating emotions, and frequent mood changes. People may report feeling happy and confident one minute, and triggered, upset and angry the next.

For some people, mood swings can be a way of coping with the intense emotions that are associated with trauma. It is common for people who are processing or trying to cope with trauma and distress to feel many things at once. Even across an average day, they might wake up feeling terrible, eventually start to feel calmer, then become upset, then become angry, then calm down again, they start to feel more motivated and back in control, feeling more positive, and then become triggered and go back to feeling exhausted and low.

However, mood swings can also be a barrier to processing and coping with trauma. If a person is unable to regulate their emotions or has difficulty maintaining stable relationships, they may have difficulty processing their trauma, talking about it, thinking about it, and may be less likely to seek out support from others. Additionally, mood swings (and the consequences those mood swings may have for others) can lead to feelings of guilt, shame, self-blame and isolation, which can further exacerbate the negative effects of trauma (and the mood swings).

Narrow mindedness

A common trauma response is a significant change in world view, which is discussed in 'Change in World View'. More specifically, some people may become more rigid, judgemental, narrow minded, and become less open to new ideas, experiences and views. There is a possibility that when this happens after trauma, it is related to fear and self-preservation. It may also be a sign that the person has become more insular, less empathic, and more focussed on themselves. None of these responses are harmful on their own, and arguably, for some people these responses may be protective and effective.

Nightmares

Nightmares are a common trauma response, experienced by many people struggling with anything from moderate distress to severe chronic trauma.

Nightmares can be a common response to trauma, particularly if the trauma has involved a threat to personal safety or well-being. Nightmares can manifest in a variety of ways, including vivid and disturbing dreams that are difficult to shake. Some people report feeling trapped in their nightmares, being paralysed, being aware that they are dreaming (lucid dreaming), having repetitive nightmares of the trauma, or having symbolic dreams about the trauma.

For some people, nightmares can be a way of processing the intense emotions and complicated memories that are associated with trauma. If a person has experienced a traumatic event that has left them feeling overwhelmed or helpless, their mind may continue to process the event through nightmares. Nightmares can also be a way of coping with repressed emotions or memories related to the trauma.

If a person is experiencing frequent nightmares, they may have difficulty getting restful sleep, become scared of going to bed or to sleep, and become sleep deprived, which can further exacerbate the negative effects of trauma on psychological and physical health. Additionally, nightmares can lead to further feelings of fear, anger, distress and sadness.

Numbness

Emotional numbness is a commonly reported response to trauma and distress. Some people describe this feeling as shock, or not feeling anything at all. For some people, the numbness feels as though nothing means anything anymore, and they no longer feel joy, sadness, fear, shock, or anger. Whilst some people are comfortable with feeling nothing, this experience causes significant distress for others, who become worried about why they are so numb, and whether it is abnormal.

Becoming obsessed with something

Becoming obsessed has become a commonly overused term to describe a strong interest or like of something or someone. However, common obsessions and compulsions after trauma include cleanliness, food intake, exercising, safety, and people.

Obsessions in their true form are usually related to control, coping, and fear. They can be a common response to trauma. After experiencing trauma, people may become fixated on certain thoughts, images, or experiences related to the trauma. This can manifest in a variety of ways, including:

Intrusive thoughts: People may experience intrusive thoughts related to the trauma, such as memories, flashbacks, or nightmares. These thoughts may be uncontrollable and may interfere with daily life.

Compulsive behaviours: People may engage in compulsive behaviours related to the trauma, such as checking, cleaning, or avoiding certain triggers. These behaviours may be driven by a need to feel in control or to avoid further harm.

Hypervigilance: People may become hypervigilant and constantly alert for potential threats or triggers related to the trauma. This can lead to a sense of being constantly on edge and may interfere with daily life.

Avoidance: People may avoid situations or people that remind them of the trauma. This can lead to a sense of social isolation and may interfere with daily life.

Obsessions can have a significant impact on a person's daily life and can interfere with their ability to function in a healthy way.

Out of body experiences (OBEs)

A type of hallucination that is fairly common is the 'out-of-body experience' (OBE). OBEs are experiences where an individual feels a disconnection between their physical body and their conscious awareness, and can view the world from a vantage point outside of their physical body. This happens when awake. For example, a person may feel that they are drifting away from their physical body, leaving it behind, and floating up towards the ceiling. From the ceiling they may be able to look down and see their physical body. OBEs can sometimes be multi-modal; someone can feel they are in a different position as compared to their physical body, and also perhaps see, hear, or feel their environment from a different perspective.

A study of over 550 healthy people found that 24% had experienced at least one OBE in their lifetime, unrelated to any health issues or substance use (Marchant & Taylor, 2021).

OBEs are commonly experienced during or after traumatic experiences (e.g. as part of a "near death experience") but can also occur without a clear cause or during non-traumatic experiences, such as during meditation.

Overachieving and overworking

Overachieving is best understood as a coping mechanism for trauma and distress. Overachieving can be a common response to trauma, particularly if the trauma has involved a loss of control, a deliberate destruction of self-worth, self-confidence or ability, or a threat to your sense of safety. Overachieving can manifest in a variety of ways, including setting high expectations for yourself, working long hours, seeking promotions, seeking awards, increasing earnings, seeking goals and other rewarding outcomes, and striving for perfection in all areas of life.

For some people, overachieving can be a way of coping with the intense emotions that are associated with trauma. If a person has experienced a traumatic event that has left them feeling helpless or out of control, they may strive to regain a sense of control through overachieving. Overachieving can also be a way of avoiding difficult emotions or situations, as it can provide a sense of distraction or accomplishment.

However, overachieving can also be a barrier to healing from trauma. If a person is constantly striving for perfection or working long hours, they may have difficulty relaxing, they might become harsh on themselves, and may neglect self-care or relationships. Additionally, overachieving can lead to feelings of burnout, distress, exhaustion, overwhelm, frustration and confusion, which can further exacerbate the negative effects of trauma.

It is important to understand and fully acknowledge that achievement and success is prized in a capitalist society. Many of us are socialised from birth to be the best, to win the prize, to get the 'A', to come first in the race – and so many of us connected self-worth and importance to achieving.

Further, there are often significant rewards for achievements, which raise from social support and celebrations through to respect, status and wealth. When a person uses a 'negative' coping mechanism for trauma and distress such as using drugs, they will not receive the same social support and respect as if they use a 'positive' coping mechanism such as overachieving and overworking, which is seen as purposeful and respectful. Despite the difference between what are perceived to be 'positive' and 'negative' coping mechanisms, they are both arising from trauma that is harming the person.

It is important therefore to understand that overachieving as a response to, or a coping mechanism for trauma is likely to be also rooted both in the nature of the trauma itself, and in social messages about success and value.

Panic

Panic is a common trauma response. Panic can be a common response to trauma, particularly if the trauma has involved a threat to life, safety or well-being.

Panic can manifest in a variety of ways, including intense feelings of fear, rapid heartbeat, sweating, blurred vision, echoed hearing, dizziness, shaking, tingling, numbness, pins and needles, and difficulty breathing. Panic can also include psychological fear, catastrophic thoughts, and a feeling that the person is going to die suddenly. For some people, panic can be a way of responding to the intense emotions that are associated with trauma. If a person has experienced a traumatic event that has left them feeling overwhelmed or helpless, they may experience panic attacks when these feelings become overwhelming or triggered by a stimulus.

Panic is the natural and normal fear response, often triggered by external stimuli such as sounds, sights, smells or people, or, triggered by internal stimuli such as memories, feelings, sensations, thoughts and emotions.

Paranoia

Paranoia is best described as a response to trauma, but this word can often be misused to describe rational and logical fears and suspicion. The original definition of the Greek word 'paranoia' was simply 'madness'. Further definitions of 'paranoia' included 'mental illness with delusions'. For this reason, it is not considered here to be a useful, trauma-informed or ethical term.

Paranoia is often used in modern language and meaning for 'the unjustified suspicion and mistrust of others'.

Suspicion and mistrust of others can be a common response to trauma, particularly if the trauma has involved a loss of trust or safety in others. It is a rational response after a person has been betrayed, lied to, controlled, manipulated or gaslit, too. These feelings of insecurity and lack of safety can manifest in a variety of ways, includes excessive suspicion of others, feelings of persecution, and a belief that others are out to harm or betray the individual.

As a coping mechanism for some people, suspicion and mistrust can be a way of protecting themselves from further harm or betrayal. If a person has experienced a traumatic event that has left them feeling vulnerable or betrayed, they may develop a heightened sense of suspicion or mistrust towards others as a way of protecting themselves from further harm. Suspicion and mistrust can provide a sense of control or security.

If a person is experiencing excessive suspicion or mistrust towards others, they may have difficulty building and maintaining healthy relationships. Additionally, paranoia can lead to feelings of isolation, fear, sadness, and anger which can further exacerbate the trauma.
For professionals working with people who are described as 'paranoid', it may be worth considering the root of the mistrust and suspicion. It is also important not to discount everything that person says just because others have

termed it 'paranoia' or 'delusional'. Suspicion and mistrust are better understood as a form of hypervigilance and self-preservation.

Peace keeping

For some people who have experienced trauma and distress, especially when subjected to violence and conflict, they may become peacekeepers as a coping mechanism.

Peacekeeping behaviour can be a common response to trauma, particularly if the trauma has involved conflict or interpersonal harm. Peacekeeping behaviour refers to behaviours and attitudes that are intended to maintain peace, harmony, and order in relationships, even if it requires suppressing their own needs or feelings, and even if it causes them harm or distress to do so. For some people, peacekeeping behaviour can be a way of coping with the aftermath of trauma by attempting to prevent any further harm or conflict. The person may adopt peacekeeping behaviour as a way of avoiding further harm and maintaining a sense of safety. Peacekeeping behaviour can also be a way of avoiding difficult emotions or situations, as it can provide a sense of control or stability whilst conflict is being avoided.

When a person has been subjected to abuse, violence, aggression, and conflict, they may develop peacekeeping behaviours or take on that role within a family or relationship in order to protect themselves or others from triggers such as violent behaviour, verbal abuse, aggression and threats.

However, peacekeeping behaviour can become a harmful and exhausting coping mechanism. If a person is constantly prioritising the needs of others over their own, and feels as though they have become the 'rock' of the family, or the person who keeps everything together, they may have difficulty expressing their own needs and feelings or developing/maintaining healthy boundaries. Additionally, peacekeeping behaviour can lead to feelings of resentment, fatigue, fear, sadness, anger, burnout, frustration, pressure and injustice which may cause further trauma and distress.

People pleasing

For some people who have experienced trauma and distress, especially when subjected to violence and conflict, they may become people-pleasers as a coping mechanism. This can be a deliberate, conscious choice, or an unconscious change in behaviour. People-pleasing behaviour is usually a way to protect the self from further harm, trauma, conflict, or confrontation. It is common where the person has been subjected to abuse or neglect.

People-pleasing is usually done to appease others, at the expense of the person's own needs, desires, and feelings. It may mean saying 'yes' to things they do not want or need, agreeing to help with things, lending money, taking care of others, taking on extra workloads, and feeling as though they cannot say no to people. This behaviour can give the person a sense of control over difficult situations, and can help them to maintain a feeling of safety and security. Despite this, it is common for people to begin feeling exhaustion, resentment, sadness, fear, pressure and burnout from people-pleasing.

Perfectionism

Perfectionism can be understood as a coping mechanism for traumatic or distressing events, especially those which made the person feel flawed, inadequate, or worthless.

Perfectionism can develop as a way to cope with the feelings of powerlessness and uncertainty that trauma can cause. For most people, it is often characterised by setting extremely high standards for themselves and striving to meet those standards at all costs. For some people, perfectionism can serve as a way to regain a sense of control in their lives after experiencing a traumatic event. By focusing on achieving perfection, they can create a sense of predictability, competence, control and order in their lives, which can feel comforting in the face of chaos and uncertainty.

However, perfectionism can also be a double-edged sword. The pressure to meet impossibly high standards can lead to intense feelings of fear, shame, and self-criticism, which can ultimately exacerbate the effects of trauma. Additionally, perfectionism can lead to a fear of failure, which can prevent people from taking risks or trying new things, further limiting their ability to process and grow from their traumatic experiences.

Perfectionism is another example of a socially acceptable coping mechanism, that can be rewarded or revered in a produce-focussed, capitalist society. In fact, many people consider perfectionism as one of their strengths. It is therefore important that professionals acknowledge the way this coping mechanism can become embedded and normalised, despite causing further distress to the person.

Persecution

Feeling persecuted is a common feeling for people who have been subjected to trauma and abuse.

Feelings of persecution or 'paranoia' (already discussed earlier) can be a common response to trauma, particularly if the trauma has involved targeting, persecution, discrimination, or a sense of threat or danger. These feelings can manifest as a belief that others are out to get you, harm you, or undermine you in some way. This can lead to suspicion, mistrust, and hypervigilance, as the individual constantly feels on guard and unable to let their guard down.

For some people, the feelings of persecution are a way of protecting themselves. These feelings can serve as a way of maintaining a sense of control or preparedness in the face of potential harm. However, these feelings can also be a source of distress, as they can lead to social isolation, and difficulty forming relationships.

For professionals working with people who feel persecuted, targeted, or victimised, it is important that they are listened to. Whilst others may have described them as paranoid, delusional or self-obsessed, it is highly likely that those who have been abused, bullied, discriminated against, and deliberately harmed were targeted, persecuted and victimised. In those cases, the feeling of persecution is arguably rational, factual, and natural. The person has become frightened of being harmed again, and their assessment that they were deliberately targeted and harmed is likely to be accurate (especially if they were abused or bullied).

Pessimistic about the future

During and after trauma and distress, it might be that some people become pessimistic about their future.

Feeling pessimistic about the future can be a common response to trauma, particularly if the trauma has involved a significant loss or has impacted the person's sense of safety or stability. This can lead to a sense of hopelessness and a belief that the future will be bleak, equally as traumatic, or uncertain.

If a person has experienced trauma that has caused them to feel pessimistic about the future, they may struggle with feelings of despair, fear, sadness, lack of motivation, numbness, and anger. They may feel as though they are unable to see a way out of their current situation, and may feel as though their options for the future are limited or non-existent. This can lead to a sense of helplessness and a loss of motivation or drive.

Phobias

Phobias are defined as an 'extreme irrational fear of, or aversion to something'. On this basis, it is important for trauma-informed professionals that the term 'phobia' is used accurately. For example, if the person is extremely frightened of something rational (such as being raped again, or having a car crash, or being stalked again), it is arguably not a phobia. Similarly, if the person is extremely frightened of an aspect, item, situation, location or experience related to the trauma, this fear is not irrational. The fear is rational, natural, and related to a trauma and potential action.

These fears are best defined as responses to trauma.

Despite some sources stating that phobias are a mental disorder, or an 'anxiety disorder', phobias that develop during or after a trauma are likely to be coping mechanisms and trauma responses. They are not disordered.

Even when a phobia appears unrelated to the original trauma, there is likely to be a common root, or connection. For example, a woman who escapes domestic and sexual violence develops a phobia of bridges. She will not walk under or over bridges, and her fear is so severe that she faints and drops to the floor if she is near a bridge. The fear of bridges was not present before the abuse and violence, but the fear of bridges also has nothing to do with the abuse and violence.

However, she is frightened that the bridge may fall on her or collapse, which she puts down to people not doing their jobs correctly to inspect bridges. She becomes frightened that professionals are not monitoring the strength of the bridge, and there is no way to know if the bridge is safe just by looking at it. In this sense, it is likely that the fear is rooted in being let down by professionals or others, and being out of control of her own safety. It may also be linked to a feeling of uncertainty and unpredictability.

Planning and controlling uncertainties

During and after distress and trauma, some people may become fearful of how unpredictable and uncontrollable people and the world is. Attempting to plan for, and control uncertainties is best understood as a coping mechanism for potential risks and danger. For some people, this may considerably affect their day-to-day life, as they may try to plan for every eventuality (which is of course, impossible). This may lead to the person feeling exhausted, insecure, unsafe, and scared.

Preoccupation with death and dying

A preoccupation with death and dying can be a response to trauma in some people. Trauma can lead to intense feelings of fear, vulnerability, and mortality, and may result in people becoming preoccupied with thoughts of death and dying (their own, and that of others). Some common signs of preoccupation with death and dying as a response to trauma may include:

Obsessive thoughts: People may have persistent and intrusive thoughts about death and dying, which can interfere with their daily activities and relationships.

Avoidance: The preoccupation with death and dying may lead people to avoid situations or people that remind them of their mortality or vulnerability. This can include avoiding hospitals, funerals, graveyards, crematoriums, and avoiding watching videos, movies or reading books which contain death and dying.

Fear: The preoccupation with death and dying can lead to heightened levels of fear and distress, as people may feel constantly on guard and hypervigilant.

Presenting as an ethnicity or culture you are not from

Presenting as an ethnicity or culture that you are not from is often referred to as cultural appropriation. This is a complex issue that involves taking elements of another culture, often without understanding the cultural significance or history behind them, and using them for your own purposes or benefit.

Cultural appropriation can be harmful because it can perpetuate stereotypes, erase the cultural contributions of marginalised groups, and exploit aspects of a culture without proper recognition or respect. It can also contribute to the erasure of the experiences and struggles of people from that culture, and can be seen as a form of cultural theft or exploitation.

If a person experiences a traumatic event, or is subjected to abuse and violence and then begins to present or tell people that they are of a different ethnicity or culture that they are not from, this is likely to be an example of someone who is changing their identity to escape or detach themselves from something traumatic. For example, a person may want to totally disconnect from their old identity because it reminds them of the trauma, or something about themselves that they dislike or resent. Similarly, a person may create a new identity for themselves for the same reason. The new identity may well be significantly different from their own, and they may attempt to emulate or imitate someone else (a public figure, celebrity, a friend or contact).

Problem solving (for others)

A common response to, and then coping mechanism for, chronic trauma and distress is to become a 'problem solver'. Some people will relate to the feeling that they find themselves in a role in which everyone around them relies on them to care for them, support them in a crisis, solve their problems, counsel them, protect them, organise for them and mediate for them.

This coping mechanism may be related to a need for control, previous helplessness, feelings of low self-worth, feelings of usefulness, a need for preparedness, high empathy, and protection of others. For some people who were not helped or supported during their own traumas and distress, they may feel obliged, or feel they have a duty to ensure that others do not suffer the way they did. Instead, they may seek to solve problems and help others, even to their own detriment and burn out.

For some people, becoming the 'problem solver' in the family or in a community may be a way to build self-worth and self-esteem by having a purpose or role in life, having felt useless or worthless during previous trauma or abuse. For others, it may be a positive way to use their own experiences and wisdom to help others.

Protecting an abuser

Protecting the abuser as a response to trauma is a complex but common trauma response that can have a variety of underlying reasons.

One common reason is that the victim may feel a sense of loyalty or attachment to their abuser, particularly if the abuse occurred in the context of a close relationship or family dynamic. Whilst the person may be able to identify how harmful and traumatic the abuse was, they may still love their abuser, too. When this occurs, it is common for victims to want to protect the abuser from prosecution, conviction and imprisonment, as they feel guilty that they would potentially cause those outcomes by reporting or disclosing. The victim may also feel a sense of guilt or responsibility for the abuse, particularly if the abuser has manipulated or gaslit them into believing that the abuse was their fault (or that they enjoyed it or wanted it).

Another reason why some people protect the abuser is that they may fear retaliation or harm if they speak out or report the abuse. This is particularly common in cases of domestic and sexual abuse, where the victim may feel trapped, and may not have access to resources or support that can help them leave the abusive relationship safely.

In some cases, protecting an abuser may also be a coping mechanism for the victim, particularly if they are struggling with complex feelings of trauma, shame, self-blame, self-doubt, and betrayal. By minimising or denying the abuse, and instead defending the abuser, the victim may be able to maintain a sense of control over their own narrative and avoid confronting the painful reality of their experience.

Proving everything

When a person has been abused, gaslit, accused of lying, or has been ignored and minimised, they may develop a coping mechanism to those traumas in which they feel the need to prove everything. This might mean taking screenshots of all text messages, voice recordings of all phone calls, keeping receipts, screenshots of social media, never deleting text messages and emails, and providing evidence or proof to partners, friends, family, co-workers and bosses.

For some people, this coping mechanism is a way to feel safe and in control. It is likely that they have experienced a situation in which they were not believed, or they did not have the evidence they needed to show someone that they were telling the truth.

For professionals working with someone who feels they need to prove everything, there are some things to consider. Firstly, it is very common for people to be asked, 'Do you have any proof of that?' when they raise any kind of concern. It is common for people to dismiss reports, rumours, information, stories, or allegations without clear proof (especially if people do not want to believe they are true). Secondly, if a person has been gaslit during abuse, they will often feel as though they don't trust their own memory, and so may feel the only way they can truly remember accurately what happened, is to record it or prove it for possible scenarios where they are challenged later.

Proving yourself to others

Feeling the need to prove yourself to others can be a common coping mechanism for people who have experienced abuse, neglect, or other forms of trauma. This can be due to a number of reasons, including:

Lack of validation: Trauma can cause a person to feel invalidated or unheard, and they may believe that the only way to get their needs met is by proving themselves. This can lead to a constant need to prove their worth, intelligence, or competence in order to gain validation from others.

Fear of rejection: Trauma can also cause a person to develop a fear of rejection, abandonment, or criticism. This can lead to a constant need to prove oneself in order to avoid being rejected or abandoned by others.

Internalised shame: People who have experienced trauma may also struggle with feelings of shame, self-doubt, self-blame, and low self-esteem. This can lead to a constant need to prove oneself in order to combat these negative beliefs and feelings.

Sense of control: Finally, feeling the need to prove yourself to others can also be a way for people to regain a sense of control in their lives. Trauma can cause a person to feel powerless or out of control, and they may believe that the only way to regain control is by proving themselves in various ways.

It's important to note that while the need to prove yourself to others can be a common response to trauma, it can also be a harmful coping mechanism. People who feel the need to constantly prove themselves to others may struggle with burnout, perfectionism, distress, fear of failure, and exhaustion.

Pushing people away

Pushing people away as a response to trauma can be a common behaviour or coping mechanism for people who have been subjected to abuse, neglect, or other forms of trauma. Trauma can cause a person to feel vulnerable and exposed, and they may believe that pushing others away is a way to protect themselves from further harm.

People who have experienced trauma or have been subjected to abuse, betrayal, neglect or manipulation may struggle with trusting others and may believe that everyone is out to hurt them. This can lead to a pattern of pushing people away in order to avoid being hurt again. Trauma can also cause a person to avoid situations or people that remind them of their trauma. They may push people away who trigger memories of their trauma, even if those people are not actually harmful.

People who have experienced trauma or been subjected to abuse and neglect may also struggle with feelings of shame, self-blame, self-doubt and guilt, which can lead to a belief that they are unworthy of love and support. This can cause them to push people away in order to avoid being seen as weak or damaged.

While pushing people away may initially feel like a way to protect the self, it can ultimately be a harmful coping mechanism that leads to social isolation, loneliness, fear, anger, resentment, and sadness.

Questioning your judgement

Questioning your judgement can be a common response to trauma, particularly if the trauma involved a situation where the individual's judgement was called into question or they made a decision that they now regret. This can lead to a lack of confidence in the ability to make decisions, even in situations where the trauma is not directly related.

In addition, trauma can cause people to feel overwhelmed and emotionally dysregulated, which can impact their ability to think clearly and make decisions. This can lead to a cycle of self-doubt and questioning, as the individual struggles to trust their own judgement.

Finally, trauma can also lead to a general sense of mistrust and cynicism, as the individual may feel that the world is a dangerous and unpredictable place. This can cause them to question their judgement in order to avoid making decisions that could potentially put them in harm's way.

Racing thoughts

Racing thoughts can be a common trauma response, particularly in people who are struggling with fear, hypervigilance, and worry. Racing thoughts are characterised by a constant flow of thoughts that seem to be moving too quickly to keep up with, making it difficult to concentrate or focus on anything else. Sometimes, people describe the thoughts as being on many different levels at once, or about many different topics at once. They may struggle to keep up, or remember what they were just thinking about.

In the context of trauma, racing thoughts may be a result of hyperarousal, which is a common response to trauma and distress. Hyperarousal is a state of heightened physical and emotional arousal, which can cause the individual to feel constantly on edge and easily triggered. This can lead to a constant stream of intrusive thoughts and memories related to the traumatic event, as well as a general sense of fear, risk, and hypervigilance.

Re-enacting the trauma

Re-enactment of trauma is a complex psychological experience that can occur in some people who have experienced trauma. It can take many different forms, including repetitive patterns of behaviour or relationships that seem to repeat the traumatic experience in some way.

There are a number of theories about why some people re-enact their trauma. One theory is that the person may be trying to gain a sense of control over the traumatic experience by repeating it in a way that they can manage or control. By recreating the traumatic experience in a controlled way, the person may be able to process the trauma and gain a sense of mastery over it.

Another theory is that re-enactment may be a way of seeking validation or understanding from others. Trauma can be an isolating experience, and the person may feel that others do not fully understand or believe their experience. By re-enacting the trauma, the person may be seeking validation or understanding from others, or trying to communicate their experience in a way that others can understand.

Finally, re-enactment may also be a result of unconscious psychological processes, such as dissociation or repressed memories. In some cases, the individual may not be aware that they are re-enacting their trauma, or may not fully understand the reasons behind their behaviour.

Regression to a childlike state or behaviour

Some people may regress to childhood as a response to trauma as a way to cope with their emotional distress. Regression is a psychological coping mechanism in which an individual reverts to an earlier stage of development in response to distress or trauma.

The exact reasons why an individual may regress to childhood as a response to trauma can vary. Trauma can be overwhelming and can leave people feeling helpless and out of control. Regressing to childhood may provide a sense of comfort and security, as people can retreat to a time when they felt safe and protected.

Childhood may represent a time when people received a lot of care and support from others. Regressing to childhood may be a way for people to seek out care and support from others, either consciously or unconsciously. Trauma can be difficult to face and process. Regressing to childhood may be a way for people to avoid dealing with their emotions and experiences, by retreating to a time before the traumatic event occurred.

Reinvention of the self

Reinvention of self as a response to trauma is a process of creating a new identity or sense of self after experiencing a traumatic event or series of events. This process can involve significant changes in behaviour, personality, beliefs, and values, as the individual seeks to distance themselves from the traumatic experience and create a new sense of identity.

The reinvention of self can take many different forms, and can be both positive and negative. Some people may use the trauma as a catalyst for positive change, such as pursuing new interests, changing careers, or developing stronger relationships with others. Others may engage in more destructive behaviour, such as substance abuse, lowering their empathy and becoming intimidating, or causing conflict between others as a way of coping with the trauma.

Reinvention of self can also be a way of creating a sense of safety and control after the trauma. By creating a new identity or sense of self, the individual may be able to distance themselves from the traumatic experience and regain a sense of control over their life.

However, reinvention of self can also be a sign of unresolved trauma. If the individual is unable to process the trauma and move on, they may continue to reinvent themselves in an attempt to escape the pain and memories associated with the trauma.

Rejecting gender roles

Rejecting gender roles as a response to trauma can be a way for people to assert their autonomy and identity after experiencing trauma. Gender roles are societal expectations and norms about how men and women should behave and express themselves, and can be limiting and oppressive for some people.

Trauma can alter a person's sense of self and challenge their beliefs and values, including their beliefs about gender roles. Rejecting traditional gender roles can be a way for people to assert their independence, break free from societal expectations, and redefine their identity.

For example, an individual who has been subjected to sexual abuse may reject traditional gender roles that assign men as aggressors and women as passive victims, and instead seek to assert their power and autonomy in non-traditional ways. Similarly, an individual who has experienced an emotional trauma such as loss, may reject societal expectations that men should suppress their emotions and instead seek to express their emotions freely.

Rejecting gender roles can also be a way to resist patriarchal power structures that contribute to systemic oppression and gender-based violence.

It is important to note that rejecting gender roles is a personal choice and not all people who experience trauma will choose to do so (and vice versa).

Rejecting politics

Rejecting politics as a response to trauma can be a way for people to cope with the overwhelming and distressing feelings that can arise after experiencing trauma. Trauma can cause people to feel disconnected from the world around them and to question their beliefs and values, including their political views.

For some people, rejecting politics may be a way to avoid triggering and distressing topics or to escape feelings of helplessness and despair that can come with engaging with politics. In some cases, people may also reject politics as a way to distance themselves from the societal structures and power dynamics that contributed to their trauma.

Additionally, rejecting politics can be a way to resist the pressure to engage in political activism or advocacy that can arise after experiencing trauma. While political engagement can be a powerful way to effect change and seek justice for survivors of trauma, it can also be overwhelming and triggering for some people.

It may also be worth noting that trauma can cause such a profound change in world view, that it may also change the political beliefs of the person entirely. Where once they might have believed and supported one approach to government of people, they may have had experiences with services, authorities, police forces and communities that changed the way they understood social and personal issues.

Rejecting religion

Rejecting religion as a response to trauma can be a way for people to cope with the emotional and psychological impact of traumatic experiences. Trauma can cause people to question their beliefs and values, including their religious beliefs, and can challenge their understanding of the world and their place in it.

For some people, rejecting religion may be a way to distance themselves from the spiritual or religious context in which the trauma occurred. In some cases, people may also reject religion as a way to cope with feelings of anger or betrayal towards a higher power or religious institution that they feel failed to protect them.

In addition, rejecting religion can be a way for people to assert their independence and autonomy, and to redefine their identity outside of the constraints of religious expectations and norms. This can be especially important for people whose religious beliefs were a significant part of their identity before experiencing trauma.

Rejection

Feelings of rejection can be a common response to trauma, particularly if the trauma involved interpersonal harm or betrayal. For some people, their feelings of rejection are accurate reflections of what happened to them, as they may have been rejected by family, friends, and ex-partners.

Trauma can cause people to feel isolated, disconnected, and rejected by others, and these feelings can persist long after the traumatic event has ended. They may feel that they cannot trust others, and so they withdraw and isolate themselves to avoid the risk of being hurt again.

For others, feelings of rejection can be a way to process and understand the shame and self-blame that can accompany trauma. They may feel that they are unworthy of love and belonging, and so they push others away in order to protect themselves from the pain of rejection.

Rejection of authority

Rejection of authority can be a response to trauma, particularly if the traumatic experience involved abuse or mistreatment by someone in a position of power or authority. Trauma can cause people to question and distrust authority figures, and to reject the notion that authority figures have their best interests at heart.

For some people, rejecting authority can be a way to assert their autonomy and independence, and to regain a sense of control over their lives. They may feel that they have been disempowered by their traumatic experiences, and rejecting authority can be a way to reclaim their sense of agency.

In addition, rejecting authority can be a way to cope with feelings of anger and resentment towards people or institutions that they feel failed to protect them from harm.

This can be particularly relevant for people who experienced trauma, bullying, or were subjected to abuse in settings such as schools, religious organisations, or other institutions where trust in authority figures was important.

Remaining single

Remaining single can be a response to trauma, particularly for people who have experienced past relationship trauma, such as if they were subjected to abuse or betrayal. Traumatic experiences can cause people to develop a fear of intimacy and a reluctance to enter into new relationships. They may worry that they will experience similar mistreatment, abuse, or harm in future relationships, and as a result, they may avoid relationships altogether.

For some people, remaining single can be a way to protect themselves from further trauma. They may feel that being single allows them to have greater control over their lives and to avoid the vulnerability and potential risk associated with intimate relationships. They may also feel that being single allows them to focus on their own healing and personal growth.

For professionals, it is important that the social significance and meaning of singledom is considered. Being single is often seen as negative, but this is only because heteronormative societies expect people to settle down, get into serious relationships and get married. This is more prominent for women than men, and single women are often faced with the belief that if they remain single for too long, no one will ever want them, or they will have less social worth.

For this reason, if the person wants to remain single, and this makes them happy, it is important that the professional does not suggest that this is abnormal behaviour. More and more people (especially younger generations) are choosing to remain single and childless, and are rejecting older, traditional forms of family structure, marriage and lifestyles. It is important that this isn't considered to be a deficit of some kind.

Replaying memories

Replaying memories can be a common response to trauma, particularly in people who have experienced repeated or ongoing traumatic events. This can manifest as intrusive thoughts, flashbacks, or nightmares that replay the traumatic event or events.

Replaying memories can serve as a way for people to process and make sense of the traumatic experience. However, it can also be a distressing and overwhelming experience that can lead to increasing fear responses and distress.

In some cases, people may intentionally or unintentionally seek out situations or triggers that replay the memories of the traumatic event. This can be a way for them to try to gain a sense of control over the traumatic experience, or to try to desensitise themselves to the memories. However, this can also be a harmful coping mechanism that can lead to retraumatisation or further harm.

Reprocessing trauma throughout life

It is common for trauma to be processed, triggered and then reprocessed many times throughout the life span. Some people are unaware of this, and feel they are 'going backwards' or 'not making progress' because they repeatedly return to certain traumas or memories that have not been resolved. Some people may make comments such as, 'I thought I had gotten over this, why has it come back up again?'

Lifelong trauma reprocessing occurs because trauma memories are constructed and reconstructed repeatedly based on later experiences, new knowledge, new understanding and insight. For example, a person may have felt that they had dealt with much of the trauma from many years of domestic abuse, but then watch a drama series that reminds them of their own relationship with their ex. Within that, there might be a new angle that has not been considered or processed, or an event that makes the person realise that also happened to them, and they had not realised before. This will likely cause another reprocessing and unpicking of the trauma.

Similarly, reprocessing can happen when new knowledge or new insight is gained. A woman may feel she has completed as much trauma processing and therapy as she needs about the sexual abuse she was subjected to as a little girl, until she has her own daughter, and her daughter reaches the same age she was when she was sexually abused. This new insight as a parent of a little girl the same age, may trigger her and cause her to relook at her own trauma through a new lens.

Importantly, trauma processing and reprocessing is natural, normal, and happens to most memories. Someone may have had years of happy memories with their grandparents, only to find that they were not telling the truth, or were hiding something from them. It is likely at that point, that they will re-examine their experiences and their relationship with their grandparents, and find old memories that they had ignored or minimised beforehand.

It is important that professionals explain that repeatedly reprocessing and revisiting a trauma is a sign is it not yet resolved or settled, but that this is normal for many people, and it may be revisited many times throughout life. The person needs to know that this is not a sign of a problem, or anything 'abnormal', and does not mean they are 'going backwards'.

Rescuing people

Becoming a rescuer, or the tendency to help and care for others at the expense of your own needs, can be a response to trauma in some people. This can be particularly common in people who have been subjected to neglect or abuse in their own lives.

The act of rescuing others can provide a sense of control and empowerment for people who have experienced trauma. By caring for others, they may feel a sense of purpose and fulfilment, and may be able to avoid feelings of helplessness or powerlessness that may be associated with their own experiences of trauma.

However, becoming a rescuer can also be a way for people to avoid confronting their own unresolved trauma. By focusing on the needs of others, they may be able to avoid dealing with their own emotions and experiences. This can lead to burnout, compassion fatigue, and a lack of self-care.

Sabotaging positive experiences and relationships

Sabotaging positive experiences can be a response to trauma for some people. This can manifest in a variety of ways, such as self-sabotage, self-destructive behaviours, or pushing away positive relationships or experiences.

One reason why this may occur is that people who have experienced trauma may struggle with feelings of shame, guilt, doubt, or unworthiness. They may feel that they do not deserve positive experiences or that they are not capable of sustaining them. In order to avoid the pain of potential disappointment or rejection, they may pre-emptively sabotage these positive experiences or relationships.

Additionally, people who have experienced trauma may struggle with trusting others or feeling safe in vulnerable situations. Positive experiences or relationships can trigger feelings of vulnerability, which can be uncomfortable or frightening for some people. As a result, they may sabotage these experiences as a way of avoiding or managing these uncomfortable feelings.

Sabotaging positive experiences can be a way for people to maintain a sense of control over their lives and their emotions, even if it is a self-defeating behaviour. However, it can also prevent people from fully experiencing the joys and rewards of positive relationships and experiences.

Safe people

After experiencing trauma, people may feel unsafe, confused, uncertain, or fearful. They may struggle to trust others or may have difficulty forming or maintaining relationships. In these cases, having safe people can be incredibly important for healing and recovery.

Safe people are those who can be trusted to provide support, empathy, and understanding without judgment or criticism. They can be family members, friends, or professionals who have a deep understanding of the impact of trauma and who are committed to helping the individual heal and recover.

One reason why safe people are important after trauma is that they can provide a sense of safety and security. Trauma can leave people feeling vulnerable, violated, and alone, but having safe people can provide a sense of comfort and stability. These safe people can offer support and validation, which can be essential for months and years.

Additionally, safe people can offer practical support. This may include helping the person with daily tasks, providing transportation to appointments or therapy sessions, or helping to advocate for their needs in various situations. This practical support can be especially important for people who may be struggling with the effects of trauma responses or coping mechanisms.

Finally, safe people can help people to build trust and develop healthy relationships. Trauma can make it difficult to trust others or to feel safe in relationships. Safe people can help people to feel valued, respected, and supported, which can be essential for building trust and fostering healthy relationships in the future.

Safe spaces

After experiencing trauma, people may feel unsafe, vulnerable, or triggered in certain environments or situations. This can make it difficult to engage in daily activities or to participate in social situations. In these cases, having safe spaces can be incredibly important for healing and recovery.

Safe spaces are physical or virtual environments where people can feel protected, supported, and free from judgment or criticism. They can be designated areas, such as support groups, therapy sessions, or crisis centres, or they can be virtual communities, such as online support groups or forums.

One reason why safe spaces are important after trauma is that they can provide a sense of safety and security. Trauma can leave people feeling vulnerable and exposed, but having safe spaces can provide a sense of comfort and stability. These safe spaces can offer support and validation, which can be essential for many.

Additionally, safe spaces can offer a sense of community and belonging. Trauma can make people feel isolated or alone, but safe spaces can provide an opportunity to connect with others who have had similar experiences. This can help people to feel less alone and more understood, which can be essential for building trust and fostering healthy relationships.

Finally, safe spaces can help people to regulate their emotions and manage their triggers. Trauma can cause people to experience intense emotions or to be triggered by certain situations or stimuli. Safe spaces can provide a controlled environment where people can learn coping skills, practice self-care, and manage their emotions in a supportive and non-judgmental environment.

Overall, having safe spaces after trauma can be incredibly important. Safe spaces can provide a sense of safety and security, a sense of community and belonging, and a place to regulate emotions and manage triggers.

Seeing ghosts

Experiencing trauma can have a profound impact on a person's psychological well-being. In some cases, it can lead to the development of post-trauma responses, such as flashbacks, nightmares, and feelings of dissociation. Some people who have experienced trauma may also report seeing or sensing the presence of ghosts or other supernatural entities.

There are different theories about why some people see ghosts after trauma. One possibility is that it could be a form of dissociation or a coping mechanism that the mind creates to deal with the trauma. Dissociation is a common response to trauma and involves a feeling of detachment from oneself or from reality. Seeing ghosts could be a way for the mind to process the trauma and create a sense of control over what happened.

Another possibility is that seeing ghosts is a way to externalise the trauma and give it a concrete form. This could make it easier to talk about and work through in therapy. For some people, seeing ghosts may also be a way to validate their experiences and feel that they are not alone in what they have been through.

Seeing or experiencing hallucinations

Hallucinations can occur as a response to trauma. Trauma can cause changes in brain function and structure that may lead to sensory misperceptions or hallucinations. These may be visual, auditory, or tactile in nature, and can be disturbing and distressing for the individual experiencing them. In some cases, hallucinations may be related to the traumatic event itself, such as seeing or hearing things that remind the person of the trauma.

Hallucinations can occur in any of our senses. This includes the senses we usually think of – vision, hearing, taste, touch, and smell – but also many other senses that are less commonly considered. Examples of the senses we can hallucinate in include:

- Visual – our vision
- Auditory – our sense of hearing
- Olfactory – our sense of smell
- Gustatory – our sense of taste
- Tactile – our sense of touch
- Proprioception – our sense of our body's movement and position in space, relative to other parts of our body
- Balance and acceleration – our sense of our body's balance, direction, and speed

- Thermoception – our sense of temperature, both internally and externally
- Nociception – our sense of pain
- Mechanoception – our sense of the mechanical manipulation of our body, or pressure, such as when part of us is being pushed, pulled, or stretched
- Interoception – our sense of the internal happenings of our body, such as our heartbeat or blood flow
- Chronoception – our sense of the passage of time

People can also have hallucinations that are specifically associated with sleep. Hypnogogic hallucinations are experienced when falling asleep, and hypnopompic hallucinations are experienced when waking up. Bereavement hallucinations are types of experiences associated specifically with the death of someone, and can include seeing, hearing, and feeling the presence of someone who has passed away (such as a friend, family member, or partner). Both sleep and bereavement hallucinations are very common in the healthy general population (Marchant & Taylor, 2021).

To understand the research about the neuroscience underpinning hallucinations, without pathologisation, please see Marchant & Taylor (2021).

Seeking approval

Seeking approval can be a response to trauma as people who have experienced trauma may feel a sense of worthlessness or inadequacy. They may seek approval from others as a way to feel validated and increase their sense of self-worth.

Seeking approval can also be a coping mechanism, as people may believe that if they are perfect or do everything right, they can avoid being criticised or rejected, which can be triggering for them. Seeking approval can also be a way for people to avoid the uncomfortable feelings associated with trauma by focusing on the approval of others instead of addressing their own needs and emotions. While seeking approval can be a natural response to trauma, it is important for people to work towards building their own self-esteem and learning to validate themselves, rather than relying solely on the approval of others.

Seeking attention

Seeking attention can be a response to trauma as people who have experienced trauma may feel a sense of isolation or disconnection from others. Seeking attention can be a way to feel seen, heard, and validated. This can be especially true for people who have experienced neglect or emotional abuse, as they may have learned that they can only get attention by acting out or being loud. Seeking attention can also be a way for people to distract themselves from their emotions or to avoid dealing with the trauma itself.

However, seeking attention can also have negative consequences, as it may lead to people engaging in attention-seeking behaviours that can be harmful to themselves or others.

Seeking belonging

Seeking a sense of belonging can be a response to trauma as people who have experienced trauma may feel a sense of disconnection or isolation from others. Trauma can disrupt a person's sense of safety, trust, and attachment, which can make it difficult for them to form and maintain healthy relationships.

In response to this disconnection, people may seek out communities or groups that they feel they belong to. This sense of belonging can provide a sense of safety and security, as well as validation and acceptance. For some people, this sense of belonging may be found in a religious community, a social group, or a support group for people who have experienced similar types of trauma.

However, seeking a sense of belonging can also have negative consequences if people become too reliant on the group for their sense of self-worth or if the group promotes unhealthy beliefs or behaviours.

Seeking cosmetic surgery

Some people may choose to have cosmetic surgery as a response to trauma in order to change a physical feature they feel self-conscious or embarrassed about due to a traumatic event or experience.

For example, if someone was bullied as a child for their nose, they may choose to have a nose job as a way to regain a sense of control over their appearance and improve their self-confidence. Similarly, if someone was in an accident or experienced a disfiguring injury, they may choose to have reconstructive surgery as a way to repair their physical appearance and move forward from the traumatic event.

For professionals, it is important to understand how socially accepted and even celebrated cosmetic surgery is. Whereas many years ago, it was seen as a serious operation, many people now see cosmetic surgery as a relatively risk-free, quick way to get the results they are looking for. Botox injections and lip fillers are available in many high-streets, for example. Due to the wide availability of cosmetic procedures, it may be easier for people to use them as a coping mechanism for trauma, distress, and body image issues than many years ago.

Seeking justice

Seeking justice is a common response to trauma, particularly if the trauma is related to a specific incident or event where someone was victimised or harmed.

Justice systems of some sort exist everywhere in the world, and it is common for humans to seek justice for the crimes and wrongdoings of others.

People can seek justice for a wide range of experiences, such as theft, physical or sexual assault, workplace harassment, bullying, or discrimination. Seeking justice may involve reporting the incident to law enforcement, pursuing action against the perpetrator or organisation involved, or advocating for policy changes to prevent similar incidents from occurring in the future.

For many people who have been subjected to abuse, crime, wrongdoing or trauma, seeking justice can be an important step towards regaining a sense of control over their lives. By taking action and holding those responsible accountable, people can reclaim their power and assert their rights. However, seeking justice can also be a challenging and emotional process, particularly if it involves confronting the perpetrator or reliving the traumatic event.

Seeking meaning of life

Experiencing trauma or being subjected to abuse, can make a person question their life's purpose and meaning, especially if the trauma caused significant disruption to their previous way of life. Some people may engage in a search for meaning as a way to make sense of their trauma and find purpose in their suffering. This search for meaning may involve exploring spirituality, religion, philosophy, or engaging in education, activism, self-reflection and introspection.

For some people, the experience of trauma may cause them to question the fairness or randomness of life, and they may become preoccupied with finding answers to the bigger questions about existence. Seeking the meaning of life can also provide a sense of control and agency in the aftermath of trauma, as it allows people to direct their energy towards something productive and meaningful. Overall, the search for the meaning of life can serve as a coping mechanism for people seeking to make sense of their trauma and find a sense of purpose and direction in their lives.

Seeking revenge

Seeking revenge can be a response to trauma as a way of trying to regain control and power in a situation where the person has been victimised or harmed. It can stem from a deep desire for justice or a need for closure, as well as feelings of anger and resentment towards the person or people who caused the trauma. In some cases, seeking revenge may be a way of coping with feelings of powerlessness and helplessness that often accompany traumatic experiences. It may also be a way of trying to prevent future harm or victimisation.

However, seeking revenge can also be harmful and may perpetuate cycles of violence and trauma. For some people, feelings of revenge are a psychological coping mechanism that will never be followed through or acted upon. It is common for people to have 'revenge fantasies', or dreams about getting revenge on their abuser or perpetrator. These fantasies usually come from a place of helplessness, lack of power, lack of control and injustice. Some common signs of revenge fantasies as a response to trauma may include:

Obsessive thoughts: People may have persistent and intrusive thoughts about seeking revenge, which can interfere with their daily activities and relationships.

Increased aggression: Revenge fantasies can lead to an increase in aggressive behaviour, as people may feel justified in acting out their desire for revenge.

Difficulty letting go: Revenge fantasies can make it difficult for people to move on from the traumatic event, as they may feel that seeking revenge is the only way to achieve closure. It is important to note that some feelings of revenge can lead to further feelings of anger, isolation, and distress, and can prevent people from fully processing their trauma.

Seeking sexual pleasure

For some people, trauma, neglect, abuse and distress may mean that they seek out sexual pleasure, sexual encounters and casual sex. This is a complex topic, as there is so much social and personal stigma and assumption around sexual pleasure seeking. Ultimately, it is vital that the seeking of sexual pleasure is consensual, healthy, informed, and not harming the person as a coping mechanism.

Sexual pleasure seeking can be due to a variety of factors, such as attempting to regain control over their body, seeking a sense of pleasure and intimacy as a way to counteract feelings of loneliness, shame or worthlessness, or attempting to recreate a traumatic situation in an effort to "master" it.

For some people, their worth and value becomes linked to sex with other people. Some people may feel that the only time anyone pays any attention to them, or wants to spend time with them, is when they offer them sex. For others, they may only feel close to people during sex. In addition, where someone has been sexually abused and exploited, they may feel that their only purpose is to be used as a sex object by other people.

It is important to note that seeking sexual pleasure is not a typical response to trauma, and any behaviour that may cause harm to self or others is not healthy or acceptable. However, some people who have experienced trauma may engage in behaviours that are sexually risky or compulsive as a way to cope with the emotional pain of their trauma.

Seeking thrills and risks

Thrill-seeking and risk-taking can be a response to trauma in some people. Trauma can lead to feelings of boredom, numbness, disconnection, or dissociation, and engaging in activities that provide a rush of adrenaline can be a way to counteract these feelings. It can also be a way to regain a sense of control and power after feeling powerless during a traumatic event. Engaging in risky behaviours or thrill seeking can also be a way to distract the self from intrusive thoughts, feelings, or memories related to the trauma. However, it is important to note that thrill-seeking and risk-taking can also be harmful and lead to negative consequences which then exacerbate trauma and distress.

Self-blame

Blaming the self as a response to trauma is a common reaction, and it can happen for a variety of reasons. People who experience trauma may blame themselves as a way to make sense of what has happened to them or to feel in control of the situation.

Self-blame is understood to manifest in two ways:

Behavioural self-blame: the blame of behaviours such as 'I should never have got in that car' or 'It was my fault for walking home alone'.

Characterological self-blame: the blame of character or personality such as 'I am so stupid and naïve' or 'This wouldn't have happened if I wasn't so friendly to people'.

They may feel responsible for the trauma or believe that they should have done something differently to prevent it. Blaming the self can also be a way of coping with feelings of shame, guilt, or powerlessness that may arise in the aftermath of trauma.

Additionally, some people who have experienced trauma may have a history of being blamed for things that were not their fault. This can lead to a tendency to blame the self as a default response, even when the trauma was not their fault. In some cases, self-blame may also be reinforced by cultural or societal messages that suggest that victims are somehow responsible for the trauma they experience. It is important to note that self-blame is not a productive or accurate response to trauma. Trauma is not the fault of the victim, and no one deserves to experience it.

Self-doubt

Self-doubt is a common response to trauma. Trauma can leave people feeling uncertain about themselves and their abilities, and they may struggle to trust their own judgment or decisions. This can lead to feelings of self-doubt and a lack of confidence in the self. Self-doubt can manifest in various ways, such as questioning their competence, second-guessing decisions, or feeling like an imposter in certain situations.

Self-analysis and questioning

Over-analysing can be a common response to trauma, as it is natural for people to try to make sense of what has happened to them. When an individual has experienced a traumatic event, they may feel overwhelmed, confused, and uncertain about how to process what they have been through. As a result, they may find themselves constantly thinking about the traumatic event, replaying it over and over in their minds and trying to understand why it happened and what it means for them.

This over-analysing can manifest in many different ways, such as constantly questioning themselves and their actions, second-guessing their decisions, and obsessively trying to make sense of what happened. This can be a way for people to try to gain a sense of control over the traumatic experience and find a way to make it fit into their understanding of the world.

However, over-analysing can also be counterproductive and lead to feelings of fear, obsession, exhaustion, and distress. It is important for people to find a balance between processing their trauma and not getting stuck in a cycle of overthinking and rumination.

Self-isolation

Isolation is a common response to trauma, as it can be difficult to trust others or feel safe around them. Some people isolate themselves as a way of protecting themselves from further harm, while others may withdraw as a way of processing their feelings and emotions. Isolation can also be a way of avoiding triggers that may remind them of their trauma. Additionally, some people may feel ashamed or embarrassed about what happened to them, and isolate themselves as a result. They may believe that others will judge them or not understand what they are going through, which can make it hard to seek support or talk about their experiences.

Self-objectification

Objectifying the self as a response to trauma refers to seeing oneself as an object rather than a person with thoughts, feelings, and needs. It can be a way for people to detach themselves from their emotions and pain and dissociate from their trauma. Objectification can also be a coping mechanism that allows people to focus on physical sensations or superficial aspects of their identity rather than confronting their emotional pain.

Objectifying the self can take many forms, such as obsessively focusing on appearance, engaging in risky behaviour, or disassociating from emotions and relationships. This response to trauma can be damaging as it can lead to feelings of emptiness, detachment, and a lack of self-worth. People may also struggle with forming and maintaining healthy relationships as they may view themselves and others as objects rather than people with emotions and needs.

Sexual objectification

Sexual objectification is a form of dehumanisation where a person is reduced to an object of sexual desire, rather than being treated as a whole person with their own agency, desires, and feelings. This form of dehumanisation is more common for women and girls due to misogyny and the pornification of the female body. Being sexually objectified can be traumatic because it can make a person feel powerless and vulnerable, as if they are not in control of their own body or how others perceive them. It can lead to feelings of shame, self-doubt, self-blame, and low self-esteem, and can also contribute to the development of fear, sadness, worthlessness, and anger. Furthermore, being subjected to sexual objectification can also increase the risk of sexual assault and other forms of sex-based violence, which can further exacerbate the trauma.

Self-sexualisation can be a response to trauma in which an individual seeks control over their own sexuality and body after experiencing sexual trauma or abuse. In some cases, people may use sexual behaviour as a way to cope with feelings of powerlessness or low self-esteem that result from the trauma. This behaviour can include dressing in certain ways, engaging in sexual activity frequently, or seeking attention or validation from others through sexual means.

Sexuality changes

It is important to note that sexual orientation is not an active choice. Some people say that they were 'born gay' and others feel it was a process of realisation throughout life. Some people do not realise they are gay, lesbian or bisexual until much later in life. However, some people who have experienced trauma of any kind may feel confusion about their sexual identity or may feel the need to explore different sexual orientations as a way of coping with their trauma. For example, someone who has been subjected to sexual trauma may feel uncomfortable with their own sexuality and may try to distance themselves from their own sexual feelings by identifying as a different sexual orientation. For other people, they realise that much of their trauma and psychological distress has come from many years of repressing or denying their sexuality, and living a mental 'double life'.

Whilst the general narrative in pro-LGBTQ+ sources is that people are born into their sexual orientation, and it is unchangeable, this does not account for the people who do feel their sexuality changed with age or experience, and that they became attracted to the same sex, or the opposite sex, after life events, traumas, or with time. For professionals then, it is important not to impose theories of sexuality on to people who need to be able to safely discuss the change in their own sexual orientation.

Sexual preferences

Changes in sexual preferences can be a complex and multifaceted response to trauma, and can vary greatly from person to person. For some people, trauma can cause them to question or change their sexual identity the kind of sex they enjoy. This may be due to feeling unsafe, feeling a need to distance themselves from the trauma, or seeking a sense of control or empowerment through sexual exploration.

For others, trauma may cause changes in sexual behaviour, preferences or desires. They may experience hypersexuality or a decreased sex drive, or find it difficult to experience pleasure during sexual activity. These changes may be due to the trauma impacting their ability to feel safe and comfortable during sexual experiences or causing a disconnection from their body and emotions.

Further, some people experience a change in what arouses them after trauma. They may notice that their sexual fantasies change, or they develop desires or fetishes they did not have before. For some people, this can be distressing and confusing (developing a sexual desire to be controlled or hurt during sex, after being sexually abused, for example). For others, they are comfortable with exploring this sexual desire with a safe partner.

This does sometimes raise complex ethical questions, though, as some people develop sexual fantasies that are arguably abusive, harmful or violent. It's important to note that changes in sexual preferences are not always a direct response to trauma and can have other causes.

Shame

Shame is a common response to trauma. Trauma can cause people to feel like they are damaged, flawed, or unworthy. They may feel ashamed of the trauma itself or the way they responded to the trauma. For example, they may feel ashamed that they froze during a traumatic event instead of fighting back or running away. Shame can also be a result of negative beliefs or messages that were internalised during the trauma or as a result of it.

People may experience shame in different ways. They may feel a sense of guilt, humiliation, or self-disgust. They may also experience physical symptoms like blushing, sweating, or an increased heart rate. Shame can lead to negative self-talk, such as harsh self-criticism or self-blame, and can make it difficult for people to seek help or support. It can also cause people to isolate themselves from others and feel like they don't deserve love, care, or compassion.

Shock

Shock is a common response to trauma. It is an immediate and overwhelming reaction to an event that threatens the person's safety or sense of self. In the immediate aftermath of a traumatic event, shock can be experienced as a feeling of numbness, disbelief, or dissociation from reality.

In the context of trauma, shock can serve as a protective mechanism, allowing the person to distance themselves from the intensity of the experience and provide some time to process what has happened. However, if shock persists for an extended period of time, it can interfere with a person's ability to cope with the trauma. It's important to note that not everyone who experiences trauma will necessarily feel shock as a response. Different people may have different emotional, physical, and psychological responses to trauma based on their unique experiences and coping mechanisms.

Shortened attention span

After experiencing trauma, some people may have a shortened attention span as a result of being hypervigilant or easily distracted. Hypervigilance is a state of being constantly on guard and perceiving threats even when there are none. This can cause the individual to have difficulty focusing on one task or thought for an extended period of time.
Additionally, trauma can activate the fight or flight response, which prepares the body to react quickly to a perceived danger. This response can cause the individual to feel restless, fidgety, and easily distracted. They may feel like they need to be alert and on the lookout for potential threats, making it difficult for them to stay focused on one thing for too long.

The impact of trauma on attention span can vary from person to person depending on the nature and severity of the trauma, as well as individual coping mechanisms and support systems. It is important to seek help from a mental health professional if shortened attention span or other symptoms of trauma persist and interfere with daily life.

Sleep disturbance

Sleep disturbance is a common response to trauma. Traumatic experiences can lead to sleep problems, such as insomnia or nightmares. Insomnia may involve difficulty falling asleep, staying asleep, or waking up too early.

Nightmares are often vivid and distressing dreams that can be a re-experiencing of the traumatic event. People who have experienced trauma may also have sleep disorders such as sleep apnoea, restless legs syndrome, or narcolepsy. These sleep disorders can result in disrupted sleep patterns and make it difficult to get enough restorative sleep. The impact of sleep disturbance can further contribute to feelings of exhaustion, irritability, and difficulty with concentration and memory.

Starting new projects

Starting new projects or taking on new challenges can be a response to trauma as it may serve as a way to distract oneself from the pain and negative emotions associated with the trauma. Engaging in new activities or learning new skills can also give a sense of accomplishment and control, which can help to counteract the feelings of helplessness that may arise from the traumatic experience. It can also provide a sense of purpose and direction for the future, which can be particularly important if the trauma has disrupted one's sense of identity or goals. Additionally, starting new projects or taking on new challenges can provide a sense of excitement or adventure that may be lacking in one's life after experiencing trauma.

Starving yourself

Some people may develop disordered eating behaviours, such as starving themselves, as a response to trauma. Trauma can cause a range of emotional and psychological distress, including fear, low mood, despair, helplessness, and feelings of powerlessness. Some people may feel a need to exert control over their bodies in response to these overwhelming feelings, and disordered eating behaviours can be a way to achieve this sense of control.

Additionally, some people may feel that their bodies are no longer safe or worthy of care after experiencing trauma, and this may lead them to engage in self-destructive behaviours, such as starving themselves or engaging in other harmful behaviours.

Strange sensations

Strange sensations can be a response to trauma, particularly if the trauma was related to physical harm or injury. These sensations may manifest as physical symptoms, such as pain, tingling, or numbness, even when there is no physical injury present. For example, someone who has experienced a traumatic car accident may experience sensations of pain or discomfort in their body even after they have fully healed. Additionally, strange sensations can manifest as psychological symptoms, such as feeling disconnected from oneself or from reality, experiencing depersonalisation or derealisation, or feeling as though the body or surroundings are not real. These sensations may be distressing and may interfere with a person's ability to function in their daily life.

Stuttering or stammering

Experiencing trauma can cause a person to develop a stutter or stammer as a result of the psychological and physiological effects it has on the body. Trauma can cause a person to feel overwhelmed and anxious, and this can lead to physical changes in the body, including changes to the voice and speech patterns. The physical effects of trauma, such as tension and hypervigilance, can also make it difficult for a person to speak smoothly and confidently, leading to a stutter or stammer. Additionally, some people may develop a stutter or stammer as a coping mechanism to deal with the emotional impact of the trauma.

Submissive (submission)

A common response to trauma, or a method of coping with trauma responses is to become more submissive and agreeable. After experiencing trauma, some people may become submissive as a response. Trauma can leave people feeling afraid and vulnerable. As a result, some people may become submissive to protect themselves from further harm.

Trauma can erode a person's ability to trust others. Some people may become submissive to avoid conflict or to prevent others from lashing out at them. Other people may have learned submissive behaviour as a coping mechanism from their abusers, or for the abuse they were subjected to for years. They may have learned that submitting to the abuser's demands was the safest way to avoid further harm.

Trauma can also have a significant impact on a person's self-esteem and self-confidence. Some people may become submissive as a way to avoid taking risks or making decisions, out of fear of failure or rejection.

Suicidal ideation or feelings

Suicidal ideation is a common response to trauma, particularly in those who have experienced severe or prolonged trauma. Trauma can have a profound effect on a person's mental health, leading to feelings of hopelessness, worthlessness, and despair. These feelings can become so overwhelming that the individual begins to consider suicide as a way to escape their pain.

Suicidal ideation can take many forms, ranging from fleeting thoughts of suicide to detailed plans for ending one's life. Some people may feel that suicide is the only way to escape the pain of their trauma or that their loved ones would be better off without them. Others may feel that they have lost all sense of purpose or meaning in their lives and that death would be a release from their suffering.

It's important to note that experiencing suicidal ideation does not necessarily mean that an individual will act on these thoughts.

Taking drugs

Taking drugs as a coping mechanism for trauma is a way for some people to temporarily escape from their painful emotions and memories. Trauma can be overwhelming and consuming, and drugs may provide a sense of relief or numbing. They may also be used to self-medicate the feelings of panic, stress, anger, sadness, fear or trauma.

Drug use can also be a way for some people to feel a sense of control, particularly if they experienced a loss of control during the traumatic event. However, drug use can be dangerous and may lead to addiction, further exacerbating trauma and distress.

Triggers (being triggered)

A trigger is defined as a stimulus that causes an unexpected or uncontrollable fear response, where the stimulus is directly or indirectly related to the trauma. Directly related triggers may include seeing images about or related to the traumatic event, smelling fragrances or smells that were present at the original trauma,

Being 'triggered' in trauma refers to the experience of having a psychological or emotional response to a reminder of a traumatic event. Triggers can be external or internal stimuli that remind an individual of their trauma, such as sights, sounds, smells, or thoughts. When triggered, people may feel fear, horror, danger, doom, panic, have flashbacks, or experience dissociation.

Triggers can be unpredictable and may vary from person to person. They can be specific to the type of trauma experienced or can be more general in nature. For example, a survivor of sexual assault may be triggered by seeing someone who looks like their perpetrator, while a survivor of a car accident may be triggered by the sound of screeching tires. Being triggered is a common response to trauma. Triggers are simply stimuli that remind the person of the trauma they have been subjected to. They are not disordered or abnormal. Triggers can be the brain or body's way of trying to protect the person from further harm, by recognising stimuli or similarities in situations.

Toxic positivity

Toxic positivity is a phenomenon where people, who may have experienced trauma or difficult life events, feel pressure to maintain a positive outlook and deny or suppress their negative emotions. This response to trauma is often a result of societal or cultural messages that promote the idea of being "positive" or "happy" as the ideal state of being. The pressure to maintain a positive outlook can sometimes lead people to ignore or dismiss their negative emotions, which can lead to further trauma and distress.

Toxic positivity can also be a result of internalised beliefs about emotions and vulnerability, where people feel shame or weakness for experiencing negative emotions. This can cause people to avoid seeking support or expressing their true feelings, which can prevent them from healing and moving forward from the trauma.

It is important to recognise that emotions, both positive and negative, are a natural and normal part of the human experience, and that suppressing or denying them can lead to further harm. Instead, seeking support and allowing oneself to feel and process all emotions can help people to heal and move forward from trauma in a healthy way.

Unable to feel satisfied

After experiencing trauma, some people may feel unsatisfied due to a number of reasons. They may have feelings of numbness or emotional detachment, making it difficult to experience pleasure or joy. They may also struggle with feelings of guilt, shame, or self-blame, which can contribute to a sense of worthlessness or inadequacy. In addition, trauma can cause changes in personal beliefs or values, leading to a sense of disillusionment or loss of purpose.

Finally, some people may struggle with their trauma responses and coping mechanisms, which can also contribute to feelings of dissatisfaction with life. It is important for people who are struggling with the after-effects of trauma to seek professional support and guidance to help them process their experiences and move forward in a healthy and positive way.

Unfairness

After experiencing trauma, it is common to feel a sense of unfairness about what happened. This feeling of unfairness can stem from a variety of sources, including:

Loss of control: Traumatic events can leave people feeling like they had no control over what happened to them. This loss of control can make it feel unfair that they were put in such a vulnerable position without the ability to protect themselves.

Betrayal: If the trauma was caused by another person, such as in cases of abuse or violence, people may feel a sense of betrayal that someone they trusted could do something so harmful to them. This can make the trauma feel even more unfair.

Sense of injustice: Trauma can be a result of circumstances beyond a person's control, such as natural disasters or accidents. People may feel like it is unfair that they were in the wrong place at the wrong time, and that others around them did not experience the same trauma.

Comparison to others: People may compare their experience of trauma to others who have not gone through similar experiences. They may feel that it is unfair that they have to carry the burden of the trauma while others are able to go through life without that same weight.

These feelings of unfairness can be difficult to navigate and may lead to a sense of bitterness or anger.

Victim blaming others

It is not uncommon for some survivors of trauma to victim blame other survivors. In fact, some studies have shown that people who have been subjected to abuse and violence will victim blame others at the same rate as people who have never experienced those crimes.

People may internalise the belief that they were responsible for the trauma they experienced. This can lead them to believe that other survivors are also responsible for their trauma, and to blame them for what happened. Some people may feel angry and frustrated about what happened to them, but may not know how to express or process those feelings in a healthy way. This can lead them to direct their anger towards other survivors, blaming them for their own trauma instead of acknowledging the responsibility of the perpetrator.

For others, facing their own trauma can be a difficult and painful process. Blaming other people who have been subjected to abuse and trauma may be a way for some people to avoid confronting their own experiences and the associated emotions. In most cultures, victim blaming is a pervasive and normalised response to trauma. It is likely that people may have internalised these cultural beliefs and perpetuate them by blaming other survivors for their own trauma.

Wanting to be dead

After experiencing trauma, some people may express a desire to be dead or have suicidal thoughts. This can be due to a variety of reasons, including:

Overwhelming emotions: Traumatic events can trigger intense emotions that may feel unbearable to the person. Feelings of fear, anger, guilt, shame, and hopelessness can become overwhelming and make the person feel like there is no way to escape their pain.

Loss of meaning or purpose: Trauma can shatter a person's sense of meaning and purpose in life. The person may feel like their life has lost all meaning or that they have lost all hope for the future.

Physical pain: Trauma can also cause physical pain and discomfort that can be difficult to manage. Chronic pain and disability resulting from the trauma can be a constant reminder of the traumatic event and make the person feel like their quality of life has significantly decreased.

Self-blame: People subjected to abuse and trauma may blame themselves for what happened, even if the trauma was not their fault. They may feel like they do not deserve to live or that their death would be a way to atone for their perceived mistakes.

Wanting to appear unattractive

After being subjected to abuse, some people may want to appear unattractive for a variety of reasons. If the abuse occurred in a romantic or sexual relationship, the person may feel that appearing unattractive will help them avoid future abuse. They may believe that if they are less physically attractive, their partner will be less likely to be interested in them and less likely to hurt them.

Some people subjected to abuse may feel a sense of guilt or shame for what happened to them, even if the abuse was not their fault. They may feel that by appearing unattractive, they are punishing themselves for what they perceive as their role in the abuse. Abuse can leave people feeling powerless and out of control. By changing their appearance to something they perceive as unattractive, they may feel like they are reclaiming some control over their lives. Due to the traumas they were subjected to, they may feel uncomfortable with the attention that comes with being physically attractive. By appearing unattractive, they may feel that they can avoid unwanted attention and stay under the radar.

It is important to note that everyone's experience with abuse is different, and there is no one 'right' way to cope with the aftermath of abuse.

Withdrawn (withdrawing)

A common trauma response or coping mechanism, becoming withdrawn serves many purposes for people who have been subjected to trauma. The person may slowly withdraw more and more, or may suddenly withdraw themselves from people, situations, events, environments, and relationships. There are many different reasons why this response or coping mechanism may be employed, including withdrawal as a fear response, a self-preservation response, a coping mechanism for worries, fears and discomfort, a way to protect the self from certain people, responses, judgements, comments, experiences, triggers, or external stimuli.

Why me?

When people experience trauma, it is common for them to ask, 'why me?' as a response. This can stem from a variety of reasons, including:

Sense of unfairness: Traumatic events can leave people feeling like they were singled out for suffering. They may feel like it is unfair that they had to go through something so painful and wonder why they were the ones who had to experience it.

Loss of control: Trauma can leave people feeling like they had no control over what happened to them. This loss of control can make them question why they had to go through something so terrible, and why they were not able to prevent it from happening.

Guilt or self-blame: People may blame themselves for what happened, even if the trauma was not their fault. They may ask "why me?" as a way of trying to understand why they were put in that situation and what they could have done differently to prevent it.

Search for meaning: Trauma can significantly impact a person's sense of meaning and purpose in life. People may ask "why me?" as a way of trying to make sense of what happened and find meaning in their suffering.

Asking "why me?" can be a natural response to trauma, but it is important for the person to understand that there is often no answer to their question, and there was not a reason that the abuse, trauma, or harm happened to them, and they may not have been able to do anything differently.

This is particularly true where the trauma was caused by a third party, as the person is not responsible for the actions and choices of the perpetrator.

Worthlessness

Trauma can have a significant impact on a person's sense of self-worth and self-esteem. After experiencing trauma, people may experience feelings of worthlessness as a response.

People who have been subjected to abuse and trauma may blame themselves for what happened, even if the trauma was not their fault. This self-blame can make them feel like they are responsible for the trauma and that they are a bad or unworthy person as a result. Trauma can leave people feeling ashamed of what happened to them or of their own reactions to the trauma. This can lead to feelings of worthlessness and a belief that they are unworthy of love, respect, or happiness.

Trauma can change a person's sense of self and their understanding of who they are. Some people may feel like they have lost a part of themselves and that they are not the same person they were before the trauma. This can lead to feelings of worthlessness and a sense of not knowing who they are or what their purpose is. Some may compare themselves to others who have not gone through similar experiences. They may feel like they are inferior to others who have not experienced the same trauma, or that their trauma makes them less worthy of love, respect, or happiness.

CHAPTER 5

Signs of trauma in infants and toddlers

Trauma in infants can be difficult to recognise, as they may not be able to communicate their experiences verbally. However, there are some signs that may indicate that an infant has experienced, or been subjected to distress or trauma.

Excessive crying or fussiness: Children who are distressed or traumatised may be more irritable or cry more frequently than other infants.

Sleep disturbances: Children who have are distressed or traumatised may have trouble sleeping or wake up frequently during the night.

Feeding difficulties: Children who are distressed or traumatised may have trouble with feeding, either refusing to eat or eating excessively.

Developmental delays: Children who are distressed or traumatised may have delays in reaching developmental milestones, such as sitting up, crawling, talking, or walking.

Hypervigilance: Children who are distressed or traumatised may be easily startled or overly sensitive to loud noises or other stimuli. They may become frightened of places, or people.

Avoidance: Children who are distressed or traumatised may avoid eye contact or physical touch, or may seem withdrawn or unresponsive.

It is important to note that not all infants who exhibit these signs have experienced trauma, and many infants may show no obvious signs of trauma at all. Any changes in health, development or behaviour should be considered.

Signs of sexual trauma in infants and toddlers

Signs of sexual abuse in infants can be difficult to recognise, as they are often non-specific and may be mistaken for other health conditions. However, some common signs of sexual abuse in infants may include:

Pain or discomfort in the genital area: Children may have pain or discomfort in the genital area, or may cry or become irritable when the area is touched. They may be reluctant to go to the toilet. They may have recurring UTIs.

Bleeding or bruising in the genital area: Children may have visible signs of infection, injury, or trauma, such as bleeding, marks, redness, itching, or bruising in the genital area.

Difficulty sitting or walking: Children may have difficulty sitting or walking due to pain or discomfort in the genital area.

Changes in behaviour: Children may exhibit changes in behaviour, such as becoming withdrawn, irritable, or scared, sad, or may exhibit regressive behaviours such as bed-wetting.

Sleeping or eating disturbances: Children may have trouble sleeping or may experience changes in their eating patterns.

Sexual or developmentally inappropriate behaviour: Children may touch or stimulate their genitals, try to touch others, or develop unusual or inappropriate behaviours. They may say words, talk sexually, talk of games or special secrets, or try to communicate about being touched or touching others.

Signs of neglect of infants and toddlers

Neglect of infants is a form of child abuse that occurs when a caregiver fails to meet a child's basic needs for food, shelter, safety, and medical care. Signs of neglect in infants may include:

Failure to thrive: Infants who are neglected may not receive adequate nutrition, which can lead to failure to gain weight or grow at a normal rate.

Poor hygiene: Infants who are neglected may have poor hygiene, such as dirty clothing or skin, uncut nails, or untreated nappy rash.

Health problems: Infants who are neglected may be at increased risk for health problems, such as infections, respiratory illnesses, or developmental delays.

Lack of supervision: Infants who are neglected may be left alone for extended periods of time, without adequate supervision or care.

Inadequate clothing or shelter: Infants who are neglected may not have adequate clothing or shelter to protect them from the elements.

Lack of emotional responsiveness: Infants who are neglected may not receive adequate emotional care, such as attention, affection, or comfort.

Coping mechanisms in young children

Just like adults, children of all ages develop coping mechanisms for trauma, abuse, and distress. Their coping mechanisms can be varied, and are also subject to the same social narratives as those of adults. For example, a young child who becomes quiet, submissive and obedient is likely to be seen as a 'good child', and therefore not considered to be traumatised. Some coping mechanisms that children may use include:

Self-harm: Children may engage in self-harm, such as hitting their head, hitting, scratching, pinching, pulling their hair, cutting, or burning, as a way to manage or cope.

Avoidance: Children may avoid situations, stimuli, people, or emotions that make them uncomfortable or scared.

Aggression: Children may act out in aggressive or violent ways as a way to cope with distress or emotions.

Issues with eating: Children may develop concerning eating patterns, such as restrictive eating, refusing to eat, hiding food, or bingeing, as a way to cope with distress.

Withdrawal: Children may withdraw from social situations or isolate themselves as a way to cope with distress or emotions.

Submission and seeking approval: Children may become more submissive, more obedient, seek approval, seek reward, and want to be seen as a 'good girl/boy' by being well behaved.

Imagination: Children may create imaginative worlds, imaginary friends, voices, alters, people, ghosts, monsters, heroes, characters, and toys as a way to cope with a distressing reality.

CHAPTER 6

Physical responses to trauma and distress

This section provides a non-exhaustive list of physiological responses to trauma and distress in humans, with explanations as to why people may suffer them after, or during experiencing or being subjected to something traumatic. Additionally, it is important to consider that an individual may be unaware of what is making them feel distressed, and so the physiological responses may not have been considered as something resulting from psychological trauma and distress.

You will notice that as you read through this section, a significant number of physiological symptoms related to psychological trauma and distress are linked to the release of hormones such as adrenaline and cortisol during states of distress, panic, worry, low mood, anxiety, anger, trauma, and more. The release of these hormones is linked to many physiological responses due to the physical changes in the body they cause.

As is the case with the entirety of this book, it is not for the intended use of any medical diagnosis or ruling out diagnosis. While many responses to trauma have psychosomatic or physiological responses, it is important that people experiencing any of the symptoms or responses in this section consult their healthcare provider due to the potential risk of them resulting from a health condition.

While this section looks at physiological symptoms of distress and trauma, the following section looks at health issues misdiagnosed as psychiatric disorders. It may be helpful to see the section of the ITIM entitled 'health issues that can be ignored or minimised in favour of suggesting that the patient is mentally ill or stressed'.

The role of cortisol

Cortisol and adrenaline are hormones produced by the adrenal glands in response to stress. These hormones play a crucial role in the body's 'fight or flight' response, which is a natural response to a perceived threat. When the body is under stress, cortisol and adrenaline are released into the bloodstream, which triggers several physiological changes, including:

- Increased heart rate and blood pressure
- Increased respiration rate
- Dilated pupils
- Increased blood sugar levels
- Suppressed immune system response

While the distress response is designed to be helpful in short-term situations, high levels of cortisol and adrenaline over time can lead to:

- High blood pressure
- Increased risk of heart disease
- Impaired immune system function
- Increased risk of infection
- Impaired memory and concentration
- Fatigue and sleep problems

Health issues related to trauma

Acne

Acne is a common skin condition that results in multiple spots (usually on the face, back, and/or chest area) that can cause pain and discomfort (NHS, 2023). Research has indicated that those who suffer with, or who have suffered previously with acne are likely to have breakouts or worsening symptoms or severity during periods of distress (Chiu et al., 2003). Some theories suggest that this is due to the relationship between psychological distress affecting the immune system which leads to prolonged healing timeframes (Kiecolt-Glaser et al., 1995).

Bedwetting/night-time incontinence/nocturnal enuresis

Bedwetting is involuntary urination during the night or while asleep (MFMER, 2017). While bedwetting is most commonly associated with children, it can occur in adults too and is sometimes linked to stress, trauma, and fear. If the cause of bedwetting does stem from some form of distress, it is likely that the bedwetting will continue for a long period after the trauma has gone. Currently, there is little literature on this and so it is important for people to consult a medical professional as bedwetting is a relatively uncommon distress response in adults (more common in children and teens) and may be linked to physiological health issues.

Blurred vision

Psychosomatic related blurred vision occurs most often when a person is in a high level of distress or panic. Increased levels of adrenaline in the body can cause pressure on the eyes causing vision to blur.

Stress can cause blurred vision in several ways:

Muscle tension: When we experience stress, our natural response is to tense up. This can cause the muscles in and around the eyes to become tense and rigid, which can lead to blurred vision.

Changes in blood flow: distress can cause changes in blood flow to the eyes, which can affect the clarity of vision. When we experience stress, our body's natural response is to increase blood pressure and heart rate. This can cause blood vessels in the eyes to constrict, which can reduce the amount of oxygen and nutrients that reach the eyes.

Eye strain: distress can lead to eye strain, which can cause blurred vision. When we are stressed, we may spend more time staring at a computer screen or reading, which can cause eye fatigue and strain.

Dry eye syndrome: distress can contribute to dry eye syndrome, which is a condition in which the eyes do not produce enough tears to keep them moist. This can cause eye irritation, redness, and blurred vision.

During a panic attack, the body experiences a surge of adrenaline and other distress hormones, which can cause several physical symptoms, including blurred vision. Here are a few reasons why panic attacks can cause vision to blur:

Hyperventilation: During a panic attack, it's common to experience hyperventilation, or rapid breathing. This can lead to a decrease in carbon dioxide levels in the blood, which can cause blood vessels in the brain to constrict. As a result, the brain may receive less oxygen, which can cause blurred vision.

Pupil dilation: A possible effect of the adrenaline surge during a panic attack is pupil dilation. This can cause the eyes to become more sensitive to light and can also affect visual acuity, leading to blurry vision.

Body aches

People who are distressed or traumatised often report body aches and pain without a clear underlying medical cause. Physical tension and sleep disturbances related to distress and trauma can cause these symptoms:

- Headaches and migraines
- Neck and back pain
- General body aches and pains

When we experience distress or trauma, our body responds by releasing distress hormones, such as cortisol and adrenaline, which can cause a range of physical symptoms, including body aches. Here are a few reasons why distress and trauma can lead to body aches:

Muscle tension: Distress and trauma can cause muscles to tense up, leading to pain and discomfort. This tension can be caused by trauma responses, which prepare the body to respond to a perceived threat.

Inflammation: Distress can cause inflammation in the body, which can contribute to muscle pain and stiffness. When the body is under stress, it may produce more cytokines, which are proteins that regulate inflammation.

Reduced sleep quality: Distress and trauma can affect our sleep quality, leading to fatigue and muscle soreness. When we don't get enough sleep, our body may become more inflamed, which can contribute to pain and discomfort.

Emotional distress: Distress and trauma can manifest as physical pain. It is generally accepted that mental distress and trauma can cause, and exacerbate physical pain (Hall-Flavin, 2023).

Chest pain & chest tightness

Chest pain and/or tightness related to distress and trauma can have multiple stems. The first is related to physical muscle tension and stiffness, which is structural. The second is a result of the combination of an increase in heart beating quicker or harder, and a tightness in chest muscles; this is very common during a panic attack. This can feel different from person to person, but can present as sharp, shooting, or stabbing pain, chest ache, tension or tightness.

During a panic attack, the body experiences a surge of adrenaline and other distress hormones, which can cause several physical symptoms, including chest pain or tightness. Here are a few reasons why panic attacks can cause chest pain or tightness:

Hyperventilation: During a panic attack, it's common to experience hyperventilation, or rapid breathing. This can cause a decrease in carbon dioxide levels in the blood, which can lead to constriction of the blood vessels in the heart and chest, causing chest pain or discomfort.

Muscle tension: During a panic attack, muscles tend to become tense, including those in the chest. This tension can lead to pain or tightness in the chest.

Fear response: Panic attacks are often triggered by a perceived threat, which can lead to a fear response. This fear response can cause the body to release adrenaline, which can increase heart rate and blood pressure, leading to chest pain or tightness.

Gastrointestinal issues: In some cases, chest pain or tightness during a panic attack may be related to gastrointestinal issues, such as acid reflux or indigestion, which can be triggered by distress.

While chest pain is a common symptom of many non-serious medical issues, it's always important for those experiencing chest pain to speak to a medical professional due to the potential severity of this.

Cognitive function decline

Cognitive function refers to what we understand to be brain activity such as memory, attention, planning, processing speed, and executive functions (Oregon State University, 2019). Current theories suggest that the interplay between cognition and emotion during a period or event of significant distress or trauma results in the prioritisation of threat detection, at the expense of cognitive function (Hayes et al., 2012).

Distress or trauma can have a significant impact on cognitive functions due to the way it affects the brain and nervous system. Here are a few ways that distress or trauma can impact cognitive functions:

Stress response: When we experience distress or trauma, our body's distress response is activated. This can cause a surge of distress hormones, such as cortisol and adrenaline, which can affect the way the brain functions.

Emotional regulation: Distress or trauma can affect our ability to regulate emotions, which can impact cognitive functions such as attention, memory, and decision-making. When we are overwhelmed by emotions, it can be difficult to focus or remember important information.

Sleep disturbances: Distress or trauma can lead to sleep disturbances and ongoing deprivation, which can significantly impact cognitive functions such as attention, memory, and learning. When we don't get enough sleep, our brain may not be able to function optimally.

Disruptive thoughts: Distress or trauma can lead to intrusive or disruptive thoughts, which can interfere with cognitive functions such as attention and memory. When we are preoccupied with distressing thoughts, it can be difficult to focus on other tasks or remember important information.

Daydreaming

Daydreaming is considered a mild form of dissociation. Memories, fantasies, problem solving, meditation, or aesthetic/poetic imaginings are some of the main formulations of what we understand daydreaming to be (Singer & McCraven, 1961). Most people daydream, and some more frequently than others; with some being positive, some negative, and some neutral.

(Developing) intolerances and sensitivities

Food intolerances and sensitivities can develop as a response to distress due to the impact of distress on the digestive system and the immune system.

Stress triggers the release of hormones such as cortisol and adrenaline, which can affect the functioning of the digestive system. When we are stressed, our body enters a "fight or flight" response, which diverts blood flow away from the digestive system and towards the muscles to prepare for physical action. This can lead to digestive issues such as bloating, constipation, and diarrhoea.

In addition, distress can weaken the lining of the gut, making it more permeable and allowing undigested food and toxins to pass into the bloodstream. This can trigger an immune response, leading to the development of food sensitivities or intolerances.

Food sensitivities and intolerances are different from food allergies, which are an immediate immune response to a specific food. Food sensitivities and intolerances are a delayed reaction, and symptoms can appear several hours or even days after consuming the food.

Symptoms of food sensitivities and intolerances can include bloating, abdominal pain, diarrhoea, constipation, skin rashes, joint pain, and headaches. Eliminating the offending food from the diet can alleviate these symptoms.

Dissociation

People who experience disassociation report strong feelings of disconnect from themselves, their surroundings, their senses, and more. While many people experience dissociation in their life, the severity of this can greatly differ.

Some people report:

- Feeling like they are dead, not alive, or not real
- Feeling like their surroundings are not real
- Feeling like they are not in their own body
- Feeling as though they are observing themselves as a third party
- Feeling as though time is moving very slowly, very quickly, or not at all.
- Feeling as though they are not in control of the actions they are performing

Disorientation

When we are stressed, our natural, automatic response is to prepare the body to respond to a perceived threat. This can cause several physical and psychological symptoms, including disorientation. Here are a few reasons why distress can cause disorientation:

Reduced blood flow to the brain: When we experience stress, blood pressure and heart rate increase. This can cause blood vessels in the brain to constrict, which can reduce blood flow to the brain. As a result, we may experience disorientation or confusion.

Hyperventilation: During stress, it's common to experience hyperventilation, or rapid breathing. This can cause a decrease in carbon dioxide levels in the blood, which can lead to dizziness, light-headedness, and disorientation.

Overwhelmed by stimuli: distress can cause us to become overwhelmed by stimuli, such as noise, crowds, or visual stimulation. When we are overwhelmed, it can be difficult to process information and maintain a sense of orientation.

Emotional distress: distress can lead to emotional distress, which can manifest as disorientation. When we are emotionally overwhelmed, it can be difficult to think clearly and maintain a sense of orientation.

Dizziness

When we are distressed or traumatised, our body may respond by activating the sympathetic nervous system, which prepares the body to respond to a perceived threat. This can cause several physical and psychological symptoms, including dizziness. Here are a few reasons why distress or trauma can cause dizziness:

Hyperventilation: During distress or trauma, it's common to experience hyperventilation, or rapid breathing. This can cause a decrease in carbon dioxide levels in the blood, which can lead to dizziness, light-headedness, and a feeling of being off-balance.

Blood pressure changes: distress or trauma can cause changes in blood pressure, which can lead to dizziness. When we are under stress, our blood pressure and heart rate increases, which can cause blood vessels in the brain to constrict, leading to dizziness.

Emotional distress: distress or trauma can cause emotional distress, which can manifest as dizziness.

Muscle tension: distress or trauma can cause muscle tension, including tension in the neck and shoulders. This tension can lead to headaches and dizziness.

Echoed or distorted hearing

Trauma and distress can cause several physical and psychological symptoms, including changes in hearing. Here are a few reasons why hearing may go echoey or distorted when in shock or trauma:

Adrenaline surge: During shock or trauma, the body releases adrenaline and other distress hormones, which can affect the way we perceive sound. Adrenaline can cause the muscles in the ear to tense up, which can lead to a feeling of fullness or pressure in the ear, and may cause sounds to become distorted or echoey.

Rapid breathing: During shock or trauma, it's common to experience rapid breathing or hyperventilation. This can cause a decrease in carbon dioxide levels in the blood, which can affect the way we perceive sound and may contribute to a feeling of being disconnected or disoriented.

Auditory processing issues: Shock or trauma can affect auditory processing. When we are in shock or trauma, it can be difficult to process and understand what we are hearing, which may contribute to a feeling of distortion or echoing.

Fainting

Fainting, also known as syncope, can be a response to distress in some cases. Fainting occurs when there is a temporary decrease in blood flow to the brain, which can cause a person to lose consciousness. While fainting is often associated with physical causes such as dehydration or low blood sugar, it can also be triggered by emotional or psychological stress.

When a person experiences stress, the 'fight or flight' response is activated, which causes a release of hormones such as adrenaline and cortisol. These hormones can cause the heart rate and blood pressure to increase, which in turn can lead to a sudden drop in blood pressure and a decrease in blood flow to the brain. This can cause a person to feel lightheaded, dizzy, or even lose consciousness.

Fainting as a response to distress is more likely to occur in people who are prone to 'anxiety' or 'panic' attacks, as these responses can cause sudden changes in heart rate and blood pressure. Other factors that can increase the risk of fainting in response to distress include dehydration, low blood sugar, or standing up too quickly.

Appetite changes (food)

Changes in appetite refer to a change the quantity and/ or variety of food a person desires. This is not to be confused with their chosen diet, though this may be the same.

Increase

An increase in appetite means that you desire a higher quantity of food than in a previous period.
An increase in the quantity of food people crave or desire may come from a plethora of psychologically-driven causes. During periods of psychological stress, trauma, uncertainty, or even excitement, and elevation, peoples body's will often be using more adrenaline and energy, resulting in desire for a greater amount of food. Increased appetite is more common when somebody is experiencing long-term distress (sometimes referred to as chronic stress) rather than short term (Ans, A.H. et al., 2018).

Decrease

A decrease in appetite means that you desire a lower quantity of food than in a previous period of time.
A decrease an appetite can equally come from a plethora of psychologically driven causes. People often report having little to no appetite particularly during periods of distress and grief. Grief and distress can impact the digestive system- likely as a result of hormonal production. Short-term periods of stress, trauma, and grief (sometimes referred to as acute stress) are more likely to cause

a decrease in appetite rather than an increase (Ans, A.H. et al., 2018).

What you consume

A change in appetite can also refer to a change in the variety of food you desire. This can often be a change in food groups such as craving more rich carbohydrates, salts, fats, or fruits and vegetables.

Changes in eating habits

Eating habits are your conscious behaviours and choices on which foods you consume, when you consume them, and the quantity you consume them in.
Eating habits can often change during or after a trauma or period of trauma as a coping mechanism for control. Feelings of powerlessness and lack of control are very common particularly when somebody has been subjected to violent or abusive actions of another, when there has been grief or loss, or after an accident.

Increase: An increase in the quantity of food a person chooses to intake may be for many different reasons, some of which being unhealthy choices, some of which being healthy, and some being neutral.

Reasons may include:

- Being comforted by the feeling of being full
- Feeling comforted by the taste of food (this is usually certain food groups which may be specific to the person, however foods that are high in fats and sugars are common).
- Wanting to change how their body looks and / or feels. Reasons for this may include:
    o Progressing from previously consuming too little
    o To help build muscle mass
    o As a form of self-harm / self-neglect

> o   To change appearance following on from an incident in which they may be a victim wherein they attribute the blame into their own appearance

Decrease: Similarly, a decrease may also be for multiple reasons; some of which being unhealthy choices, some of which being healthy, and some being neutral.

Reasons may include:

- Progressing from previously eating too much
- Attempts at changing appearance
- As a form of self-harm
- Fear of gaining weight
- Decrease in physical activity

Erectile Dysfunction

Trauma and distress can cause erectile dysfunction (ED) due to a number of reasons.

One possible explanation is that trauma and distress can cause changes in the levels of hormones, such as cortisol and testosterone, that are involved in sexual function. Trauma and distress can lead to an increase in cortisol levels, which can reduce testosterone levels, leading to ED.

Another possible explanation is that trauma and distress can lead to changes in the autonomic nervous system, which is responsible for regulating sexual function. Trauma and distress can cause the sympathetic nervous system, which is responsible for the 'fight or flight' response, to become overactive, leading to a decrease in blood flow to the penis, making it difficult to achieve or maintain an erection.

Trauma can also increase fear, worry, sadness and distress which can contribute to erectile dysfunction. These factors can make it difficult to relax and enjoy sexual experiences, leading to difficulty achieving or maintaining an erection.

Flushed skin or 'going red'

Flushed skin, particularly on the face and neck area are common responses to emotions such as anger, fear, and embarrassment. This happens when blood vessels dilate to increase blood flow for oxygen delivery when adrenaline is released. Blood vessels in the face and cheek area are closer to the surface than other body parts, which created the 'flushed' appearance most commonly in these parts of the body.

Hair loss

Hair loss is common during and after period of distress and trauma. Telogen effluvium, Trichotillomania, and Alopecia areata are all associated with distress (Daniel K. Hall-Flavin, 2021). Telogen effluvium occurs during significant distress wherein large amounts of hair follicles are pushed into a 'resting phase' while simultaneously 'shedding' excessively (Chang, 1997).

Another possible explanation is that trauma can cause a hormonal imbalance that can lead to hair loss. Trauma can cause the body to produce excess cortisol, which is a stress hormone. High levels of cortisol can disrupt the normal hair growth cycle and lead to hair loss. In addition, trauma can also cause inflammation and damage to the scalp, which can disrupt the normal function of hair follicles and lead to hair loss.

It's worth noting that hair loss due to trauma is usually temporary and the hair will often regrow once the underlying cause is addressed. Trichotillomania is the urge that a person cannot resist to pull out strands or clumps of hair; usually from the head, eyelashes, or eyebrows (NHS, 2021). Alopecia areata is the condition wherein the immune system attacks the hair follicles causing hair loss (Daniel K. Hall-Flavin, 2021) often in clumps on the scalp (Street, 2021).

Headaches

Headaches can be caused by stress and trauma. One possible explanation is that trauma and distress can cause the body to produce stress hormones like cortisol and adrenaline. These hormones can cause the blood vessels in the brain to constrict or dilate, leading to a headache.

Headaches are a feeling of pain, discomfort, and/or pressure in a person's head and/or face. Feelings of distress often cause people to tense up parts of their body; often in areas such as the head, face, neck, and shoulders leading to headaches being a common distress response (MFMER, 2022). Distress and trauma-related headaches can also be caused by crying, pulling facial expressions, sleep deprivation, diet, dehydration, and more.

Hyperventilating

Hyperventilation that is related to distress or fear is often a sign of a panic attack. It refers to a rapid increase in breathing; whether in rate and/or depth.

One of the ways the body responds to fear, shock, trauma, and distress is by increasing the breathing rate, which can cause a person to hyperventilate. Hyperventilation occurs when a person breathes rapidly and shallowly, causing an increase in oxygen intake and a decrease in carbon dioxide levels in the blood. This decrease in carbon dioxide levels can cause symptoms such as dizziness, light-headedness, and tingling in the fingers and toes. These symptoms can then trigger further trauma, leading to a cycle of hyperventilation and panic.

It's important to note that hyperventilation during a panic attack is not dangerous, but it can be uncomfortable and distressing. Due to an increase in oxygen the body takes in when hyperventilating during a panic attack, it can leave the person dizzy, faint, trembling, sweating, tingling, and with cramps (St John Ambulance, 2021).

IBS (Irritable Bowel Syndrome)

Irritable Bowel Syndrome or 'IBS' is a common digestive disorder affecting the large intestine. While the exact cause is unknown, many studies have shown that the condition is strongly linked to distress and trauma, and likely worsens during stressful or traumatic periods. Some theories suggest it is closely linked to the brain-gut axis which is responsible for regulating the function of the digestive system.

Stress can increase inflammation in the gut, which can contribute to symptoms such as abdominal discomfort and pain, bloating, diarrhoea and/or constipation. People suffering with IBS can experience further distress as a result of the condition, which can contribute to a cycle of distress and worsening symptoms.

Inability to orgasm or climax

Trauma and distress can affect the ability to orgasm or climax due to a number of reasons.

One possible explanation is that trauma and distress can cause psychological factors such as fear, distress, sadness, worry, distraction, and irritability which can make it difficult to relax and enjoy sexual experiences. These factors can interfere with the sexual response cycle, which includes desire, arousal, plateau, orgasm, and resolution.

Another possible explanation is that trauma and distress can cause changes in the levels of hormones, such as cortisol and testosterone, that are involved in sexual function. Trauma and distress can lead to an increase in cortisol levels, which can reduce testosterone levels, leading to a decrease in sexual desire and difficulty achieving orgasm.

Trauma and distress can also lead to physical factors that can affect sexual function, such as chronic pain, fatigue, and changes in physical health.

Inability to yawn

The inability to yawn, or to complete a yawn has been linked with stress, fear, and stressful periods. This can be a strange, distressing and frustrating experience, which can last days or weeks. There are multiple theories which explain why this occurs, one being due to the body's muscles being in a tense state preventing them to stretch and relax enough to complete a yawn (BetterSleep, 2022).

Insomnia

Insomnia is classed as a sleep disorder characterised by difficulty falling asleep, staying asleep, or both. It can also refer to poor sleep quality, such as waking up frequently during the night, waking up too early in the morning, or feeling unrefreshed upon waking.

 people who have experienced trauma may have difficulty falling asleep or staying asleep due to intrusive thoughts, flashbacks, or memories related to their trauma. distress can also contribute to insomnia by increasing arousal and vigilance, making it difficult to relax and fall asleep. Chronic distress can lead to the activation of the distress response system, which can interfere with sleep quality and duration. Insomnia can have significant impacts on overall health and well-being, leading to daytime fatigue, impaired cognitive function, and increased risk of other health problems.

Irregular/stopped periods & menstrual cycles

Stress can disrupt the menstrual cycle in several ways, leading to irregular periods, changes in the duration or flow, periods stopping for an amount of time, and other menstrual symptoms.

The menstrual cycle is regulated by a complex interplay of hormones, including oestrogen, progesterone, follicle-stimulating hormone (FSH), and luteinizing hormone (LH). distress can affect the production and regulation of these hormones, leading to changes in the menstrual cycle.

Stress and trauma can have a significant impact on menstrual cycles due to the way they affect the body's hormonal balance and reproductive system. Here are a few ways that distress and trauma can impact menstrual cycles:

Hormonal changes: distress and trauma can disrupt the balance of hormones in the body, including those that regulate the menstrual cycle. Chronic distress can lead to an increase in cortisol levels, which can affect the production of reproductive hormones like oestrogen and progesterone.

Irregular cycles: distress and trauma can cause menstrual cycles to become irregular or unpredictable. This may be due to changes in hormone levels, as well as changes in the body's distress response.

Amenorrhea: In some cases, distress and trauma can cause amenorrhea, which is the absence of menstrual periods. This may be due to a disruption in the production of reproductive hormones.

Painful periods: distress and trauma can contribute to painful periods, known as dysmenorrhea. This may be due to increased tension in the muscles of the uterus and pelvic region, as well as changes in hormone levels.

Premenstrual symptoms: distress and trauma can also exacerbate premenstrual symptoms, such as mood swings, fatigue, and bloating.

Muscle spasms

People often report feelings of tension and ache in their body in particular periods of stress, trauma, or worry. This is due to changes in muscle tension and tone. distress can cause muscles to tense up, which can lead to discomfort, pain, and spasms.

This is likely to be caused by increased levels of cortisol and adrenaline (known as 'stress hormones') in their body which can cause muscles to tense up in preparation for physical action.

Chronic distress can lead to persistent muscle tension and spasms, particularly in the neck, shoulders, back, and limbs. This can contribute to pain and discomfort, as well as headaches and other physical symptoms.

Nerve pain

Nerve pain, also known as neuropathic pain, is often described by people as, but not limited to, shooting, burning, tingling, and numbness.

Stress and psychological trauma are linked to nerve pain due to the body's distress response involving the activation of the sympathetic nervous system. Increased levels of cortisol and adrenaline during these states affect nerve function and sensitivity. Stress can also exacerbate existing nerve pain, making it more intense and difficult to manage. This can lead to a cycle of pain and stress, as the pain itself can cause further distress and fear.

Palpitations

A racing or pounding heartbeat refers to a faster and/or harder heartbeat than a person's 'normal'. During situations where a person feels threatened, scared, or stressed, the body will release hormones such as adrenaline causing the heart to beat faster and harder (NHS Inform, 2023).

One possible explanation is that trauma and distress can trigger the 'fight or flight' response of the body, which is a natural response to stress that prepares the body to respond to a perceived threat. This response causes an increase in the release of stress hormones such as adrenaline and cortisol, which can cause the heart to beat faster and stronger, leading to palpitations.

Another possible explanation is that trauma and distress can cause changes in the body's autonomic nervous system, which is responsible for regulating the heart rate. When a person is under stress, the sympathetic nervous system can become overactive, leading to an increase in heart rate and palpitations.

Stress can also lead to other factors that can contribute to palpitations, such as dehydration, lack of sleep, and changes in diet or physical activity. While palpitations caused by stress are usually harmless, they can be uncomfortable and distressing.

Physiological weakness

Physiological weakness is a common response to distress and trauma that can affect many parts of the body. distress triggers the release of hormones such as cortisol, adrenaline, and norepinephrine, which can lead to physical changes in the body such as weakness or fatigue.

Physiological weakness can the muscles, the cardiovascular system, and the respiratory system. Some common symptoms of physiological weakness in response to trauma and distress may include:

- **Muscle weakness:** Trauma and distress can cause tension and tightness in the muscles, which can lead to muscle weakness or fatigue.
- **Fatigue:** Trauma and distress can cause a feeling of exhaustion or tiredness, making it difficult to carry out everyday activities.

- **Rapid heartbeat:** Trauma and distress can cause the heart to beat faster, which can lead to a feeling of weakness or dizziness.

- **Shortness of breath:** Trauma and distress can cause shallow breathing or hyperventilation, which can lead to a feeling of weakness or light-headedness.

- **Headaches:** Trauma and distress can cause tension headaches, which can lead to a feeling of weakness or discomfort in the head and neck.

Physiological weaknesses as a response to trauma and distress can vary in severity and duration, depending on the individual's distress response and coping mechanisms.

Shakes/tremors

Tremors are involuntary muscle movements that can occur in different parts of the body, including the hands, arms, legs, or torso. Tremors can range in severity from mild shaking to severe convulsions. This can be brought on by fear, distress, and trauma due to the effect they can have on the nervous system. The release of cortisol and adrenaline during these psychological states can cause physical changes in the body, including muscle tension and increased heart rate, which can lead to shakes and tremors. Shakes and tremors are usually symptoms of hyperarousal.

Sleep disturbance

Trauma can disrupt the body's natural sleep-wake cycle and cause a range of sleep disturbances, including difficulty falling asleep, staying asleep, and waking up too early. When an individual experiences, or is subjected to trauma, they are likely to become hypervigilant.

Hypervigilance can also lead to nightmares and flashbacks during sleep, which can further disrupt sleep and exacerbate trauma-related symptoms, and sometimes leave people avoiding or worried about falling asleep. Additionally, distress and trauma can impact the production of certain hormones and neurotransmitters that regulate sleep, such as cortisol and serotonin, further contributing to sleep disturbances.

Stomach Pain

Pain and discomfort in the abdominal region are common during periods of stress, worry, and trauma, and for a myriad of reasons. Hormones such as cortisol and adrenaline are released when people are in a state of distress which can cause a variety of physiological responses. This includes the release of stomach acid, which can irritate the lining of the stomach and cause pain.

Stress can also impact the functioning of the digestive system, leading to changes in gastrointestinal motility (responsible for digestion) and the composition of gut microbiota. This may cause a range of digestive symptoms, including pain, bloating, constipation, and diarrhoea. With this said, distress and trauma may cause a person to engage in unhealthy coping mechanisms, such as overeating or consuming alcohol, which can further exacerbate stomach pain.

Sweating/becoming clammy

Most people report sweating when feeling scared, embarrassed, worried, or stressed. As is the same with many physiological trauma responses, the body releases hormones associated with distress such as cortisol and adrenaline. This results in physical responses, including increased heart rate, blood pressure, and sweating or becoming clammy.

Sweating is a natural response to regulate body temperature, but it can also be triggered by emotional responses, such as fear. When a person experiences stress, their body temperature may rise, which can lead to sweating as a way to cool down the body.

Throat tightness

Throat tightness is a physical sensation that can occur in response to stress. It is typically experienced as a feeling of constriction or tightness in the throat and may be accompanied by difficulty swallowing or breathing. Throat tightness can be caused by a variety of factors, including muscle tension, fear responses, or stress.

When the body perceives a threat or stressor, it activates the sympathetic nervous system, which triggers a cascade of physiological changes designed to prepare the body for action. These changes can include increased heart rate, elevated blood pressure, and muscle tension, including in the muscles of the throat. Throat tightness can also be a sign of fear, which often accompanies stress. When a person is anxious or scared, they may experience physical symptoms like sweating, trembling, and difficulty breathing, which can in turn exacerbate feelings of distress and tension.

Throat or mouth dryness

The distress response triggers the sympathetic nervous system, which causes the body to release adrenaline and other distress hormones. These hormones can cause a range of physiological changes, including a decrease in saliva production, which can lead to dry mouth and throat. Additionally, distress and trauma can cause muscle tension, including tension in the muscles of the face and throat, which can also contribute to feelings of dryness or discomfort in these areas.

Thrush

Thrush is a type of fungal infection that can occur in various parts of the body, including the mouth, throat, genitals, and skin folds. While there is no direct evidence linking distress to thrush, it is possible that distress can indirectly contribute to its development.

Stress can weaken the immune system, making the body more susceptible to infections, including thrush. distress can also disrupt the balance of microorganisms in the body, including the natural bacteria and fungi that inhabit our skin, mouth, and gut. This disruption can create an environment that is more favourable for the growth of candida, the fungus responsible for thrush. Furthermore, distress can cause hormonal imbalances that can affect the body's ability to regulate blood sugar levels. High levels of sugar in the bloodstream can promote the growth of candida, which feeds on sugar.

Tics and twitches

Developing tics and twitches as a response to distress is a common phenomenon that can occur in many people. distress is a normal part of life and can be caused by a variety of factors such as work, school, relationships, or financial problems.

Tics are sudden, repetitive, non-rhythmic movements or sounds that are difficult to control. They can take many forms, such as eye blinking, facial grimacing, head jerking, or shoulder shrugging. Tics can also involve vocalizations, such as throat clearing, grunting, or shouting.

Twitches on the other hand, are involuntary muscle contractions that can cause small movements or jerks in different parts of the body. Twitches can occur in various body parts, such as the face, arms, legs, or trunk. In some cases, this physical response to distress can manifest as tics and twitches. This may be due to heightened levels of adrenaline & cortisol released in the body due to the increased state of arousal that distress can cause, leading to a lack of control over one's movements.

Fortunately, most stress-related tics and twitches are temporary and tend to go away once the stressor is removed or the person learns to manage their stress. In some cases, relaxation techniques, such as deep breathing, meditation, or yoga, can be helpful in reducing distress and improving tic symptoms.

Tinnitus

Tinnitus is a condition characterised by ringing, buzzing, or other sounds in the ears or head that have no external source. It can be caused by a variety of factors, including exposure to loud noises, age-related hearing loss, ear infections, or neurological disorders. While distress is not a direct cause of tinnitus, it can exacerbate existing tinnitus symptoms and make them more noticeable. distress can cause the body to release hormones that can increase blood pressure, heart rate, and muscle tension, all of which can contribute to tinnitus symptoms.

In addition, distress can also make it more difficult to cope with tinnitus, which can lead to a vicious cycle of distress and tinnitus symptoms. For example, if a person is experiencing high levels of stress, they may find it more difficult to ignore or manage their tinnitus, which can lead to increased distress levels. It's important to note that tinnitus can be a complex condition, and there may be multiple underlying factors contributing to its development and persistence.

Tiredness

Tiredness or fatigue is a common physical response to distress and trauma. The body releases higher amounts of adrenaline and cortisol when an individual is in psychological states such as stress, fear, and trauma. These hormones can cause physical changes in the body, such as increased heart rate, rapid breathing, and tense muscles. This is to enable people to detect, assess, and protect themselves from danger quickly.

In the short term, this response can be helpful in dealing with stressful situations. However, if distress is chronic or long-term, it can take a toll on the body, leading to fatigue and exhaustion.

Stress and trauma can disrupt sleep patterns, making it difficult to get a good night's sleep. In addition, distress can cause physical tension and muscle tightness, leading to physical fatigue. The mental and emotional strain of dealing with distress can also be exhausting, draining a person's energy, and leaving them feeling tired and lethargic.

Vaginismus

Vaginismus is a medical condition in which the muscles of the vagina involuntarily contract, making penetration painful or impossible. It can be a distressing and embarrassing condition that can have a significant impact on a woman's sexual health and quality of life.

Vaginismus can be caused by a variety of factors, including trauma or fear related to sex, past sexual trauma or abuse, medical conditions that cause pain during intercourse, or a lack of knowledge about the anatomy of the vagina.

Symptoms of vaginismus may include:

- Pain or discomfort during penetration
- Inability to insert a tampon or undergo a pelvic exam
- Difficulty with sexual arousal or orgasm
- Muscle spasms or tightness in the vaginal area
- Treatment for vaginismus may involve a combination of physical therapy, psychological counselling, and education about sexual anatomy and function.

Research has found that vaginismus spasms are primarily caused by fear, trauma, fear of pain, fear of penetration, previous injury, or sexual violence experiences (McEvoy et al., 2020).

Distress and trauma related flare-ups of pre-existing illnesses or conditions

Existing illnesses can flare up around distress for a number of reasons. First, distress can weaken the immune system, making it easier for viruses and bacteria to infect the body and cause illness. Additionally, distress can trigger inflammation in the body, which can exacerbate existing conditions such as arthritis, asthma, and inflammatory bowel disease.

Stress can also affect hormonal balance, causing the release of hormones such as cortisol and adrenaline. These hormones can increase heart rate and blood pressure, constrict blood vessels, and divert blood flow away from the digestive and immune systems. This can weaken the digestive system, making it harder for the body to absorb nutrients and fight off infections.

In addition, distress can also affect behaviours that can contribute to illness, such as poor diet, lack of exercise, and inadequate sleep. For example, during times of stress, people may be more likely to eat unhealthy foods, smoke cigarettes, or drink alcohol, all of which can contribute to illness. Overall, distress can have a wide range of negative effects on the body, which can exacerbate existing illnesses and make them more difficult to manage.

Herpes

Herpes is a viral infection that can be triggered or worsened by stress. There are two types of herpes virus: herpes simplex virus type 1 (HSV-1) and herpes simplex virus type 2 (HSV-2).

HSV-1 is usually associated with cold sores or fever blisters on or around the mouth, while HSV-2 is typically associated with genital herpes. However, either type of herpes virus can infect both the mouth and the genitals. Stress can weaken the immune system, making it easier for the herpes virus to reactivate and cause an outbreak. Stressful events such as illness, emotional stress, or even physical distress due to a strenuous workout or lack of sleep can trigger an outbreak of herpes.

During an outbreak, the herpes virus can cause painful blisters or sores on the affected area, such as the mouth or genitals. The blisters eventually burst, leaving behind painful ulcers that can take several days to heal. It is important to note that herpes can be transmitted even when there are no visible symptoms, so practicing safe sex and avoiding close contact during an outbreak can help prevent the spread of the virus. There is currently no cure for herpes, but antiviral medications can help manage outbreaks and reduce their severity.

Crohn's Disease

Crohn's disease is a chronic inflammatory bowel disease that can be aggravated by stress. While the exact cause of Crohn's disease is unknown, it is believed to be a result of a combination of genetic, environmental, and immune system factors.

Stress can trigger or worsen Crohn's disease by affecting the immune system and digestive system. When people are stressed, the body releases hormones such as cortisol and adrenaline, which can weaken the immune system and cause inflammation in the digestive system. Inflammation in the digestive system is a key feature of Crohn's disease. The chronic inflammation can lead to the development of scar tissue, narrowing of the intestinal walls, and ulcers, which can cause a range of symptoms including abdominal pain, diarrhoea, fatigue, and weight loss.

While distress alone is not believed to cause Crohn's disease, it can exacerbate the symptoms and increase the risk of flare-ups.

Eczema

Stress can trigger or exacerbate eczema by affecting the immune system and skin barrier function. When people are stressed, the body releases hormones such as cortisol, which can weaken the immune system and increase inflammation in the body. This can lead to flare-ups of eczema symptoms.

In addition, distress can also affect the skin barrier function, which is important for retaining moisture and protecting the skin from irritants and allergens. A weakened skin barrier can allow irritants and allergens to penetrate the skin and trigger eczema flare-ups.

Symptoms of eczema can include red, dry, and itchy patches of skin, as well as inflammation, scaling, and blisters. distress management techniques such as meditation, yoga, exercise, and therapy can help reduce distress and manage eczema symptoms.

Health issues that may be ignored, minimised, or pathologised

Whilst distress and trauma can cause a wide range of illnesses and physiological symptoms, there is also an inverse relationship in which genuine medical issues are ignored or minimised by telling the patient they are suffering from stress, or mental disorders.

This section provides information about some of the most common health issues and medical complaints that are mistaken or reframed as mental health or purely psychosomatic.
It is important that people can access the right diagnostic tests and advice at the right time, especially if they are experiencing concerning symptoms.

Breast implant illness

Breast implant illness (BII) is a term used to describe a variety of symptoms that some women with breast implants experience, including fatigue, joint pain, skin rashes, and cognitive difficulties. While breast implant illness is not an official medical diagnosis, many women who have undergone breast augmentation or reconstruction have reported experiencing these symptoms.

The exact causes of breast implant illness are not well understood, but some theories suggest that it may be related to immune system reactions to the implants themselves or to the materials used in the implants.

Symptoms of breast implant illness can range from mild to severe and can include:

- Fatigue
- Joint pain
- Muscle pain
- Skin rashes

- Cognitive difficulties
- Sadness, distress, and fear
- Hair loss
- Insomnia
- Gastrointestinal problems

Due to the lack of research and understanding of BII, women may not be believed or understood when they try to explain their symptoms, or their suspicions that their health issues are related to their breast implants.

Many women who have had reactions to their breast implants have been ignored, and have been told they have health anxiety, delusions, or other mental disorders (Lee et al., 2020). This has been discussed in medical literature since 2000. In Dush (2002) despite women having evidence of a range of serious health complications, and radiological proof of breast implant rupture and leakage, the authors still concluded that women with BII are more likely to be mentally ill because they have low self-esteem which caused them to have cosmetic surgery in the first place. It was not considered that the women were distressed by their health complications from the implants and resulting medical procedures.

Cancer symptoms

Cancer is a group of diseases characterised by the abnormal growth and spread of cells in the body. Normally, cells in the body grow and divide in a controlled way to form new cells as needed. However, cancer cells can grow and divide uncontrollably, forming tumours or invading nearby tissues and organs.

Cancer can occur in any part of the body and can affect people of all ages. There are many different types of cancer, each with its own set of symptoms and treatment options. Some common types of cancer include:

Breast cancer, lung cancer, prostate cancer, colorectal cancer, skin cancer, cervical cancer, lymphoma cancer, leukaemia, bladder cancer, and kidney cancer.

Due to cancer being such a diverse disease, the symptoms can be wide ranging. Cancer could show up in any symptom from a persistent cough to a scab that won't heal. Despite this, women are more likely than men to have their concerns about cancer ignored, minimised, or framed as mental disorders.

A study by Din et al. (2015) found that women waited much longer than men for a cancer diagnosis in six out of the eleven types of cancer that were studied. This was not due to women waiting longer than men to report their symptoms to their GP, but because they were not referred for accurate tests, or taken seriously, at the point of raising their concerns with their doctor.
Another study in 2013 found that women who presented to their doctor with clear symptoms of bladder cancer would have to present at least three times with the same concerns before their doctor would refer them to a specialist (Lyratzopoulos et al., 2013).

Researchers have repeatedly found that women are likely to have their cancer identified at a much later stage than men, (Barbiere et al., 2011; Taylor, 2022)

Studies have found that 5-year survival rates of several cancers can be significantly lower for women than men, despite men being more likely to be diagnosed with cancer. For example, 57% of men survive bladder cancer versus 44% of women (Lyratzopoulos et al., 2013). Interestingly, the highest five year survival rates are found in male cancers such as testicular cancer (97%) and prostate cancer (88%).

By contrast, female cancers appear to have worsening survival rates, with Cancer Research predicting an increase in annual deaths by 2040, from uterine cancer (+39%), vulval cancer (+54%), and ovarian cancer (+2%).

Much of these issues stem from misogyny. Women only make up 38% of cancer trials, and much medical research is still based on males as the 'default' body (Jagsi et al., 2009). There is still a deeply rooted belief that women are deviations from the norm when it comes to testing and research in medicine (usually due to beliefs about their fertility).

Women are more likely to be seen to be exaggerating their health issues, and more likely to be told that they are hormonal, or that their symptoms are purely psychosomatic (Katz Institute for Women's Health, 2023).

Cardiac symptoms

Compared to men, women are 50% more likely to receive the wrong diagnosis following a heart attack, and women who were misdiagnosed had about a 70% increased risk of death after 30 days compared with those who had received a correct diagnosis (Wu et al., 2016). Women are much more likely to be told that they have anxiety, and sent home from hospitals and emergency departments (Taylor, 2022).

One study showed women who received coronary bypass surgery were only half as likely to be prescribed painkillers, as compared to men who had undergone the same procedure, due to a belief that women exaggerate their pain (UPI, 1989).

Cardiac problems refer to any condition or disease that affects the heart, blood vessels, or the circulatory system. Some common types of cardiac problems include:

Coronary artery disease: A condition in which the blood vessels that supply the heart with blood and oxygen become narrowed or blocked.

Heart attack: A medical emergency that occurs when blood flow to a part of the heart is blocked, leading to damage or death of heart muscle.

Arrhythmia: A condition in which the heart beats too quickly, too slowly, or irregularly.

Heart failure: A condition in which the heart is unable to pump blood effectively to meet the body's needs.

Valvular heart disease: A condition in which the heart valves do not function properly, leading to problems with blood flow.

Aortic aneurysm: A condition in which the wall of the aorta (the body's largest artery) weakens and bulges, potentially leading to a rupture or tear.

Peripheral artery disease: A condition in which the blood vessels in the arms or legs become narrowed or blocked, leading to pain or discomfort.

The most important part of correct treatment is accurate and timely diagnosis, which is impaired by professionals' personal beliefs that women will exaggerate symptoms, or that their symptoms are 'all in their head'. The New England Journal of Medicine found that women are seven times more likely than men to be misdiagnosed and discharged in the middle of having a heart attack (Nabel, 2000).

Endometriosis

Endometriosis is a medical condition in which the tissue that normally lines the inside of the uterus (endometrium) grows outside of the uterus, often on the ovaries, fallopian tubes, and the tissue lining the pelvis. This can cause inflammation, scarring, and pain. Endometriosis affects an estimated 1 in 10 women during their reproductive years and can cause significant physical and emotional distress.

The exact cause of endometriosis is not well understood, but it is believed to be related to a combination of genetic and environmental factors. Symptoms of endometriosis can vary widely, but may include:

- Painful periods

- Pain during sex
- Chronic pelvic pain
- Painful bowel movements or urination
- Infertility or difficulty getting pregnant
- Fatigue
- Gastrointestinal problems
- Endometriosis is typically diagnosed through a combination of a medical history, physical exam, and imaging tests such as ultrasound or MRI.

Until the early 1990s, women of childbearing age were kept out of trial studies due to medical and liability concerns about exposing pregnant women to drugs and risking damage to their foetuses (UK Parliament, 2021).

Less is known about conditions that only affect women, including common gynaecological conditions that can have severe impacts on health and wellbeing. For example, on average it takes 7 to 8 years for women to receive a diagnosis of endometriosis, with 40% of women needing 10 or more GP appointments before being referred to a specialist (UK Parliament, 2021).

Despite one in ten women of reproductive age having endometriosis (176 million women worldwide), women are routinely told that their symptoms are psychological, that they are mentally ill or that they exaggerate their pain (Taylor, 2022). Of the thousands of women who took part in the APPG review on endometriosis in 2020, 58% of them had been to their GP about their symptoms at least 10 times, 53% visited A&E with severe symptoms and 21% saw doctors in hospital more than 10 times before being diagnosed.

Women reported that they were consistently told that their physical symptoms were depression, anxiety, panic attacks – or simply, made up. The report found that many women were prescribed cognitive behavioural therapy (CBT) instead of referring them to gynaecologists or specialist endometriosis centres.

Ehlers Danlos

Ehlers-Danlos syndrome (EDS) is a group of genetic disorders that affect the body's connective tissues, which provide support and structure to the skin, bones, blood vessels, and other organs. There are many different types of EDS, each with its own set of symptoms and patterns of inheritance. The most common types of EDS include:

Classical EDS: Characterised by skin that is smooth, velvety, and stretchy, as well as joint hypermobility and a tendency toward easy bruising.

Hypermobility EDS: Characterised by joint hypermobility, skin that is soft and velvety, and chronic joint pain.

Vascular EDS: Characterised by a thin and translucent skin that bruises easily, as well as a high risk of arterial and organ rupture.

Kyphoscoliosis EDS: Characterised by a curvature of the spine, as well as joint hypermobility and muscle weakness.

Dermatosparaxis EDS: Characterised by skin that is fragile and easily torn, as well as joint hypermobility and hernias.

EDS is caused by mutations in genes that affect the production, processing, or structure of collagen, the main component of connective tissue.

Despite this, patients with long-term pain and decreased functionality often display distress and trauma responses, independently of the EDS diagnosis. They are likely to be diagnosed with psychiatric disorders instead of EDS. Another point is that EDS is associated with multiple conditions like dysautonomia, which can cause a broad spectrum of physical complaints that can mimic 'anxiety disorder' symptoms. For instance, patients experiencing intense heart rate changes could be misdiagnosed with panic attacks. Another example could be the extreme tiredness caused by sleep deprivation could be mistaken as depression (Bulbena et al., 2017).

Due to a general lack of understanding and knowledge of EDS, and the way symptoms can present as a wide range of varied issues, psychiatrists and other mental health professionals can often misdiagnose people with EDS with personality disorders and anxiety disorders (Ehlers-Danlos Society, 2023).

Dysautonomia is often misdiagnosed as a psychiatric disorder because it can appear as anxiety, panic, ADHD, and hypomania. Autonomic dysfunction results from a depletion of energy due to chronic sympathetic nervous system responses. People often have very poor sleep quality due to chronic pain, which then leads to fatigue, exhaustion, and the inability to manage stress. This depletion puts them into mental and physical distress on a daily basis.

Chronic hyperarousal can then create the appearance of an anxiety disorder, or if they have surges of adrenaline due to autonomic dysfunction, they can appear to be having a panic attack. This state of hyperarousal can manifest as restlessness or hyperactivity, which can be mistakenly diagnosed as ADHD. Sometimes their ability to continue to function on very little sleep is mistaken for hypomania. Since they are so tired, they often make mistakes, misplace things, forget things, and have trouble concentrating, and thus look like they are suffering from ADD (Tsafrir, 2022).

This leads to many people who need support and advice about EDS being led to believe that they are mentally ill, or have neurodevelopmental disorders.

Brain tumour

A brain tumour is a mass or growth of abnormal cells in the brain or spinal cord. There are many different types of brain tumours, and they can be either benign (non-cancerous) or malignant (cancerous).

Brain tumours can cause a variety of symptoms, depending on their location, size, and rate of growth. Some common symptoms may include:

- Headaches
- Seizures
- Vision or hearing problems
- Weakness or numbness in the limbs
- Difficulty with balance or coordination
- Changes in mood or personality
- Memory problems
- Speech difficulties

The exact cause of brain tumours is not well understood, but some factors that may increase the risk of developing a brain tumour include exposure to radiation, family history of brain tumours, and certain genetic conditions.

Brain tumours are often perceived to be so rare that symptoms do not warrant investigation. Doctors will instead diagnose headaches, migraines, other forms of seizures, mental health disorders, spinal issues, or hormonal imbalances. In 2016, the Brain Tumour Charity released a report on the treatment of brain tumours in the UK. The report stated that 1 in 3 patients had visited their doctor more than 5 times before being taken seriously. Almost 25% of the sample were not diagnosed for over a year.

Women were again more likely than men to wait over 10 months for a diagnosis of a brain tumour and were significantly more likely to have been to their doctor more than five times to report that they thought they had a brain tumour.

Brain tumours can be misdiagnosed as mental health issues because the symptoms of a brain tumour can be like those of a mental health disorder.

For example, a brain tumour can cause changes in mood, behaviour, and cognition, which professionals can then mistakenly diagnose as schizophrenia, depression, anxiety, or other mental health disorders. These symptoms can include difficulty concentrating, memory problems, and changes in appetite and sleep.

In addition, brain tumours can cause physical symptoms such as headaches, seizures, and balance problems, which can also be mistaken for mental health symptoms. These physical symptoms can sometimes be subtle, making them difficult to identify and diagnose.

Encephalitis

Encephalitis is a medical condition characterised by inflammation of the brain. It can be caused by a variety of factors, including viral infections, bacterial infections, or autoimmune reactions. Encephalitis can be a serious and potentially life-threatening condition that requires prompt medical attention.

Symptoms of encephalitis can vary widely, but may include:

- Fever
- Headache
- Stiff neck
- Confusion or disorientation
- Seizures
- Hallucinations
- Personality changes
- Weakness or paralysis

One of the most common misdiagnoses of patients with encephalitis is schizophrenia. Encephalitis is an autoimmune disease which causes swelling in the brain. That swelling can lead to behaviours and thought patterns that doctors may not explore further, because they assume the changes are psychiatric (Deng & Yeshokumar, 2020). Similarly, encephalitis can be misdiagnosed as bipolar, anxiety, and delusional disorder (Pagan, 2021; Taylor, 2022).

In children, encephalitis can be misdiagnosed as autism (Salvi, 2013), or in some cases, used to suggest that the mothers of those children have mental disorders themselves, and are fabricating the illness of their child (Taylor, 2022.)

Musculoskeletal issues

Musculoskeletal issues refer to any condition or injury that affects the bones, muscles, joints, tendons, or ligaments in the body. Musculoskeletal issues can be caused by a variety of factors, including repetitive strain, poor posture, overuse, trauma, or underlying medical conditions.

Some common musculoskeletal issues include:

Arthritis: A condition characterised by inflammation and pain in the joints.

Osteoporosis: A condition in which the bones become weak and brittle, increasing the risk of fractures.

Tendinitis: Inflammation of a tendon, usually caused by overuse.

Carpal tunnel syndrome: A condition in which the median nerve in the wrist is compressed, causing pain, numbness, and weakness in the hand and wrist.

Herniated disc: A condition in which the soft tissue inside a spinal disc bulges out, causing pain and pressure on nearby nerves.

Strains and sprains: Injuries to muscles or ligaments caused by overstretching or tearing.

Scoliosis: A condition in which the spine curves to one side, causing uneven hips or shoulders.

When it comes to chronic pain, 70% of the people it impacts are women, but 80% of pain studies are conducted on male mice or human men (Kiesel, 2017). A 2018 study analysing journal papers on sex, gender and pain published in the UK, US and Europe since 2001 revealed that terms like 'sensitive', 'malingering', 'complaining' and 'hysterical' are applied more frequently to pain reports from women (For review, see Samulowitz et al, 2018).

Vitamin and mineral deficiencies

A vitamin or mineral deficiency occurs when a person does not consume enough of a specific vitamin or mineral, or when the body cannot absorb or use a vitamin or mineral properly. Vitamins and minerals are essential nutrients that the body needs to function properly, and deficiencies can lead to a range of health problems.

Common vitamin deficiencies include:

Vitamin D deficiency: Can lead to bone weakness, fatigue, and an increased risk of certain cancers and autoimmune disorders.

Vitamin B12 deficiency: Can lead to anaemia, fatigue, and neurological symptoms such as numbness and tingling.

Vitamin C deficiency: Can lead to scurvy, a condition characterised by bleeding gums, joint pain, and fatigue.

Common mineral deficiencies include:

Iron deficiency: Can lead to anaemia, fatigue, and weakness.

Calcium deficiency: Can lead to osteoporosis, a condition in which the bones become weak and brittle.

Magnesium deficiency: Can lead to muscle weakness, fatigue, and abnormal heart rhythms.

Vitamin deficiencies can be misdiagnosed as mental disorders because the symptoms of some vitamin deficiencies can be like those of mental health disorders.

For example, a deficiency in vitamin B12 can cause symptoms such as fatigue, irritability, and difficulty concentrating, which can be mistaken for symptoms of depression or anxiety. Similarly, a deficiency in vitamin D can cause symptoms such as fatigue, mood swings, and difficulty sleeping, which can also be mistaken for symptoms of a mental health disorder. In addition, some vitamin deficiencies can cause neurological symptoms such as numbness and tingling in the extremities, which can be mistaken for symptoms of a mental health disorder.

Polycystic Ovary Syndrome

Polycystic ovary syndrome (PCOS) is a hormonal disorder that affects women of reproductive age. It is characterised by the presence of small cysts on the ovaries, as well as hormonal imbalances that can cause a range of symptoms.

Symptoms of PCOS can vary widely, but may include:

- Irregular menstrual periods
- Excess hair growth on the face, chest, or back
- Acne
- Weight gain
- Difficulty getting pregnant
- Darkening of the skin around the neck or underarms
- Hair loss or thinning on the scalp

Polycystic ovary syndrome (PCOS) can be misdiagnosed as a mental disorder because some of the symptoms of PCOS can cause trauma responses, distress, and coping mechanisms which may mirror symptoms which are considered psychiatric.

For example, PCOS can cause low mood, feelings of fear and distress, mood changes, and panic which can then be misdiagnosed as psychiatric disorders (Bailey et al., 2014). Similarly, PCOS can cause fatigue, sleep disturbances and deprivation, and changes in appetite, which can also be misdiagnosed as a mental health disorder.

In addition, some of the physical symptoms of PCOS, such as weight gain and acne, can also contribute to low self-esteem and mood disturbances, which can further complicate the diagnosis.

Multiple sclerosis

MS stands for Multiple Sclerosis, which is a chronic autoimmune disease that affects the central nervous system, including the brain, spinal cord, and optic nerves. The immune system mistakenly attacks the protective covering of nerve fibres, called myelin, leading to inflammation, damage, and scarring.

Symptoms of MS can vary widely, but may include:

- Fatigue
- Muscle weakness or stiffness
- Numbness or tingling in the limbs
- Blurred or double vision
- Difficulty with coordination or balance
- Problems with memory or concentration
- Bladder or bowel dysfunction
- Low mood and fear

A study in 2009 found that 16% of people with MS were diagnosed first with psychiatric disorders (Skegg et al., 2009). One of the conclusions of the study was that women with MS present with 'histrionic behaviour' and are therefore more likely to be considered mentally disordered. This led professionals to ignore physical symptoms, and continue down their assumption that the woman had a psychiatric disorder rather than MS.

A 2016 study in Neurology also found that 11% of people with MS were diagnosed with conversion disorders and other psychological disorders which assumed that their psychological trauma or distress had been converted into a physical issue with no medical cause (Solomon et al., 2016). In their study, they found that misdiagnosis was common, and 33% of people were misdiagnosed for over 10 years. Again, there was a clear sex difference. Their sample consisted of 100 people who had their MS misdiagnosed as something else. 85% of patients who were misdiagnosed were female.

Nerve damage

Nerve damage, also known as neuropathy, is a condition that occurs when the nerves that transmit signals between the brain and the rest of the body are damaged or disrupted. This can lead to a range of symptoms, depending on the location and severity of the nerve damage.

Symptoms of nerve damage may include:

- Numbness or tingling in the limbs
- Muscle weakness or paralysis
- Pain or burning sensations
- Sensitivity to touch or temperature changes
- Difficulty with coordination or balance
- Loss of reflexes
- Bladder or bowel dysfunction
- Digestive problems

Nerve damage can be misdiagnosed as a mental disorder because some of the symptoms of nerve damage can be similar to those of certain mental health disorders.

For example, nerve damage can cause symptoms such as numbness, tingling, and weakness, which can be mistaken for symptoms of anxiety or panic disorder. Similarly, nerve damage can cause chronic pain, fatigue, and changes in sleep patterns, which can also be mistaken for symptoms of a mental health disorder.

In addition, nerve damage can cause changes in mood and behaviour due to the impact on a person's quality of life, which can further complicate the diagnosis.

Thyroid issues

Thyroid issues refer to a range of medical conditions that affect the thyroid gland, a small butterfly-shaped gland located in the neck that produces hormones that regulate the body's metabolism.

Common thyroid issues include:

Hypothyroidism: A condition in which the thyroid gland does not produce enough thyroid hormone, leading to symptoms such as fatigue, weight gain, cold intolerance, and constipation.

Hyperthyroidism: A condition in which the thyroid gland produces too much thyroid hormone, leading to symptoms such as weight loss, increased heart rate, anxiety, and heat intolerance.

Thyroid nodules: Abnormal growths or lumps in the thyroid gland that can be benign (non-cancerous) or malignant (cancerous).

Thyroiditis: Inflammation of the thyroid gland, which can be caused by autoimmune disorders, infection, or other factors.

Goiter: A swelling of the thyroid gland that can be caused by iodine deficiency, autoimmune disorders, or other factors.

Thyroid issues can be misdiagnosed as mental disorders because some of the symptoms of thyroid disorders can be similar to those of certain mental health disorders.

For example, an overactive thyroid (hyperthyroidism) can cause symptoms such as worry, irritability, and nervousness, which can then be misdiagnosed as symptoms of a mental disorder. Similarly, an underactive thyroid (hypothyroidism) can cause symptoms such as low mood, fatigue, and difficulty concentrating, which can also be misdiagnosed as a disorder. In addition, thyroid disorders can cause changes in sleep patterns, weight changes, and changes in appetite, which can also be mistaken for symptoms of a psychiatric disorder.

These issues have been recognised as far back as 1981, in which McGaffee et al. wrote a paper outlining their concerns that people with hypothyroidism were being misdiagnosed with psychiatric illnesses including psychosis. This was causing serious health complications due to the thyroid issues never being addressed. In 2003, Heinrich and Grahm wrote an article which presented the case study of a woman who was misdiagnosed with psychosis due to reporting auditory and visual hallucinations. She was medicated with risperidone, but when the doctors realised she had hypothyroidism and treated her correctly, the symptoms disappeared. The woman chose to discontinue the risperidone herself.

Diabetes

Diabetes is a chronic medical condition in which the body cannot properly process glucose (sugar), which is the body's primary source of energy. There are two main types of diabetes:

Type 1 diabetes: This type of diabetes is caused by an autoimmune reaction that destroys the cells in the pancreas that produce insulin, a hormone that regulates blood sugar levels. People with type 1 diabetes must take insulin injections or use an insulin pump to manage their blood sugar levels.

Type 2 diabetes: This type of diabetes is caused by a combination of genetic and lifestyle factors, including obesity, lack of exercise, and poor diet. People with type 2 diabetes may be able to manage their blood sugar levels with diet and exercise, oral medications, or insulin injections.

Symptoms of diabetes may include:

- Increased thirst and hunger
- Frequent urination
- Fatigue
- Blurred vision
- Slow-healing wounds or infections

- Tingling or numbness in the hands or feet

Diabetes can be misdiagnosed as a mental disorder because some of the symptoms of diabetes can be like those of mental disorders.

High blood sugar levels in diabetes can cause symptoms such as fatigue, irritability, and difficulty concentrating, which can then be mistaken for depression or anxiety disorders. Similarly, low blood sugar levels in diabetes can cause symptoms such as confusion, dizziness, and mood swings, which can also be misdiagnosed as psychiatric disorders. In addition, diabetes can cause physical symptoms such as changes in appetite, weight loss or gain, and changes in sleep patterns, which can further complicate the diagnosis.

Some recent studies have shown that children with type 1 diabetes are likely to be diagnosed with ADHD (LeBow, 2016). Continuing with the sex-based theme of females being more likely to be misdiagnosed, Simms (2016) reported that girls with diabetes were more likely to be diagnosed with psychiatric disorders than boys. Diabetes Australia reports that up to 50% of people with diabetes will be diagnosed with depression and anxiety (2023). Overall, the prevalence of co-morbid diagnosed depression in the UK has risen from 29% in 2006 to 43% in 2017, and in the USA from 22% to 29% (Diabetologia, 2022).

Crohn's disease

Crohn's disease is a chronic inflammatory bowel disease (IBD) that can affect any part of the digestive tract, from the mouth to the anus. It is a condition in which the immune system mistakenly attacks healthy tissues in the digestive tract, leading to inflammation, ulceration, and scarring. Symptoms of Crohn's disease can vary widely, but may include:

- Abdominal pain and cramping
- Diarrhoea
- Fatigue

- Weight loss
- Loss of appetite
- Anaemia
- Fever
- Mouth sores

Valenti and Friedman (2020) wrote 'Believe me: How trusting women can change the world', in which they included a story of a woman with Crohn's who was disbelieved and gaslit over many years. Due to her pain being minimised and ignored, when she presented to doctors in severe pain, she was accused of attempting to access prescription painkiller drugs.

In 2021, a study by Blackwell et al. found that 1 in 10 people repeatedly visited their doctor for over five years before they received an accurate diagnoses of Crohn's disease. The results also found that some people had been reporting concerns to their doctors for over a decade before they were accurately diagnosed. Importantly, those patients who had previously been diagnosed with psychiatric disorders first, were forced to wait 25% longer for referral to a specialist than others (Blackwell et al., 2021).

Macular degeneration

Macular degeneration is a medical condition that affects the macula, which is the central part of the retina in the eye that allows us to see fine details clearly. Macular degeneration is a leading cause of vision loss in older adults and can affect one or both eyes.

There are two main types of macular degeneration:

Dry macular degeneration: This is the more common type of macular degeneration and occurs when the macula thins and small deposits of waste material called drusen accumulate in the retina, causing vision loss.

Wet macular degeneration: This is less common but more severe type of macular degeneration and occurs when abnormal blood vessels grow under the macula, leaking blood and fluid, which can cause rapid vision loss.

Symptoms of macular degeneration may include:

- Blurred or distorted vision
- Difficulty seeing details or colours
- Dark or empty areas in your central vision
- Difficulty recognising faces or reading

Macular degeneration can be misdiagnosed as a mental illness because some of the symptoms of macular degeneration can be similar to those of psychiatric disorders.

For example, macular degeneration can cause symptoms such as difficulty seeing, distorted vision, and loss of central vision, which can lead to difficulty with daily activities and a decrease in quality of life. Some people with macular degeneration also see shapes, colours, figures, and movements in their vision that can be incorrectly diagnosed as delusions or hallucinations.

One study found that misdiagnosis occurred in 1 in 4 cases of macular degeneration (Neely et al., 2017), and patients were told their eyesight was fine. Macular degeneration is just one of the medical conditions that can mimic or be misdiagnosed as dementia in older patients. This is usually due to patients talking about seeing things that are not there (Bright Focus Foundation, 2021).

Urinary tract infections

A UTI (Urinary Tract Infection) is an infection that affects any part of the urinary system, including the kidneys, bladder, ureters, and urethra. UTIs are most commonly caused by bacteria, but can also be caused by viruses or fungi.

Symptoms of a UTI may include:

- Pain or burning during urination

- Frequent urge to urinate
- Strong or foul-smelling urine
- Cloudy or bloody urine
- Pain in the lower abdomen or back
- Fever or chills

UTIs in women are likely to be misdiagnosed or ignored. One study found that women with UTIs had been in pain and suffering for so long that they had developed significant trauma responses (OpenDemocracy, 2023). The NHS in the UK only included chronic UTIs on their website as a legitimate illness in 2022.

Chieng et al. (2023) found that women were three times as likely to be misdiagnosed and that some women were left for over 12 years without correct diagnosis. Founder of the UTI Clinic in London, Catriona Anderson stated that 'a culture of normalisation of female pain' is behind the discriminatory behaviour of professionals. She stated that men who report symptoms of UTI are likely to be given a course of antibiotics immediately, but when women report the same symptoms, 'they are told it is all in their head'.

Other health issues not listed

As can be appreciated, this section is not exhaustive and could not possible be. Due to the power of psychiatric disorder, and the suggestion of mental illness in place of physical health complaints, it is common for people with hundreds of possible health issues to be told that they have psychiatric illnesses.

It is however of note, that the evidence base for the majority of health issues listed here suggests a sex-based discrimination in which women and girls were more likely to be misdiagnosed, ignored, or framed as mentally ill. This is consistent with other literature surrounding the pathologisation of women and girls (Taylor, 2022).

CHAPTER 7

Useful tools and resources

This section of the book includes some quick, easy-to-use tools to think more about the trauma and distress of your clients. Some of the tools can be used with your client, but others are for your own reflection whilst thinking about the traumas, distress and coping mechanisms that may be impacting the person you are supporting.

We have included:

Exploring coping mechanisms	p. 352
Baseline trauma tool	p. 354
Ecological model of trauma and distress	p. 358
Maslow's Hierarchy of Needs	p. 360
Mapping out traumas and stressors	p. 361
Beliefs about self	p. 362
Counterfactual thinking tool	p. 363
Exploring intersectionality in trauma and distress	p. 364
Understanding the trauma response	p. 365
Exploring trauma responses	p. 366
Belief in a Just World tool	p. 367
Trauma self-blame tool	p. 368
Harmful responses to trauma tool	p. 369

Exploring coping mechanisms

A set of basic questions/prompts for professionals to discuss coping mechanisms with their client.

1. Could you list what you feel you are coping with (or trying to cope with) at the moment?

2. What do you feel you are not coping with?

3. How do you feel you are coping at the moment?

4. What are your healthy coping mechanisms?

5. What are your neutral coping mechanisms?

6. What are your unhealthy coping mechanisms?

For each coping mechanism identified, consider;

7. When do you use this coping mechanism?
   Are there any specific times/patterns?
   (Before or after certain activities, events, attending places)

8. When did you start using this as a coping mechanism?

9. What coping mechanism did you use before?

10. How does the coping mechanism make you feel?

11. Do you feel that the coping mechanism improves your psychological state? If so, how long for?

12. What do you feel this coping mechanism provides?

13. Has what this coping mechanism provides to you changed over time? Has the purpose or meaning of it changed (during and after the trauma)?

14. Does this coping mechanism make you feel any of the following;

- In control
- Inspired/hopeful
- Distracted
- Excited
- Calm
- Sad
- Anxious
- Supported
- Lonely
- Self-punished
- Helps to express how I feel

Considering baseline trauma and distress

This tool helps professionals to consider how much trauma and distress the client has already been exposed to due to global systems of oppression, abuse, power, and threat.

Working from the perspective that human life, particularly in consideration with modern society, is traumatic and distressing, we have categorised baseline human traumas. Here are some things to consider before using this tool:

Prejudice

Much of the global population live in societies with strong prejudices; with racism, sexism, and/ or classism statistically affecting most people. Those most likely to be subjected to/ affected by racism are Black, Asian, and people of ethnic minority (sometimes referred to as 'the global majority'). Fifty-one percent of the population are female, and the vast majority of societies are considered to be patriarchal, wherein males hold the majority of power, and females likely to be subjected to 'sex-based' or 'gender-based' abuse. Additionally, most societies around the world have a social class system, with a minority at the top who prosper, leaving the majority with fewer opportunities to advance or climb.

The three most common forms of prejudice referred to in this section are likely to feed into the other human baseline traumas in this tool.

Fear

Whilst fear as an emotion serves to keep humans alive, it is naturally a distressing and traumatic emotion. Some of the most common fears are practical and rooted in human-nature, however some are counterintuitive, and often manufactured by societal governing.

Grief

Humans are naturally social, and have lived in communities for millennia. This allows us to connect, and thrive fulfilling basic needs. When there is loss through death, circumstantial change, or relationship breakdown, humans are likely to feel a great level of distress.

Hopelessness

While considering baseline human traumas, it's important to understand the interplay between modern-day societies and human's natural responses to trauma. The growing rate of globalisation has resulted in global economies, cultures, and populations becoming interlinked. Humans have increased levels of awareness of suffering, natural disasters, and tragedies globally than ever before. Understanding the scale of global suffering may be considered a level of trauma in itself, and arguably one which a human's natural empathic response to would struggle to comprehend, cope with, or think about.

Additionally, overarching societal prejudices that a person may be impacted by may contribute to feelings of hopelessness due to the disadvantages they face.

Abuse

Being subjected to different forms of abuse is common, and there are many implications of this. Consider norms, victim blaming, self-blame, prejudice, and denial while looking at this with your client.

Questions to consider when using the Baseline Trauma Tool

- Does your client ever feel distressed by any of the following?
- How might these specific intersections explain their feelings, trauma responses, and coping mechanisms?
- How many of the baseline traumas has your client been subjected to/experienced?

- Are any of the baseline traumas chronic and likely to continue (racism, for example)?
- Are there any of these traumas that your client will never be subjected to? Does this affect them in any way?
- What is/has been the impact of invalidating these traumas?
- Was the client aware of any of these baseline traumas?

Baseline Trauma Tool

	Likely to be affected	Has already experienced
Racism	☐	☐
Sexism	☐	☐
Classism	☐	☐
Other kinds of prejudice: Homophobia, transphobia, biphobia, ableism, antisemitism, Islamophobia, weight-based prejudice, etc.	☐	☐
Fear		
Fear of own or others' mortality, dying, death, or illness	☐	☐
Fear of being subjected to hate crime	☐	☐
Fear of failure or not achieving life goals	☐	☐
Fear of poverty/remaining in poverty	☐	☐
Grief		
Death of loved one	☐	☐
Relationship breakdown (partner)	☐	☐
Relationship breakdown (family)	☐	☐
Death of a pet	☐	☐
Hopelessness		
Awareness of global atrocities and/or natural disasters	☐	☐
Poor career prospects/uncertainty	☐	☐
Empathy and awareness of global suffering of others, without a solution	☐	☐
Abuse		
Being subjected to domestic or sexual abuse	☐	☐
Being bullied	☐	☐

Ecological model of trauma and distress

The model below has been adapted from Bronfenbrenner's ecological systems model and Taylor's ecological model of victim blaming experiences.

This model can be used to explore the origins and influences of trauma, distress, narratives, abuses, power, control, and oppression in the lives of our clients.

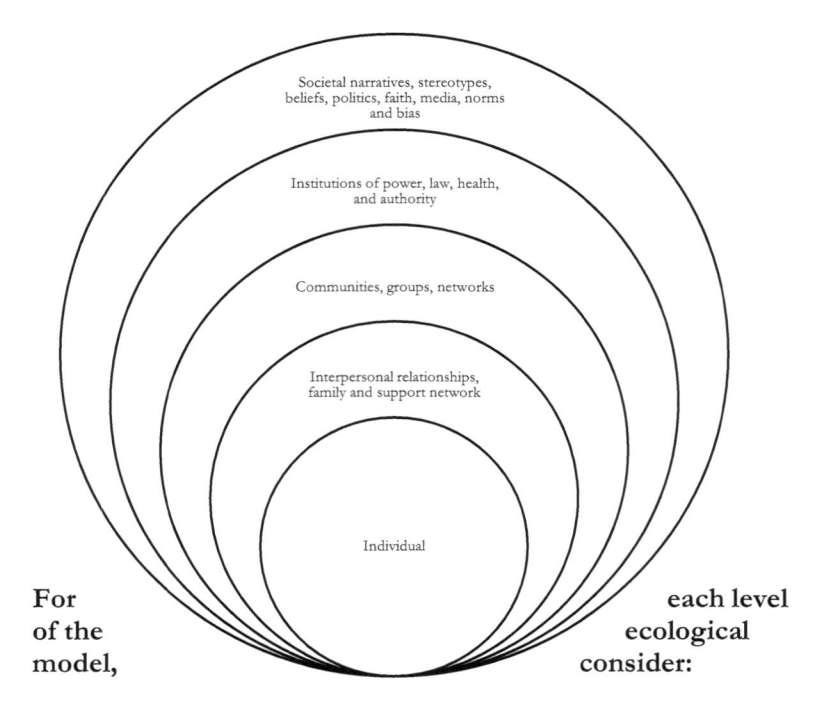

Societal narratives, stereotypes, beliefs, politics, faith, media, norms and bias

Institutions of power, law, health, and authority

Communities, groups, networks

Interpersonal relationships, family and support network

Individual

For each level of the ecological model, consider:

- Where is the harm of your client coming from?
- Where are their narratives about themselves coming from?
- Which systems are traumatising or distressing them?
- Which systems are oppressing or controlling them?
- How are the systems related, or influencing each other?

Taylor, J. & Shrive, J. (2023)

- Where do they feel safest?
- Where are they able to seek support?
- Which systems are already involved and are they working?
- How have the macrosystems (societal narratives, beliefs etc.) impacted the client during their distress and trauma?

Maslow's Hierarchy of Needs

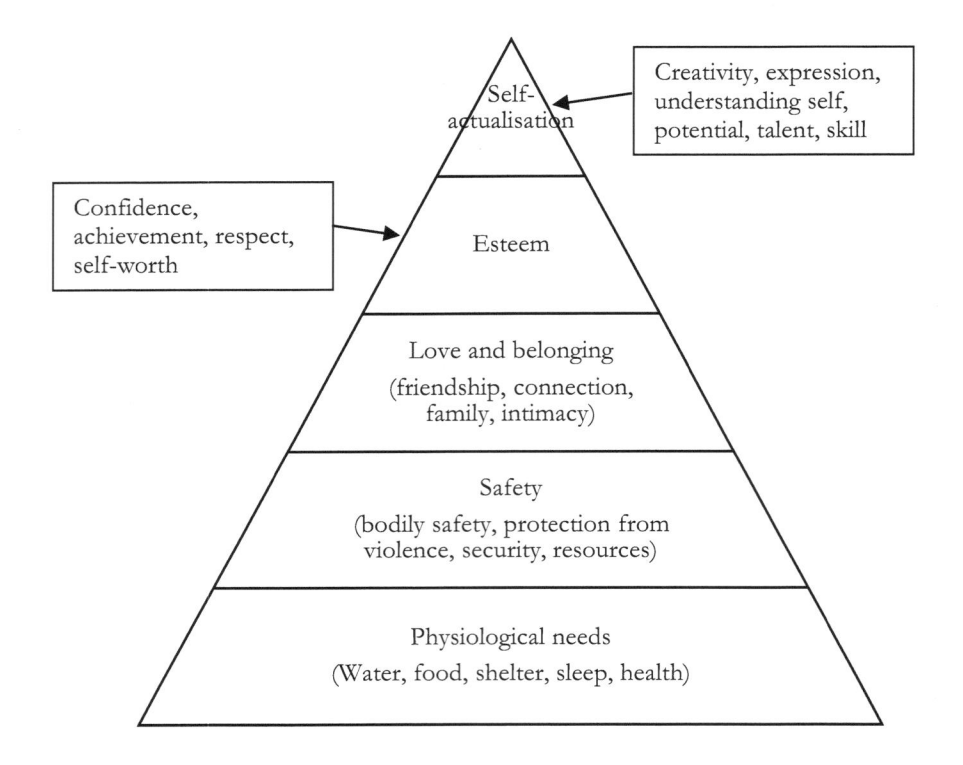

- **Self-actualisation**: Creativity, expression, understanding self, potential, talent, skill
- **Esteem**: Confidence, achievement, respect, self-worth
- **Love and belonging** (friendship, connection, family, intimacy)
- **Safety** (bodily safety, protection from violence, security, resources)
- **Physiological needs** (Water, food, shelter, sleep, health)

This model is presented as a tool for thinking about what basic needs are not being met for your client, and how this might be contributing to their distress and trauma. People who do not have their foundational needs met (such as physiological needs and safety) are likely to be distressed.

Mapping out traumas and stressors

A simple but effective tool to help your client to understand or explore everything that is impacting their wellbeing is to physically map it out like the diagram below. Be aware that for some people, there may be 20 or more issues impacting them.

Consider asking:

1. What is bothering you at the moment?
2. What is bothering you in the back of your head?
3. What feeling/emotion does each one of these experiences invoke?

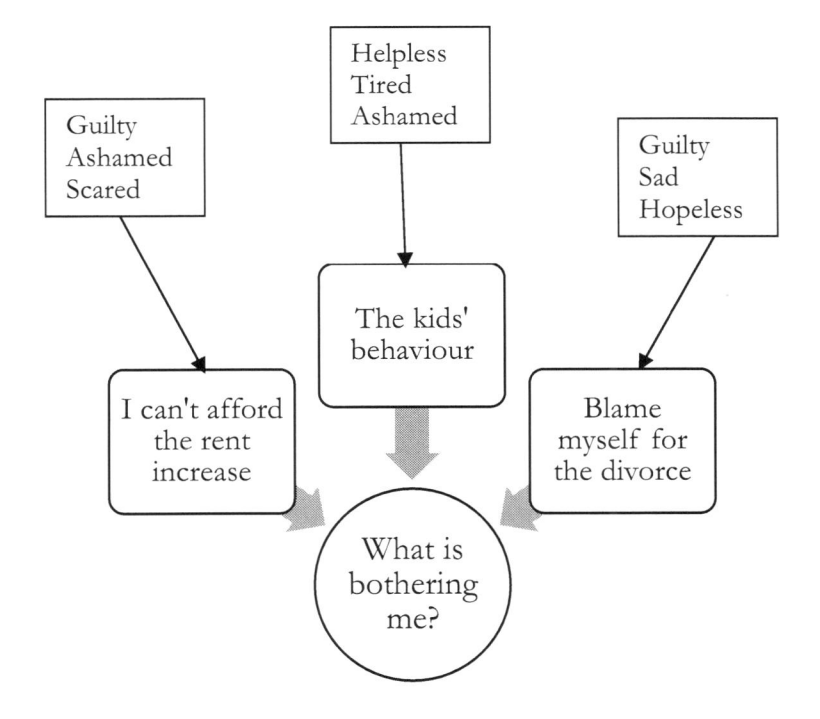

```
    Guilty              Helpless           Guilty
    Ashamed             Tired              Sad
    Scared              Ashamed            Hopeless
       │                   │                  │
       ▼                   ▼                  ▼
   I can't afford      The kids'          Blame
   the rent            behaviour          myself for
   increase                               the divorce
             ╲            │            ╱
              ╲           ▼           ╱
               →    What is    ←
                    bothering
                       me?
```

Beliefs about self: Prompts and questions

A selection of possible prompts or questions for your client, to explore beliefs about self, or accepted narratives about self.

1. Do you believe that you cannot achieve your goals or dreams?
2. Do you believe you need to be punished or harmed for things you have done wrong in life?
3. Do you believe you need to be perfect, or the best?
4. Do you believe belief that the negative aspects of your life outweigh the positives?
5. Do you have negative expectations for your future?
6. Do you believe you need to present a certain way for others to accept you or love you?
7. Do you believe you need to hide parts of yourself to be accepted by others?
8. Do you believe you need to seek approval or permission from others?
9. Do you believe that being liked, respected, and approved of by others is more important than anything else?
10. Do you believe that you should give up your needs for the sake of others?
11. Do you believe you should submit to the demands of others in order to make them happy, or to avoid conflict?
12. Do you believe you will often or always fail at something new?
13. Do you believe you are terrible at making decisions or judgements about a situation?
14. Do you believe you are damaged, unlovable, flawed, or broken?
15. Do you believe that everyone is abusive, dangerous, or looking to exploit you?
16. Do you believe that everyone will abandon you or leave you eventually?

Counterfactual thinking tool

Counterfactual thinking and perceived control are cognitive biases which may play a role in the distress and trauma of your client. Use this tool to consider whether this way of thinking may be present, and whether it may be distressing the person.

Does your client:	Yes	No
Reason backwards to try to find a reason why the trauma happened to them	☐	☐
Say 'If only I had never, then none of this would have happened.'	☐	☐
Attempt to identify a reason or catalyst for the trauma or distress, even if irrelevant	☐	☐
Attribute cause to something that did not cause the trauma or distress	☐	☐
Attribute cause to their own behaviour or character that did not cause the trauma or distress	☐	☐
Change something about themselves based on their belief that it caused the trauma or distress	☐	☐
Change their behaviour or lifestyle based on their belief that it caused the trauma or distress	☐	☐

It is important to consider whether these beliefs seem to make the client feel safer, more in control, guilty, blameworthy, worried, or unsafe.

Exploring intersectionality in trauma and distress

Use this simple tool to consider what additional factors arising from intersecting oppression may be (a) impacting/causing the traumas of your client, (b) exacerbating the traumas of your client, (c) creating barriers for your client to seek support or receive adequate support, and (d) influencing the way services and professionals are perceiving, portraying, and supporting your client.

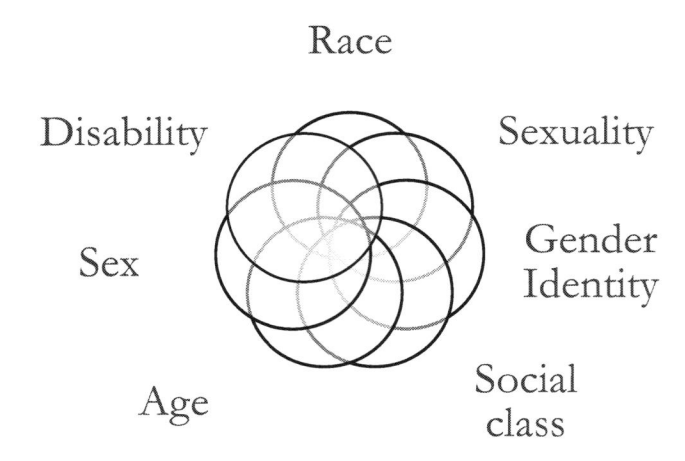

Race

Disability

Sexuality

Sex

Gender Identity

Age

Social class

Intersectionality includes many more overlapping and intersecting factors. You may also need to consider:

Religion, language, education level, perceived attractiveness, wealth, body size, skin colour, citizenship status, housing, indigeneity, culture, accent, and appearance.

Understanding the trauma response

This tool presents an easy-to-use model of how to break down common intersecting responses to trauma and distress, and how to understand them in more depth. This may help people to understand the many impacts trauma and distress can have on their body, mind, life, relationships, and beliefs.

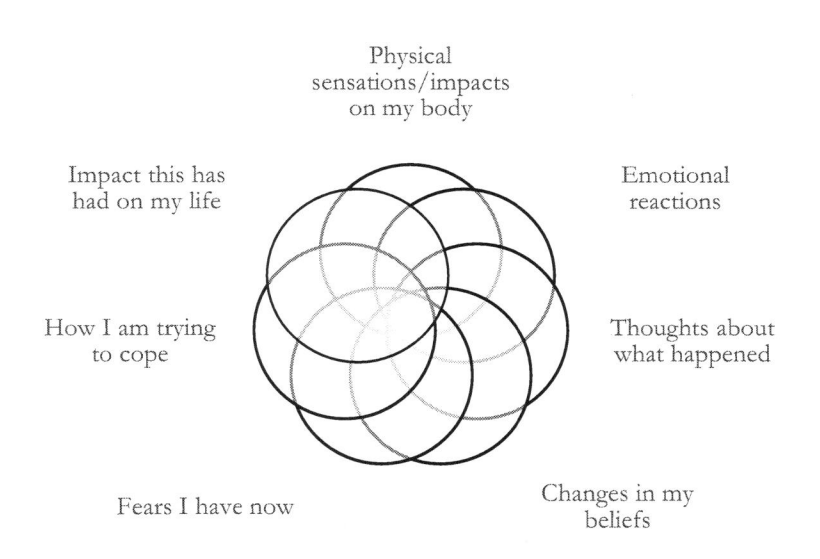

Physical sensations/impacts on my body

Impact this has had on my life

Emotional reactions

How I am trying to cope

Thoughts about what happened

Fears I have now

Changes in my beliefs

Exploring trauma responses

Use this simple tool to explore the responses to trauma at multiple stages of trauma processing, from the moment the trauma began to the present day.

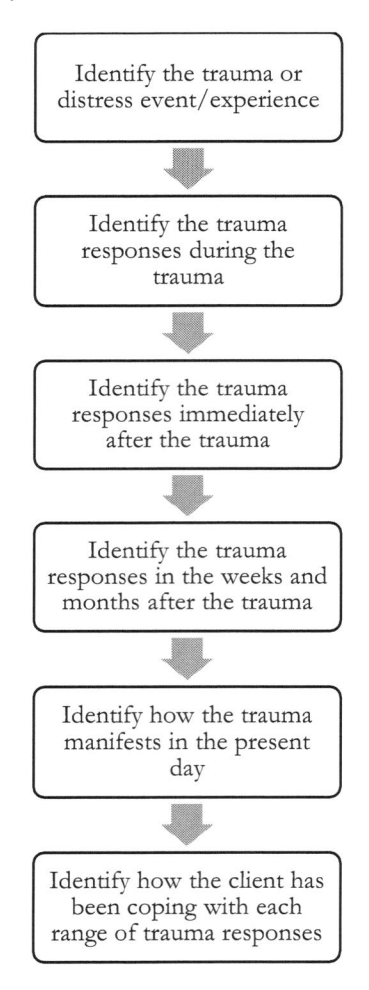

```
┌─────────────────────────────┐
│   Identify the trauma or    │
│  distress event/experience  │
└─────────────────────────────┘
              ↓
┌─────────────────────────────┐
│     Identify the trauma     │
│    responses during the     │
│           trauma            │
└─────────────────────────────┘
              ↓
┌─────────────────────────────┐
│     Identify the trauma     │
│   responses immediately     │
│      after the trauma       │
└─────────────────────────────┘
              ↓
┌─────────────────────────────┐
│     Identify the trauma     │
│  responses in the weeks and │
│   months after the trauma   │
└─────────────────────────────┘
              ↓
┌─────────────────────────────┐
│  Identify how the trauma    │
│  manifests in the present   │
│             day             │
└─────────────────────────────┘
              ↓
┌─────────────────────────────┐
│ Identify how the client has │
│   been coping with each     │
│  range of trauma responses  │
└─────────────────────────────┘
```

Belief in a Just World Tool

Belief in a Just World is a cognitive bias which may play a role in the distress and trauma of your client. Use this tool to consider whether this way of thinking may be present, and whether it may be distressing the person.

Does your client think/say:	Yes	Is this belief harming them?	Is this belief helping them?
Everything happens for a reason	☐	☐	☐
I must have done something terrible in a past life	☐	☐	☐
Bad things happen to bad people and good things happen to good people	☐	☐	☐
I must have bad karma	☐	☐	☐
I must be being punished for the bad things I have done in my life	☐	☐	☐
What goes around comes around in the end	☐	☐	☐
You get what you deserve in life	☐	☐	☐
I deserved what happened to me	☐	☐	☐

Trauma self-blame tool

Self-blame is a common experience for people who have experienced many kinds of trauma and distress. It may play a role in exacerbating the distress and trauma of your client. Use this tool to consider whether this way of thinking may be present, and whether it may be distressing the person.

Does your client:	Yes	No
Believe they did something to cause the trauma or distress	☐	☐
Change things about themselves, that they feel caused the trauma or distress	☐	☐
Over-analyse the incident or experience, looking for something to blame themselves for	☐	☐
Overstate their control or power in a situation where they were powerless	☐	☐
Apply knowledge they now have to their former selves in trauma, and blame themselves for not knowing what to do	☐	☐
Place unreasonable expectations on themselves to have foreseen, prevented or stopped the trauma or distress	☐	☐
Believe or say that they feel they 'let' the trauma or distress happen to them	☐	☐
Ruminate on 'what ifs', and what could have been different	☐	☐
Talk of being convinced, encouraged, or manipulated into blaming themselves by others	☐	☐

Taylor, J. & Shrive, J. (2023)

Harmful responses to trauma tool

When a person discloses their trauma or distress to someone else, it is common for them to receive a harmful response. It may cause further distress to receive a response like this. Use this tool to consider whether your client has experienced harmful responses to their experiences, and who from.

Has your client experienced:	From support network	From services
Being told that their trauma or distress did not happen, they are exaggerating, or lying	☐	☐
Being outcast, ignored, isolated, or removed from a group or setting	☐	☐
Being shamed, ridiculed, mocked, or made to feel stupid about their trauma or distress	☐	☐
Being blamed, and told that their experiences were caused by themselves	☐	☐
Being repositioned as the aggressor, abuser, bully, or perpetrator in a situation where they were the victim	☐	☐
Their confidentiality, secrets, or anonymity broken by someone who they confided in	☐	☐
Being threatened with violence, death, or harm if they talk about what happened	☐	☐
Positioned as mentally ill, disordered, delusional or non-credible	☐	☐
Being subjected to punishment, punitive measures, or restrictions due to disclosure	☐	☐

CHAPTER 8

Side effects, withdrawal, and complaints about medication

Introduction

Whilst many professionals reading this book will not be prescribers or doctors, they are likely to work with clients who discuss psychiatric medication, side effects, withdrawal impacts and other concerns about their treatment (present or past).

This section intends to give basic information about commonly reported side effects, withdrawal impacts and complaints about common medication used in psychiatry, so professionals feel informed and able to discuss these experiences with their clients.

Further, many people feel their medication has made them feel worse. They may disclose to professionals that their medication made them tired, low, irritable, unable to enjoy life, unable to enjoy sex, unwell and even suicidal. Whilst the voices and experiences of clients can be ignored by others, it is important as trauma-informed professionals, that we validate and listen to people who feel their medication is making them feel worse.

When clients ask for advice about tapering or ending the use of their previously prescribed psychiatric medication, it is always best practice to direct them back to their registered health provider to discuss safe tapering and reduction of dosages. If your client suddenly stops their medication, they may experience severe withdrawal effects that can make them feel very unwell.

Antidepressants

'Antidepressants' are medications used by psychiatrists to treat 'depression', 'anxiety', and other psychiatric diagnoses. They can have harmful side effects. 'Antidepressant' is a marketing term. Some potential harmful side effects of antidepressants include:

Suicidal thoughts and behaviour: In some people, antidepressants increase the risk of suicidal thoughts and behaviour, particularly in young adults and children.

Sexual dysfunction: Antidepressants can cause a variety of sexual side effects, including decreased libido, erectile dysfunction, and difficulty achieving orgasm.

Weight gain: Some antidepressants can cause weight gain, which can contribute to other health problems.

Nausea and vomiting: Antidepressants can cause nausea and vomiting, which can be especially problematic for people with pre-existing digestive problems.

Insomnia and other sleep disturbances: Antidepressants can disrupt sleep patterns, causing insomnia, sleep deprivation, or other sleep disturbances.

Headaches: Antidepressants can cause headaches in some people.

Increased risk of bleeding: Some antidepressants can increase the risk of bleeding, particularly when taken with other medications.

Serotonin syndrome: In rare cases, antidepressants can cause a condition called serotonin syndrome, which is characterised by high levels of serotonin in the brain and can cause symptoms such as agitation, confusion, and high blood pressure.

Anti-psychotic drugs

'Antipsychotics' are medications used by psychiatrists to treat 'psychotic symptoms' such as delusions, hallucinations, and 'disordered' thinking. 'Antipsychotic' is a marketing term. Most of these medications are tranquillisers, and anti-convulsant drugs.

They can also have harmful side effects. Some potential harmful side effects of antipsychotics include:

Extrapyramidal symptoms (EPS): EPS are movement disorders that can occur as a side effect of antipsychotic medications. These can include tremors, muscle stiffness, and involuntary movements.

Weight gain: Some antipsychotics can cause significant weight gain, which can lead to other health problems. This is why some people need regular blood tests whilst taking them.

Diabetes: Antipsychotics can increase the risk of developing diabetes, particularly in people who are already at risk.

Sexual dysfunction: Antipsychotics can cause a variety of sexual side effects, including decreased libido and difficulty achieving orgasm.

Sedation and drowsiness: Antipsychotics can cause sedation and drowsiness, which can be especially problematic for people who need to be alert and focused.

Increased risk of cardiovascular problems: Some antipsychotics can increase the risk of cardiovascular problems, including high blood pressure, irregular heartbeat, and heart attack.

Hyperprolactinemia: Some antipsychotics can increase levels of the hormone prolactin, which can cause breast enlargement and lactation in both men and women.

Neuroleptic malignant syndrome (NMS): NMS is a rare but potentially life-threatening condition that can occur as a side effect of antipsychotic medications. Symptoms can include fever, muscle rigidity, and altered mental status.

Melatonin supplements

Melatonin supplements are sometimes used to treat insomnia and other sleep disorders. While melatonin is generally considered safe, it can have some harmful side effects, including:

Daytime drowsiness: Taking too much melatonin or taking it too close to the intended wake-up time can cause daytime drowsiness and difficulty concentrating.

Vivid dreams or nightmares: Melatonin can cause vivid dreams or nightmares in some people.

Headaches: Melatonin can cause headaches in some people.

Nausea: Melatonin can cause nausea in some people.

Dizziness: Melatonin can cause dizziness in some people.

Mood changes: Melatonin can cause changes in mood, including fear, sadness, low mood, irritability, anger, and fatigue.

Blood pressure changes: Melatonin can cause changes in blood pressure, particularly in people with pre-existing cardiovascular problems.

Hormonal changes: Melatonin can affect levels of other hormones in the body, which can have a variety of effects.

Beta-blockers

Beta blockers are a class of medication that are sometimes used to treat symptoms of 'anxiety disorder', such as rapid heartbeat and trembling. They can have harmful side effects. Some potential harmful side effects of beta blockers for anxiety include:

Fatigue and dizziness: Beta blockers can cause fatigue and dizziness, which can make it difficult to function normally.

Hypotension: Beta blockers can cause a drop in blood pressure, which can be especially problematic for people with pre-existing cardiovascular problems.

Bronchospasm: Beta blockers can cause constriction of the airways, making it difficult to breathe. This can be especially problematic for people with asthma or other respiratory conditions.

Insomnia and vivid dreams: Beta blockers can disrupt sleep patterns, causing insomnia or vivid dreams.

Mood changes: Beta blockers can cause changes in mood, including low mood, irritability, and apathy.

Masking of hypoglycaemia symptoms: Beta blockers can mask symptoms of low blood sugar, making it more difficult for people with diabetes to manage their condition.

Sexual dysfunction: Beta blockers can cause sexual side effects, including decreased libido and difficulty achieving orgasm.

Stimulant medications

Stimulant medications, such as amphetamines and methylphenidate, are sometimes used for 'ADHD' and narcolepsy. These medications can also have harmful side effects. Some potential harmful side effects of stimulant medications for mental health include:

Addiction and abuse: Stimulant medications can be addictive and are sometimes abused for their stimulant effects.

Cardiovascular problems: Stimulant medications can increase heart rate and blood pressure, which can be problematic for people with pre-existing cardiovascular problems.

Insomnia: Stimulant medications can disrupt sleep patterns, causing insomnia, sleep deprivation, or other sleep disturbances.

Loss of appetite: Stimulant medications can cause loss of appetite and weight loss, which can be especially problematic for children who need proper nutrition for growth and development.

Mood changes: Stimulant medications can cause changes in mood, including irritability, anxiety, and agitation.

Hallucinations: In rare cases, stimulant medications can cause hallucinations and delusions.

Seizures: Stimulant medications can lower the seizure threshold, increasing the risk of seizures in some people.

Sedative medications

Sedatives are a class of medication that are sometimes used to treat 'anxiety', insomnia, and certain 'mood disorders'. They can have harmful side effects. Some potential harmful side effects of sedatives for mental health include:

Dependence and withdrawal: Sedatives can be addictive and can cause withdrawal symptoms if stopped abruptly.

Respiratory depression: Sedatives can cause slow and shallow breathing, which can be life-threatening in some cases.

Memory impairment: Sedatives can cause memory impairment and can interfere with the ability to learn and remember new information.

Drowsiness and impaired coordination: Sedatives can cause drowsiness and impaired coordination, making it difficult to function normally.

Confusion and cognitive impairment: Sedatives can cause confusion and cognitive impairment, particularly in older adults.

Increased risk of falls: Sedatives can increase the risk of falls, particularly in older adults.

Sexual dysfunction: Sedatives can cause sexual side effects, including decreased libido and difficulty achieving orgasm.

Benzodiazepines

Benzodiazepines are a class of medication that are sometimes used by psychiatrists to treat a range of 'mental health conditions' and 'mood disorders'. This class of medication can also have harmful side effects. Some potential harmful side effects of benzodiazepines in mental health include:

Dependence and withdrawal: Benzodiazepines can be addictive and can cause withdrawal symptoms if stopped abruptly.

Respiratory depression: Benzodiazepines can cause slow and shallow breathing, which can be life-threatening in some cases.

Memory impairment: Benzodiazepines can cause memory impairment and can interfere with the ability to learn and remember new information.

Drowsiness and impaired coordination: Benzodiazepines can cause drowsiness and impaired coordination, making it difficult to function normally.

Confusion and cognitive impairment: Benzodiazepines can cause confusion and cognitive impairment.

Increased risk of falls: Benzodiazepines can increase the risk of falls, particularly in older adults.

Sexual dysfunction: Benzodiazepines can cause sexual side effects, including decreased libido and difficulty achieving orgasm.

Paradoxical reactions: In some cases, benzodiazepines can cause paradoxical reactions, such as increased fear, increased distress, agitation, and aggression.

ECT (electroconvulsive therapy)

ECT (electroconvulsive therapy) is a medical treatment used primarily for what doctors label 'severe depression', 'bipolar disorder', and 'schizophrenia' that involves passing electric current through the brain to induce a seizure. ECT often has harmful side effects. Some harmful side effects of ECT include:

Memory loss: ECT can cause memory loss, particularly of events that occurred around the time of treatment.

Confusion and cognitive impairment: ECT can cause confusion and cognitive impairment, particularly immediately following treatment.

Headache: ECT can cause headaches in some people.

Muscle pain: ECT can cause muscle pain and soreness, particularly in the jaw and neck.

Cardiovascular problems: ECT can cause changes in heart rate and blood pressure, which can be problematic for people with pre-existing cardiovascular problems.

Nausea and vomiting: ECT can cause nausea and vomiting in some people.

Dental problems: ECT can cause dental problems, particularly if it is administered frequently or over a long period of time.

CHAPTER 9

Understanding bias and oppression in psychiatry

Overdiagnosis of marginalised groups of people

Overdiagnosis of mental health issues in marginalised groups refers to the tendency to diagnose mental disorders more frequently in people from marginalised communities than in the general population. Mental health professionals may hold unconscious biases or make assumptions about people from marginalised communities, leading them to over-diagnose mental disorders. This can perpetuate stereotypes and stigmatise marginalised communities.

Further, professionals may not be trained to recognise or understand the cultural and contextual factors that impact mental health in marginalised communities, including oppression, microaggressions, discrimination, inequality, and poverty. This can lead to a misinterpretation of experiences and an inaccurate psychiatric diagnosis.

People from marginalised communities may be more likely to be subjected to poverty, discrimination, and other forms of systemic oppression, which can contribute to their trauma and distress. However, these challenges may be misinterpreted as mental disorders, personality disorders, and psychiatric diagnoses rather than a response to systemic injustices.

In addition, people from marginalised communities may face barriers to accessing mental health services, such as lack of insurance or transportation. As a result, many people may not seek or receive the support they need for trauma and distress, leading to more trauma, and more marginalisation.

Racism in mental health and psychiatry

Racism in psychiatry refers to the ways in which systemic racism and bias can impact care and support for people from marginalised racial and ethnic groups. Here are a few examples of racism in psychiatry:

Misdiagnosis: People from marginalised racial and ethnic groups may be misdiagnosed with psychiatric disorders due to biases and assumptions about their behaviour and cultural background. For example, symptoms of trauma may be misinterpreted as aggression or hyperactivity in Black or Latino people.

Lack of cultural sensitivity: Mental health professionals may not be trained to recognise or understand the cultural and contextual factors that impact psychological wellbeing in people from marginalised racial and ethnic groups. This can lead to a misinterpretation of experiences and an inaccurate psychiatric diagnosis.

Stigma and discrimination: People from marginalised racial and ethnic groups may be subjected to stigma and discrimination from mental health professionals, which can impact their willingness to seek support and the quality of care they receive.

Limited access to care: People from marginalised racial and ethnic groups may face barriers to accessing services, such as lack of insurance or transportation.

Homophobia in mental health and psychiatry

Homophobia in psychiatry and mental health refers to the ways in which systemic biases and discrimination can impact the care and support of people who identify as LGBTQ+. Here are a few examples of homophobia in psychiatry and mental health:

Misdiagnosis: People who identify as LGBTQ+ may be misdiagnosed with personality disorders and psychiatric disorders due to biases and assumptions about their sexual orientation or gender identity. For example, gender non-conforming people may be misdiagnosed with gender dysphoria or bipolar disorder due to misunderstandings or stereotyping of their experiences. Bisexual women may be diagnosed with borderline personality disorder due to a belief that they have a 'confused sexuality'.

Stigma and discrimination: People who identify as LGBTQ+ may be subjected to stigma and discrimination from mental health professionals, which can impact their willingness to seek support and the quality of care they receive. This can lead to a higher risk of trauma and isolation among LGBTQ+ people.

Lack of sensitivity: Mental health professionals may not be trained to recognise or understand the unique experiences and needs of people who identify as LGBTQ+. This can lead to a misinterpretation of experiences and an inaccurate psychiatric diagnosis.

Misogyny in mental health and psychiatry

Misogyny in psychiatry and mental health refers to the ways in which systemic biases and discrimination can impact the care and support of women and girls. Here are a few examples of misogyny in psychiatry and mental health:

Misdiagnosis: Women may be misdiagnosed with psychiatric disorders, personality disorders and attachment disorders due to biases and assumptions about women, gender roles, and roles in society. For example, trauma responses may be misinterpreted as hysteria or emotional instability.

Stigma and discrimination: Women may be subjected to stigma and discrimination from mental health professionals, which can impact their willingness to seek support and the quality of care they receive.

Lack of cultural sensitivity: Mental health professionals may not be trained to recognise or understand the unique experiences, traumas, and needs of women. This can lead to lifelong psychiatric diagnoses.

Classism in mental health and psychiatry

Classism in psychiatry and mental health refers to the ways in which systemic biases and discrimination can impact the care and support of people from lower socio-economic backgrounds. Here are a few examples of classism in psychiatry and mental health:

Limited access to care: People from lower socio-economic backgrounds may face barriers to accessing mental health services, such as lack of insurance or transportation. As a result, they may not be able to access support for their trauma or distress.

Lack of cultural sensitivity: Mental health professionals may not be trained to recognise or understand the unique experiences and needs of people from lower socio-economic backgrounds. This can lead to a misinterpretation of experiences and an inaccurate psychiatric diagnosis.

Stigma and discrimination: People from lower socio-economic backgrounds may be subjected to stigma and discrimination from mental health professionals, which can impact their willingness to seek support and the quality of care they receive.

Misdiagnosis: People from lower socio-economic backgrounds may be misdiagnosed with psychiatric disorders and behavioural disorders due to biases and assumptions about their socio-economic status. For example, trauma responses may be misinterpreted as a lack of motivation or laziness.

Gender role stereotypes in mental health and psychiatry

Gender role stereotypes in mental health and psychiatry refer to the ways in which societal expectations about gender roles and behaviours can impact the diagnosis and treatment of perceived mental disorders. Here are a few examples of gender role stereotypes in mental health and psychiatry:

Misdiagnosis: Women may be misdiagnosed with psychiatric disorders due to biases and assumptions about their gender roles and gender expression. For example, trauma responses may be misinterpreted as hysteria or emotional instability.

Stigma and discrimination: People who do not conform to traditional gender roles may be subjected to stigma and discrimination from mental health professionals, which can impact their willingness to seek support and the quality of care they receive.

Lack of cultural sensitivity: Mental health professionals may not be trained to recognise or understand the unique experiences and needs of people who do not conform to traditional gender roles. This can lead to a misinterpretation of experiences and responses, and a misdiagnosis of a psychiatric disorder.

There is significant historic and current evidence that psychiatric diagnosis is based around oppression, stereotyping and marginalisation. Women are still the most likely group to be diagnosed with most psychiatric disorders, for example.

Several 'mental health disorders' are more likely to be diagnosed in in females than in males, including:

'Depression': Depression is more likely to be diagnosed in females than in males. Psychiatric literature argues that this may be due to hormonal differences, social and cultural factors, and differences in coping strategies.

'Anxiety disorders': Anxiety disorders, including generalised anxiety disorder, panic disorder, and social anxiety disorder, are more commonly diagnosed in females than in males. The psychiatric literature suggests that this may be due to differences in brain structure and function.

'Eating disorders': Eating disorders, such as anorexia nervosa and bulimia nervosa, are more common in females than in males. This may be due to cultural pressures to conform to narrow beauty standards, as well as biological and psychological factors.

'Post-traumatic distress disorder (PTSD)': PTSD is more commonly diagnosed in females than in males, particularly among those who have been subjected to sexual trauma. The psychiatric literature suggests that this may be due to differences in brain structure and function, as well as differences in exposure to traumatic events.

'Borderline personality disorder (BPD)': BPD is more commonly diagnosed in females than in males. The psychiatric literature suggests that this may be due to hormonal differences, as well as differences in coping strategies and emotional regulation.

Several mental health disorders are more common in males than in females, including:

'Autism spectrum disorder (ASD)': ASD is more prevalent in males than in females. Please note that many professionals now prefer to use ASC (autism spectrum conditions), and it is widely rejected as a 'mental disorder'.

'Attention deficit hyperactivity disorder (ADHD)': ADHD is more commonly diagnosed in males than in females. Psychiatric literature suggests that this may be due to differences in brain structure and function, as well as social and cultural norms.

'Substance use disorders': Substance use disorders, including alcohol and drug addiction, are more commonly diagnosed in males than in females.

'Conduct disorder': Conduct disorder, which involves aggression, antisocial behaviour, and violation of social norms, is more commonly diagnosed in males than in females.

'Schizophrenia': Schizophrenia is more commonly diagnosed in males than in females, although the difference is less pronounced than in other disorders.

This section is important to consider, as gender roles are so influential in mental health and psychiatry that the 'disorders' most commonly diagnosed in males are typically related to masculine traits and behaviours, and the most commonly diagnosed disorders in females are typically related to emotional distress and misogynistic conceptions of femininity.

CHAPTER 10

Understanding approaches to supporting traumatised and distressed people

Introduction

This section provides a collection of information about approaches to supporting clients who are struggling with their trauma or distress. Everyone is unique, what works for some will not work for others.

It is important to remember that some people are not ready for trauma therapy, or an intervention which requires any form of disclosure or detailed exploration of what happened to them. Instead, there are other ways they can meaningfully engage and find purpose without traditional therapy.

It is also worth considering that for some people, therapy will never be something they want to engage in, and so alternatives must be available and considered.

Creating a trauma-informed environment

A trauma-informed environment is a setting, such as a workplace, school, or healthcare facility, that recognises the potential for trauma in people and strives to provide a safe and supportive environment for those who have experienced trauma. A trauma-informed environment is based on the principles of trauma-informed care, which include safety, trustworthiness, choice, collaboration, and empowerment.

In a trauma-informed environment, staff are trained to recognise the signs of trauma and to respond in a way that is sensitive and supportive. This may include providing a calm and non-threatening environment, respecting people' boundaries and choices, and avoiding re-traumatisation.

Some key components of a trauma-informed environment may include:

Safety: Ensuring physical and emotional safety for people who have experienced trauma, and creating a safe and supportive environment that promotes healing.

Trustworthiness: Building trust with people who have experienced trauma by providing transparent and clear communication, and avoiding actions that may be perceived as threatening or harmful.

Choice: Allowing people who have experienced trauma to have a say in their care and treatment plans, and providing options and choices when possible.

Collaboration: Working together with people who have experienced trauma, as well as other providers and agencies, to provide holistic and coordinated care.

Empowerment: Helping people who have experienced trauma to regain a sense of control and empowerment, and promoting resilience and recovery.

Overall, a trauma-informed environment is a space that recognises and responds to the impact of trauma on people, and strives to promote healing and recovery through a supportive and collaborative approach.

Power Threat Meaning Framework (PTMF)

The Power Threat Meaning Framework (PTMF), by Johnstone and Boyle (2019) is an alternative framework for understanding and responding to emotional distress, mental health, and related problems. The PTMF was developed over the course of five years by a group of senior psychologists (Lucy Johnstone, Mary Boyle, John Cromby, David Harper, Peter Kinderman, David Pilgrim and John Read) and campaigners (Jacqui Dillon and Eleanor Longden).

The PTMF proposes that emotional distress and mental health difficulties are best understood in the context of the individual's personal and social experiences, including experiences of trauma, abuse, oppression, and inequality. The framework emphasises the role of power, threat, and meaning in shaping people's experiences of distress and offers an alternative to the medical model of diagnosing and treating mental health problems.

According to the PTMF, emotional distress and mental health difficulties are understandable responses to experiences of powerlessness, threat, and adversity. These experiences can be caused by a range of factors, including social inequality, oppression, interpersonal violence, and other forms of trauma.

The PTMF proposes that understanding the meaning and function of emotional distress and mental health difficulties can be more useful than focusing on diagnostic labels. The framework offers a range of tools and resources for helping people to explore and understand their experiences, develop new meanings and narratives, and find ways to manage distress in more empowering ways.

Overall, the Power Threat Meaning Framework offers an excellent alternative perspective on mental health and emotional distress that prioritises the individual's personal and social experiences and offers a more holistic approach to understanding and responding to mental health difficulties.

The ITIM builds upon the foundations built by the PTMF.

Therapies

This section contains a collection of basic descriptions of therapies and approaches to trauma for professionals who may need further information.

It is important to remember that for some people, therapies are life-changing and positive experiences, and for others, they can be harmful and oppressive experiences. There is no one-size-fits-all therapy, and people may not find comfort in traditional talking therapies at all.

What is EMDR?

EMDR, or Eye Movement Desensitization and Reprocessing, is a psychotherapy approach that is used in trauma and mental health. EMDR is a structured approach that involves a series of phases and techniques, and is typically delivered by a mental health professional who is trained in the approach.

The core technique of EMDR involves the use of bilateral stimulation, which can be accomplished through eye movements, tapping, or sounds. During a typical EMDR session, the client will be asked to recall a traumatic memory or experience while engaging in bilateral stimulation. This is thought to help the client process the memory and reduce the intensity of the associated emotions and physical sensations.

EMDR also involves a series of phases that are designed to prepare the client for processing, identify and target specific memories or experiences, and integrate the processed information into the client's broader understanding of themselves and their experiences.

The efficacy of EMDR has been supported by numerous studies and meta-analyses, which have found that EMDR can be an effective approach for trauma. However, EMDR may not be appropriate for everyone, and it can cause people to feel triggered and unsafe.

What is person centred therapy?

Person-centred therapy is a type of psychotherapy that emphasises the individual's subjective experience and personal growth. Person-centred therapy is based on the belief that people have the inherent capacity for growth and self-actualisation, and that the therapist's role is to create a supportive and non-judgmental environment in which the individual can explore their thoughts, feelings, and behaviours.

Person-centred therapy was developed by Carl Rogers in the 1950s, and is often referred to as Rogerian therapy. Some key concepts and techniques used in person-centred therapy include:

Unconditional positive regard: This involves the therapist providing a non-judgmental, accepting, and supportive environment in which the individual can explore their experiences without fear of rejection or criticism.

Empathy: Person-centred therapy emphasises the therapist's ability to understand and relate to the individual's subjective experience, and to communicate this understanding in a supportive and validating way.

Authenticity: Person-centred therapy emphasises the therapist's ability to be genuine and authentic in their interactions with the individual, and to communicate their own experiences and emotions in a transparent and honest way.

Focus on the present moment: Person-centred therapy encourages people to focus on their present experiences and emotions, rather than dwelling on past traumas or future worries.

What is CBT?

CBT stands for Cognitive Behavioural Therapy, which is a type of psychotherapy that is based on the idea that our thoughts, emotions, and behaviours are interconnected, and that by changing the way we think and behave, we can improve our mental health and well-being.

CBT is typically delivered in a structured, short-term format and involves a collaborative relationship between the therapist and the individual. The therapist works with the individual to identify and challenge negative thought patterns and beliefs, and to develop new, more adaptive ways of thinking and behaving.

Some common techniques and interventions used in CBT include:

Cognitive restructuring: This involves helping people identify and challenge negative thought patterns and beliefs that may be contributing to their distress, and replace them with more adaptive and positive ways of thinking.

Exposure therapy: This involves gradually exposing people to situations or stimuli that trigger anxiety or fear, in order to reduce the intensity of the associated emotions and physical sensations.

Behavioural activation: This involves helping people develop new, more adaptive behaviours that are consistent with their values and goals, and that can help to improve their mood and overall well-being.

Relaxation and distress reduction techniques: This involves teaching people strategies such as deep breathing, progressive muscle relaxation, or mindfulness to help them manage distress and anxiety.

What is DBT?

DBT stands for Dialectical Behaviour Therapy, which is a type of psychotherapy that is designed to help people manage intense emotions, develop healthy coping mechanisms, and build stronger relationships. DBT is often used to 'treat' people with diagnoses of 'borderline personality disorder', but can also be effective for other mental health needs that involve difficulties with emotion regulation.

DBT was developed by psychologist Marsha Linehan in the 1980s, and is based on the principles of cognitive-behavioural therapy (CBT) and mindfulness. Some key concepts and techniques used in DBT include:

Dialectics: This involves the idea that opposing ideas can both be true at the same time, and that people can learn to hold two seemingly contradictory ideas in mind and find a middle ground.

Mindfulness: This involves the practice of being present in the moment and accepting one's thoughts, feelings, and experiences without judgment.

Distress tolerance: This involves developing healthy coping mechanisms to manage intense emotions, such as breathing exercises, relaxation techniques, and distraction.

Interpersonal effectiveness: This involves developing communication and relationship-building skills, such as assertiveness, active listening, and boundary-setting.

DBT is typically delivered in a structured format that involves both individual therapy and group therapy sessions. The therapist works with the individual to identify specific areas of difficulty and develop strategies to manage those difficulties. DBT also involves the use of homework assignments, skills training, and phone coaching to help people practice and reinforce the skills they learn in therapy.

What is narrative therapy?

Narrative therapy is a type of psychotherapy that emphasises the importance of personal stories and the meaning that people assign to their experiences. Narrative therapy is based on the idea that the stories we tell about ourselves and our experiences shape our identity and our perception of the world around us.

Narrative therapy was developed by Michael White and David Epston in the 1980s, and is often used in mental health. Some key concepts and techniques used in narrative therapy include:

Externalising problems: This involves separating the individual from the problem they are experiencing, and viewing the problem as an external entity that can be explored and addressed.

Re-authoring stories: This involves helping people to examine and re-write their personal stories in a way that emphasises their strengths and resources, and reduces the power of negative or self-defeating narratives.

Deconstruction: This involves questioning and challenging dominant cultural narratives and social constructions, in order to explore the individual's experience from a more critical perspective.

Remembering: This involves exploring and integrating neglected or forgotten aspects of the individual's personal history or identity, in order to promote a more holistic and authentic sense of self.

Narrative therapy is typically delivered in a collaborative and non-judgmental environment, in which the therapist works with the individual to explore their personal stories and experiences, and to identify ways to re-author or re-interpret those stories in a more positive and empowering way. The goal of narrative therapy is to help people develop a greater sense of self-awareness, resilience, and agency, and to promote a more positive and meaningful sense of self and identity.

What is play therapy?

Play therapy is a type of psychotherapy that is used primarily with children to help them process and communicate their emotions, thoughts, and experiences in a safe and supportive environment. Play therapy uses a variety of play-based techniques and activities, such as drawing, storytelling, role-playing, and games, to help children express and work through their feelings and experiences.

Play therapy is based on the idea that play is a natural form of communication for children, and that through play, children can express their emotions and explore their world in a way that is developmentally appropriate and safe. Play therapy is typically delivered by a trained therapist who works with the child to identify areas of difficulty and develop therapeutic goals and interventions.

Some key concepts and techniques used in play therapy include:

Therapeutic relationship: This involves building a supportive and non-judgmental relationship between the child and therapist, in which the child feels safe to express themselves and explore their experiences.

Play-based techniques: This involves using a variety of play-based activities and techniques to help children express and work through their feelings and experiences, such as art, music, storytelling, and role-playing.

Parent involvement: This involves involving parents or caregivers in the play therapy process, in order to help them support their child's emotional and developmental needs.

Play therapy has been found to be an effective approach for a wide range of distress and trauma responses, and behavioural issues. The goal of play therapy is to help children develop healthy coping mechanisms, build resilience, and develop positive relationships with others.

What is psychodynamic therapy?

Psychodynamic therapy is a form of talk therapy that is based on the theories and principles of psychoanalysis, which was developed by Sigmund Freud in the late 19th and early 20th centuries. Psychodynamic therapy aims to help people become more self-aware by exploring the unconscious thoughts, emotions, and experiences that may be influencing their behaviour and mental health.

Psychodynamic therapy typically involves a longer-term approach than some other forms of therapy, and focuses on building a strong therapeutic relationship between the individual and therapist. The therapist works with the individual to explore their thoughts, feelings, and experiences, often through free association (in which the individual speaks freely about whatever comes to mind) and dream analysis.

Some key concepts and techniques used in psychodynamic therapy include:

Unconscious mind: This involves the idea that there are unconscious thoughts, feelings, and experiences that influence our behaviour and emotions, and that by exploring these unconscious factors, people can gain a greater understanding of their mental and emotional life.

Defence mechanisms: This involves the idea that people use defence mechanisms, such as repression, denial, and projection, to protect themselves from difficult emotions or experiences.

Transference: This involves the idea that the individual may transfer their feelings and emotions from past relationships onto the therapeutic relationship, providing a way to work through past issues and develop healthier relationships.

Interpretation: This involves the therapist's interpretation of the individual's thoughts, feelings, and behaviours, in order to help the individual gain insight into their underlying motivations and patterns.

Psychodynamic therapy is used in a wide range of traumas, particularly those that involve difficulties with self-awareness and interpersonal relationships. The goal of psychodynamic therapy is to help people gain a deeper understanding of themselves and their emotions, and to develop healthier ways of coping with life's challenges.

Alternatives to therapy

Meditation

Meditation can be a helpful tool in the approach to trauma by promoting relaxation, and increasing self-awareness and emotional regulation. Here are some ways that meditation can help trauma:

Promotes relaxation: Trauma can cause a constant state of hypervigilance, fear, and stress, which can lead to physical and emotional exhaustion. Meditation can help reduce the physiological and psychological symptoms of distress and promote relaxation by calming the nervous system.

Reduces fear and low mood: Meditation has been shown to reduce feelings of fear and low mood, which are common in people who have experienced trauma.

Increases self-awareness: Trauma can cause a disconnection from the body and emotions, making it difficult to identify and manage emotions. Meditation can help people develop a greater awareness of their thoughts, feelings, and physical sensations, which can promote self-regulation and emotional healing.

Increases emotional regulation: Trauma can cause people to feel overwhelmed and triggered by emotions, making it difficult to regulate emotional responses. Meditation can help people learn to observe and accept their emotions without judgment, and develop healthier ways of managing emotions.

Enhances compassion and empathy: Trauma can cause people to feel disconnected from others and experience feelings of isolation. Meditation can help people develop greater compassion and empathy for themselves and others, which can help promote a sense of connection and healing.

Writing and journalling

Writing and journaling can be a helpful tool in the support for trauma by providing a safe and private space for people to process their thoughts and emotions, express themselves, and gain insight into their experiences. Here are some ways that writing and journaling can help trauma:

Helps to process emotions: Writing and journaling can help people identify and process difficult emotions related to trauma, such as fear, anger, and sadness. By writing about their experiences, people can gain a deeper understanding of their emotional responses and work through them in a healthy way.

Provides a sense of control: Trauma can make people feel helpless and out of control. Writing and journaling can provide a sense of control and agency over their experiences, as people can choose what to write about and how to express themselves.

Encourages self-reflection: Writing and journalling can help people reflect on their experiences, thoughts, and emotions, and gain insight into patterns and behaviours that may be contributing to their distress.

Reduces fear and low mood: Writing and journalling have been shown to reduce fear, worry and low mood which are common in people who have experienced trauma.

Helps with memory processing: Trauma can affect memory processing, making it difficult for people to remember details of their experiences. Writing and journaling can help people recall and organise their memories, which can promote healing and recovery.

Art

Art therapy can be a helpful tool in the support for trauma by providing a safe and creative outlet for people to express and process their thoughts and emotions related to their experiences. Here are some ways that art can help trauma:

Provides a non-verbal means of expression: Trauma can be difficult to talk about, and people may feel overwhelmed or triggered when trying to express their emotions verbally. Art therapy provides a non-verbal means of expression, allowing people to express their experiences and emotions through art materials, such as paint, clay, or collage.

Promotes self-expression and exploration: Art therapy encourages people to explore and express their thoughts and emotions in a creative and non-judgmental way, allowing for greater self-awareness and self-expression.

Encourages mindfulness and relaxation: Art therapy can be a meditative and relaxing practice, promoting mindfulness and a sense of calm.

Promotes healing and recovery: Art therapy can help people process and integrate their experiences, leading to a greater sense of healing and recovery.

Exercise

Exercise can be a helpful tool in the support for trauma by promoting physical and mental health, reducing feelings of worry, fear, low mood, despair, and improving self-esteem and self-confidence. Here are some ways that exercise can help trauma:

Reduces feelings of fear and low mood: Exercise has been shown to reduce feelings of fear and low mood, which are common in people who have experienced trauma.

Promotes relaxation and distress relief: Exercise can help reduce distress and promote relaxation due to the physiological impact on the body.

Improves sleep: Trauma can affect sleep quality and quantity, leading to fatigue and other health issues. Exercise can improve sleep quality and promote restful sleep.

Increases self-esteem and self-confidence: Trauma can affect self-esteem and self-confidence, leading to feelings of shame, guilt, and worthlessness. Exercise can improve self-esteem and self-confidence by promoting physical health and a sense of accomplishment.

Promotes physical health: Trauma can lead to physical health issues, such as chronic pain and fatigue. Exercise can improve physical health and reduce the risk of chronic diseases, such as heart disease and diabetes.

Music

Listening to music can be a helpful tool in the support for trauma by providing a source of comfort, promoting relaxation, reducing feelings of low mood, anger, fear, worries, despair, and facilitating emotional expression and processing. Here are some ways that music can help trauma:

Promotes relaxation and distress relief: Music can have a calming effect on the nervous system, promoting relaxation and distress relief.

Facilitates emotional expression and processing: Music can help people express and process difficult emotions related to trauma, such as sadness, anger, and fear.

Provides a source of comfort: Trauma can cause people to feel isolated and disconnected from others. Music can provide a sense of comfort and connection, especially when listening to music that resonates with their experiences.

Enhances mindfulness and self-awareness: Listening to music mindfully, with a focus on the present moment, can enhance mindfulness and self-awareness, promoting a greater sense of emotional regulation and self-reflection.

Reading books

Reading books can be a helpful tool for processing trauma by providing a source of comfort, promoting relaxation, facilitating emotional expression and processing, and increasing self-awareness and understanding. Here are some ways that reading books can help trauma:

Provides a source of comfort: Reading books can provide a sense of comfort and connection, especially when reading books that resonate with the individual's experiences.

Promotes relaxation and distress relief: Reading can have a calming effect on the nervous system, promoting relaxation and distress relief.

Facilitates emotional expression and processing: Reading books about trauma can help people express and process difficult emotions related to their experiences, such as sadness, anger, and fear.

Increases self-awareness and understanding: Reading books about trauma can increase self-awareness and understanding of the individual's experiences, leading to a greater sense of clarity and insight.

Provides a sense of hope and inspiration: Reading books about trauma can provide a sense of hope and inspiration, showing people that they are not alone in their experiences and that recovery is possible.

Social prescribing

Social prescribing is a healthcare approach that involves linking patients with non-medical resources and support in their community to help improve their overall health and wellbeing. Rather than prescribing medication, a healthcare professional may recommend 'social prescriptions' that connect the patient with community-based resources such as exercise classes, art therapy, community gardening, or volunteering opportunities.

Social prescribing recognizes that many factors contribute to a person's health and wellbeing, including social, economic, and environmental factors, and that healthcare providers alone cannot address all of these factors. By connecting patients with community resources, social prescribing aims to improve patients' physical and mental health, reduce healthcare costs, and increase their sense of social connectedness and overall quality of life.

Social prescribing programs may be offered by healthcare providers, community-based organisations, or government agencies. They often involve collaboration between healthcare providers, community organisations, and local government agencies to identify and address the unique needs of each patient and community.

Social prescribing can be a helpful tool to process and address trauma by providing people with access to community-based resources and support that can address the social and emotional factors that contribute to their trauma. Here are some ways that social prescribing can help trauma:

Promotes social connectedness: Trauma can cause people to feel isolated and disconnected from others. Social prescribing can help people connect with others in their community, promoting social support and reducing feelings of isolation and loneliness.

Provides access to non-medical resources: Social prescribing can connect people with non-medical resources and support in their community, such as art therapy, support groups, or mindfulness classes, which can help them process and cope with their trauma.

Encourages physical activity and healthy habits: Trauma can have a negative impact on physical health and well-being. Social prescribing can encourage people to engage in physical activity and healthy habits, such as yoga, exercise classes, or nutrition counselling, which can improve their overall health and well-being.

Promotes self-care and self-awareness: Social prescribing can promote self-care and self-awareness by encouraging people to engage in activities that promote mindfulness, relaxation, and emotional regulation.

Increases access to mental health resources: Social prescribing can increase access to trauma-informed resources, such as therapy or counselling, that can help people manage their distress.

Activism

Engaging in activism can be a helpful tool to process trauma by providing people with a sense of purpose and agency, promoting social connectedness and support, and facilitating the processing and expression of difficult emotions related to their trauma. Here are some ways that engaging in activism can help trauma:

Provides a sense of purpose and agency: Trauma can cause people to feel powerless and helpless. Engaging in activism can provide a sense of purpose and agency, empowering people to take action and make a difference in their community.

Promotes social connectedness and support: Engaging in activism can help people connect with others who share similar experiences and values, promoting social support and reducing feelings of isolation and loneliness.

Facilitates emotional expression and processing: Engaging in activism can provide a platform for people to express and process difficult emotions related to their trauma, such as anger, sadness, or fear.

Increases awareness and understanding of trauma: Engaging in activism can increase awareness and understanding of trauma and its impact on people and communities, promoting empathy and reducing stigma.

Promotes positive change: Engaging in activism can promote positive change in society and contribute to a greater sense of social justice and equality, which can be empowering and healing for people who have experienced trauma.

Equine therapy

Equine therapy, also known as equine-assisted therapy or horse therapy, is a type of therapy that involves interactions with horses to promote emotional growth and healing. It can be a helpful tool to process trauma by providing people with a non-judgmental and nonverbal form of support that can help them process and cope with their trauma. Here are some ways that equine therapy can help trauma:

Provides a non-judgmental and nonverbal form of support: Horses are sensitive animals that respond to people's emotional states and behaviours without judgment or verbal feedback. This can provide people with a safe and non-judgmental space to explore their emotions and develop coping skills.

Promotes mindfulness and emotional regulation: Equine therapy can promote mindfulness and emotional regulation by encouraging people to focus on the present moment and become aware of their emotions and physical sensations.

Facilitates the processing of difficult emotions: Equine therapy can facilitate the processing of difficult emotions related to trauma, such as fear, anger, or sadness, by providing a safe and supportive space to express and work through these emotions.

Increases self-awareness and empathy: Equine therapy can increase self-awareness and empathy by encouraging people to observe and understand the horses' behaviour and emotions, which can translate to greater self-awareness and empathy for others.

Encourages physical activity and healthy habits: Equine therapy often involves physical activity and can encourage people to engage in healthy habits such as exercise and spending time outdoors, which can promote overall health and well-being.

Gardening and allotments

Gardening can be a therapeutic and healing activity for people who have experienced trauma. Here are some ways that gardening can help with trauma:

Promotes relaxation: Gardening can promote mindfulness and relaxation by encouraging people to focus on the present moment and engage in a calming activity that involves connecting with nature.

Provides a sense of control and agency: Trauma can cause people to feel powerless and helpless. Gardening can provide a sense of control and agency by allowing people to create and nurture something, and see the results of their efforts.

Offers a creative outlet: Gardening can offer a creative outlet for people to express themselves and process difficult emotions related to their trauma.

Promotes physical activity and healthy habits: Gardening often involves physical activity and can encourage people to engage in healthy habits such as exercise and spending time outdoors, which can promote overall health and well-being.

Facilitates social support and connection: Gardening can facilitate social support and connection by providing people with a shared activity that can be enjoyed with others, such as in community gardens or gardening clubs.

Volunteering

Volunteering for a cause can be a helpful tool to process trauma and mental health by providing people with a sense of purpose and agency, promoting social connectedness and support, and facilitating the processing and expression of difficult emotions related to their trauma. Here are some ways that volunteering for a cause can help with trauma and mental health:

Provides a sense of purpose and agency: Trauma can cause people to feel powerless and helpless. Volunteering can provide a sense of purpose and agency, empowering people to take action and make a difference in their community.

Promotes social connectedness and support: Volunteering can help people connect with others who share similar values and goals, promoting social support and reducing feelings of isolation and loneliness.

Facilitates emotional expression and processing: Volunteering can provide a platform for people to express and process difficult emotions related to their trauma, such as anger, sadness, or fear.

Increases self-esteem and sense of accomplishment: Volunteering can increase peoples' self-esteem and sense of accomplishment by providing opportunities to use their skills and make a positive impact in their community.

Promotes positive change: Volunteering can promote positive change in society and contribute to a greater sense of social justice and equality, which can be empowering and healing for people who have experienced trauma.

About VictimFocus

VictimFocus is a leading research, training, and consultancy organisation working internationally to challenge, change, and influence tens of thousands of professionals, and millions of members of the public to rethink their understanding of victim blaming, self-blame, victim stereotyping, misogyny, racism, classism, interpersonal violence, psychological trauma, pathologisation, victim care, and victim's rights.

VictimFocus operates for social good. Profits are reinvested into free research, resources, campaigns, toolkits and approaches that support government, services, professionals and the public to change the way they think, feel and behave when responding to violence, abuse and trauma in society.

Contact us at admin@victimfocus.org.uk

About the authors

Dr Jessica Taylor is a Chartered Psychologist, PhD Forensic Psychology, Director of VictimFocus, Sunday Times Bestselling Author, public speaker, trainer, and researcher. She specialises in trauma-informed approaches to abuse, violence, trauma, distress, and oppression. Her work focusses on the psychology of victim blaming and victim prejudice, and the way those subjected to abuse and trauma are likely to be reframed as disordered or mentally unstable.

Jaimi Shrive is a Doctoral Researcher undertaking a PhD in Politics, specialising in the way international and national politics changes the way governments respond to violence and abuse committed against women and girls. She is a trainer, public speaker, and writer, creating educational resources for professionals who work in trauma, abuse and violence. She is the co-author of several public and confidential reports on the impact of violence, abuse, vicarious trauma, and misogyny in policing, and social care services.

With thanks to reviewers

We acknowledge and thank our reviewers for their time, expertise, ideas, criticisms, and suggestions. Each of you helped us to shape this book into what has been presented here. Thank you so much for your support and insight.

Name	Role
Catherine MacKay	Senior Clinician and EMDR Therapist
Dr Roger McFillin	Licensed Psychologist, Executive Director, Center for IBH
Amanda Naylor	CEO of Manchester Youth Zone
Kevin Gritton	CEO of Multi Academy Trust
Jason Hamilton*	Detective Inspector RASSO
Sarah McGrath	CEO of Women For Women France
Marie-Eve Martel	Criminologist and Independent VAWG Expert
Summer Grace	Patient and NHS Professional
Mandeep Sandhu	Service Manager and Social Worker
Fiona Gwinnett	CEO of Wight DASH
Elaine Smylie	Signs of Safety Co-Ordinator
Danielle Georgiou-Read	BA Hons Psychology, PG Cert. Family Therapy & Systemic Practice Forensic and Investigative Psychology MSc, BSc Hons Psychology
Caitlin Spencer*	Survivor and Professional
Bramley Clarence	Research Manager, VictimFocus
Laura Caress	Independent HR Specialist
Dr Charlotte Proudman	Barrister and Academic
Emma Barwell	Independent Social Worker
Carol Wick	MS, LMFT, President, Sharity Global
Kelly Joynes	Coach and Trainer in Trauma and Mental Health

With thanks to VictimFocus Scrutiny Panel Members
With thanks to VictimFocus Ethics Panel Members

Pseudonym

Bibliography

Age and Gender Variations in Cancer Diagnostic Intervals in 15 Cancers: Analysis of Data from the UK Clinical Practice Research Datalink
Din NU, Ukoumunne OC, Rubin G, Hamilton W, Carter B, et al. (2015) Age and Gender Variations in Cancer Diagnostic Intervals in 15 Cancers: Analysis of Data from the UK Clinical Practice Research Datalink. PLOS ONE 10(5): e0127717. https://doi.org/10.1371/journal.pone.0127717

Acne, NHS choices. NHS. Available at: https://www.nhs.uk/conditions/acne/ (Accessed: February 6, 2023).

All Party Parliamentary Group on Endometriosis (2020) Endometriosis in the UK: time for change. Retrieved from https://www.endometriosis-uk.org/sites/endometriosis-uk.org/files/files/Endometriosis%20APPG%20Report%20Oct%202020.pdf

Anda, R., Porter, L. & Brown, D. (2020) 'Inside the Adverse Childhood Experience Score: Strengths, Limitations, and Misapplications', American Journal of Preventative Medicine, Volume 59, Issue 2, p293 – 295

BBC (2018) 'Everybody was telling me there was nothing wrong' The Health Gap, BBC https://www.bbc.com/future/article/20180523-how-gender-bias-affects-your-healthcare

Bentall, R. (2003) Madness Explained: Psychosis and human nature, Penguin Books

Bentall, R. (2009) Doctoring the mind: Why psychiatric treatments fail, Penguin Books

BetterSleep (2022) What about yawns? BetterSleep. BetterSleep. Available at: https://www.bettersleep.com/blog/what-about-yawns/#:~:text=Frequent%20incomplete%20yawning%20can%20also,dysfunction%20in%20your%20nervous%20system. (Accessed: February 10, 2023).

Blackwell, S Saxena, N Jayasooriya, A Bottle, I Petersen, M Hotopf, C Alexakis, R C Pollok, (2021) POP-IBD study group, Prevalence and Duration of Gastrointestinal Symptoms Before Diagnosis of Inflammatory Bowel Disease and Predictors of Timely Specialist Review: A Population-Based Study, Journal of Crohn's and Colitis, Volume 15, Issue 2, February 2021, Pages 203–211, https://doi.org/10.1093/ecco-jcc/jjaa146

BMA (2021) Sexism in Medicine, British Medical Association

BMJ (2020) Letter to the president of the Royal College of Psychiatrists (370:m2657)

Bowlby, J. (1969) Attachment and Loss: Volume 1. Attachment, New York, Basic Books.

Bowlby, J. (1988) A Secure Base: Parent - Child Attachment and Healthy Human Development, New York, Basic Books.

Bronfenbrenner, U. (1979). The ecology of human development: Experiments by nature and design. Cambridge, MA: Harvard University Press.

Bronfenbrenner, U. (1986). Ecology of the family as a context for human development: Research perspectives. Developmental Psychology, 22, 723-742.

Bronfenbrenner, U. (1995). Developmental ecology through space and time: A future perspective. In P. Moen, G. H. Elder, Jr., and K. Luscher (Eds.), Examining lives in context: Perspectives on the ecology of human development (pp. 619-647). Washington, DC: APA Books.

Bucher, J. & Manasse, M. (2011) When Screams Are Not Released: A Study of Communication and Consent in Acquaintance Rape Situations, Women & Criminal Justice 21(2):123-140 DOI: 10.1080/08974454.2011.558801

Cancer Research (2023) Cancer mortality for common cancers, Cancer mortality statistics

Carr, S. & Spandler, H. (2019) 'Hidden from history? A brief modern history of the psychiatric "treatment" of lesbian and bisexual women in England'. The Lancet Psychiatry, 6(4), 289–290.

Chang, F.-L.C. (1997) Telogen effluvium, DermNet. Available at: https://dermnetnz.org/topics/telogen-effluvium (Accessed: February 8, 2023).

Chen, E. H., Shofer, F. S., Dean, A. J., Hollander, J. E., Baxt, W. G., Robey, J. L., Sease, K. L. & Mills, A. M. (2008) 'Gender disparity in analgesic treatment of emergency department patients with acute abdominal pain'. The Lancet Psychiatry. Academic emergency medicine: official journal of the Society for Academic Emergency Medicine, 15(5), 414–418. https: / / doi.org / 10.1111 / j.1553 - 2712.2008.00100.x

Cleeland et al., (1994) 'Pain and Its Treatment in Outpatients with Metastatic Cancer', N Engl J Med 1994; 330:592 - 596 DOI: 10.1056 / NEJM199403033300902

Cleghorn, E. (2021) The gender pain gap has gone on for too long – it's time we closed it, New Scientist

Columbia School of Nursing (2014) Psychiatric Complications in Women with Polycystic Ovary Syndrome Most Often Linked to Menstrual Irregularities, Columbia University Irving Medical Center

Chiu, A., Chon, S.Y. and Kimball, A.B. (2003) "The response of skin disease to stress," Archives of Dermatology, 139(7). Available at: https://doi.org/10.1001/archderm.139.7.897.

Daniel K. Hall-Flavin, M.D. (2021) Can stress make you lose your hair? Mayo Clinic. Mayo Foundation for Medical Education and Research. Available at: https://www.mayoclinic.org/healthy-lifestyle/stress-management/expert-answers/stress-and-hair-loss/faq-20057820#:~:text=Yes%2C%20stress%20and%20hair%20loss,follicles%20into%20a%20resting%20phase. (Accessed: February 8, 2023).

Davies, J. (2014) Cracked: Why psychiatry is doing more harm than good, Icon Books, UK

Davies J. (2017) 'How Voting and Consensus Created the Diagnostic and Statistical Manual of Mental Disorders (DSM - III)'. Anthropology & Medicine, 24(1), 32–46. https://doi.org/10.1080/13648470.2016.1226684

Deacon B. J. (2013) 'The biomedical model of mental disorder: a critical analysis of its validity, utility, and effects on psychotherapy research'. Clinical Psychology Review, 33(7), 846–861. https://doi.org/10.1016/j.cpr.2012.09.007

Deng, P. & Yeshokumar, A. (2020) Autoimmune Encephalitis: What Psychiatrists Need to Know, Psychiatric Times

DSM - V (2013) American Psychiatric Association Diagnostic and statistical manual of mental disorders: DSM - 5. 5th edn. Washington, D.C.: American Psychiatric Publishing.

Eaton, J. (2019) 'Logically, I know I am not to blame, but I still feel to blame': Exploring and measuring victim blaming and self-blame of women subjected to sexual violence and abuse, University of Birmingham

Eaton, J. (2018) Sexual Exploitation and Mental Health of Adults, Research in Practice, Dartington Press

Eaton, J. & Holmes, D. (2017) Child Sexual Exploitation: An Evidence Scope, Research in Practice, Dartington Press

Ellis, J. (2021) Medical conditions that can mimic dementia. Bright Focus Foundation. Retrieved March 1, 2023, from https://www.brightfocus.org/alzheimers/article/medical-conditions-can-mimic-dementia

Farley, M. and Butler, E. (2012) Prostitution and Trafficking, Prostitution Research & Education. Available at: https://prostitutionresearch.com/

Farley, M. et al. (1998) "Prostitution in five countries: Violence and post-traumatic stress disorder," Feminism & Psychology, 8(4), pp. 405–426. Available at: https://doi.org/10.1177/0959353598084002

FBI (2023) Facts and statistics, 2021 Hate Crime Statistics. The United States Department of Justice. Available at: https://www.justice.gov/hatecrimes/hate-crime-statistics (Accessed: March 1, 2023)

Freud, S. (1913) 'The claims of psycho - analysis to scientific interest' S.E. 13 165–190

GOV.UK (2022) Get help for radicalisation concerns, GOV.UK. Available at: https://www.gov.uk/guidance/get-help-if-youre-worried-about-someone-being-radicalised#:~:text=Radicalisation%20means%20someone%20is%20being,more%20about%20what%20terrorism%20means. (Accessed: February 2023)

Grauerholz, L. (2000). An ecological approach to understanding sexual revictimization: Linking personal, interpersonal, and sociocultural factors and processes. Child Maltreatment, 5, 5-17

Hall-Flavin, D.K. (2023) Pain and depression: Is there a link? Mayo Clinic, mayoclinic.org

Hate crime, England and Wales, 2021 to 2022 (2022) GOV.UK. Available at: https://www.gov.uk/government/statistics/hate-crime-england-and-wales-2021-to-2022/hate-crime-england-and-wales-2021-to-2022 (Accessed: February 2023)

Hayes, J.P., VanElzakker, M.B. and Shin, L.M. (2012) Emotion and cognition interactions in PTSD: A review of neurocognitive and neuroimaging studies, Frontiers. Frontiers. Available at: https://www.frontiersin.org/articles/10.3389/fnint.2012.00089/full#:~:text=The%20emotional%20experience%20of%20psychological,emotionality%20has%20on%20cognitive%20functioning. (Accessed: February 8, 2023)

Heinrich, T. and Grahm, G. (2003) Hypothyroidism Presenting as Psychosis: Myxedema Madness Revisited, Prim Care Companion J Clin Psychiatry. 2003; 5(6): 260–266. doi: 10.4088/pcc.v05n0603

Jackson, G. (2015) Pain and Prejudice: A call to arms for women and their bodies, Piatkus

Jagsi R, Motomura AR, Amarnath S, Jankovic A, Sheets N, Ubel PA. Under-representation of women in high-impact published clinical cancer research. Cancer. 2009 Jul 15;115(14):3293-301. doi: 10.1002/cncr.24366. PMID: 19507175.

Johnstone, L. & Boyle, M. (2018) The Power Threat Meaning Framework: Towards the identification of patterns in emotional distress, unusual experiences and troubled or troubling behaviour, as an alternative to functional psychiatric diagnosis, The British Psychological Society

Kiecolt-Glaser, J.K. et al. (1995) "Slowing of wound healing by psychological stress," The Lancet, 346(8984), pp. 1194–1196. Available at: https://doi.org/10.1016/s0140-6736(95)92899-5.

Lancet (2016) 'Sex and gender differences in mental disorder', VOLUME 4, ISSUE 1, P8 - 9

Lerner, M. J. (1980). The belief in a just world. New York: Plenum Press.

Lerner, M. J. (1997) What does the belief in a just world protect us from? The dread of death or the fear of undeserved suffering? New York, Plenum Press.

von Lersner, U., Elbert, T. & Neuner, F. Mental health of refugees following state-sponsored repatriation from Germany. BMC Psychiatry 8, 88 (2008). https://doi.org/10.1186/1471-244X-8-88

Marchant, R. & Taylor, J. (2021) Understanding and supporting people who experience hallucinations, VictimFocus

McEvoy, M., McElvaney, R. & Glover, R. (2021) Understanding vaginismus: a biopsychosocial perspective, Sexual and Relationship Therapy, DOI: 10.1080/14681994.2021.2007233

MFMER (2017) Bed-wetting, Mayo Clinic. Mayo Foundation for Medical Education and Research. Available at: https://www.mayoclinic.org/diseases-conditions/bed-wetting/symptoms-causes/syc-20366685 (Accessed: February 6, 2023).

MFMER (2022) Headaches: Reduce stress to prevent the pain, Mayo Clinic. Mayo Foundation for Medical Education and Research. Available at: https://www.mayoclinic.org/diseases-conditions/tension-headache/in-depth/headaches/art-20046707#:~:text=It's%20not%20a%20coincidence%20%E2%80%94%20headaches,in%20children%20and%20young%20adults. (Accessed: February 6, 2023).

Moncrieff J, Cohen D (2006) 'Do Antidepressants Cure or Create Abnormal Brain States?' PLoS Med 3(7): e240. https: / / doi.org / 10.1371 / journal. pmed.0030240

Moshman D. (2013) 'Adolescent rationality', Advances in Child Development and Behavior, 45, 155–183. https: / / doi.org / 10.1016 / b978 - 0 - 12 - 397946 - 9.00007 - 5

Moor, A., Ben-Meir, E., Golan-Shapira, D. & Farchi, M. (2013) Rape: A Trauma of Paralyzing Dehumanization, Journal of Aggression, Maltreatment & Trauma, 22:10, 1051-1069, DOI: 10.1080/10926771.2013.848965

Moller, A., Sondergaard, H.P., Helstrom L. (2017) Tonic immobility during sexual assault – a common reaction predicting post-traumatic stress disorder and severe depression. Acta Obstet Gynecol Scand 2017; DOI: 10.1111/aogs.13174

Neely DC, Bray KJ, Huisingh CE, Clark ME, McGwin G, Owsley C. Prevalence of Undiagnosed Age-Related Macular Degeneration in Primary Eye Care. JAMA Ophthalmol. 2017;135(6):570–575. doi:10.1001/jamaophthalmol.2017.0830

NHS (2021) Trichotillomania (hair pulling disorder), NHS choices. NHS. Available at: https://www.nhs.uk/mental-health/conditions/trichotillomania/#:~:text=Trichotillomania%2C%20also%20known%20as%20trich,in%20teenagers%20and%20young%20adults. (Accessed: February 8, 2023).

NHS Inform (2023) Are you having panic attacks? NHS inform. Available at: https://www.nhsinform.scot/healthy-living/mental-wellbeing/anxiety-and-panic/are-you-having-panic_attacks#:~:text=The%20physical%20symptoms%20of%20a,your%20muscles%20to%20tense%20up. (Accessed: February 7, 2023).

Oregon State University (2019) Cognitive function in brief, Linus Pauling Institute. Available at: https://lpi.oregonstate.edu/mic/health-disease/cognitive-function-in-brief#:~:text=Cognition%20basically%20means%20using%20your,problem%20solving%2C%20and%20multitasking). (Accessed: February 8, 2023).

Read J, Cunliffe S, Jauhar S, McLoughlin D M. (2019) 'Should we stop using electroconvulsive therapy?' BMJ 2019; 364 :k5233 doi:10.1136 / bmj.k5233

Read, J. & Dillon, J. (2014) Models of Madness: Psychological, Social and Biological Approaches to Psychosis, 2nd (revised) edition. ISPS series Published by Routledge, Hove, UK

Salter, M. (2012) 'The Role of Ritual in the Organised Abuse of Children', Child Abuse Review https: / / doi.org / 10.1002 / car.2215

Samulowitz, A., Gremyr, I. Eriksson, E. & Hensing, G. (2018) "Brave Men" and "Emotional Women": A Theory-Guided Literature Review on Gender Bias in Health Care and Gendered Norms towards Patients with Chronic Pain, Pain Res Manag. 2018; 2018: 6358624. Published online 2018 Feb 25. doi: 10.1155/2018/6358624

Segrest, M. (2020) Administrations of Lunacy: Racism and the Haunting of American Psychiatry at the Milledgeville Asylum, New Press

Singer, J.L. and McCraven, V.G. (1961) "Some characteristics of adult daydreaming," The Journal of Psychology, 51(1), pp. 151–164. Available at: https://doi.org/10.1080/00223980.1961.9916467.

Solomon, A. et al. (2016) The contemporary spectrum of multiple sclerosis misdiagnosis: A multicenter study, Neurology. 2016 Sep 27; 87(13): 1393–1399. doi: 10.1212/WNL.0000000000003152

Somer, E., Abu-Rayya, H.M. and Brenner, R. (2020) "Childhood trauma and maladaptive daydreaming: Fantasy functions and themes in a multi-country sample," Journal of Trauma & Dissociation, 22(3), pp. 288–303. Available at: https://doi.org/10.1080/15299732.2020.1809599.

St John Ambulance (2021) Hyperventilation - first aid advice: St john ambulance, First Aid Advice | St John Ambulance. Available at: https://www.sja.org.uk/get-advice/first-aid-advice/breathing-difficulties/hyperventilation/ (Accessed: February 8, 2023).

Street, T. (2021) Can stress cause hair loss? Can Stress Cause Hair Loss? | Lloyds Pharmacy Online Doctor UK. Available at: https://onlinedoctor.lloydspharmacy.com/uk/hair-loss-advice/can-stress-cause-hair-loss (Accessed: February 8, 2023).

Suicide by occupation, England: 2011 to 2015. Office for National Statistics. Retrieved March 1, 2023, from https://www.ons.gov.uk/peoplepopulationandcommunity/birthsdeathsandmarriages/deaths/articles/suicidebyoccupation/england2011to2015

Taylor, J. (2022) Sexy But Psycho: How patriarchy uses women's trauma against them, Little Brown, Hachette, UK

Taylor, J. (2020) Why Women are Blamed for Everything: Exposing victim blaming, Little Brown, Hachette, UK

Timimi, S. (2021) Insane Medicine: How the Mental Health Industry Creates Damaging Treatment Traps and How you can Escape Them

Tsafrir, J. (2022) Ehler's Danlos Syndrome and Psychiatric Symptoms
The perils of misdiagnosing EDS as a primary psychiatric condition, Psychology Today

Upham, B. (2022) 16 Conditions Commonly Mistaken for Multiple Sclerosis, Everyday Health

Ussher, J. (2013) Diagnosing difficult women and pathologising femininity: Gender bias in psychiatric nosology, Feminism and Psychology, 23 (1) 63-69, DOI: 10.1177/0959353512467968

Wighton, K. (2020) Long delays for diagnosis of ulcerative colitis and Crohn's disease, Imperial College London

Women and Equalities Committee, (2016) Sexual harassment and sexual violence in schools, Third report of session 2016-17, House of Commons

Printed in Great Britain
by Amazon